Praise for *In the Wake of Madness:*

"Joan Druett pulls off an unlikely feat: she delivers both a primer on nineteenth-century whaling, complete with *Moby-Dick* resonances, *and* a genuine nautical thriller, a page-turner. She takes us along on this doomed voyage, building to a climax that is shocking and very satisfying."
—RICHARD ZACKS, author of *The Pirate Hunter: The True Story of Captain Kidd*

"Masterfully weaves the history of whaling and sailing with a detailed murder investigation." —*Richmond Ti...* *?ispatch*

"[Druett] draws a fine picture of the floating c... ...ers and deserters." —*T... ...s Book Review*

"A nautical murder mystery." —*USA Today*

"Those who enjoy maritime history, whaling, and Melville should embark on the *Sharon* book voyage for a thrilling ride."
—*Good Old Boat*

"A fascinating historical, action-packed tale of high seas adventure."
—*The Westerly Sun*

"Gripping. . . . Brings alive Herman Melville's description of the high seas and of the characters who inhabit the vessels that sail it."
—*The Sunday Oklahoman*

"Stunning. [Druett] writes about maritime history with the delicious ease and nail-biting suspense of a crack mystery novelist."
—*The Standard-Times*

"This book would make a wonderful movie. . . . First-rate"
—*ForeWord* magazine

"Druett has written an interesting work of creative non-fiction. Readers won't need to read beyond the introduction to know what's going to happen. Her hook is not what, but how this tragedy happened. It's more than enough to keep readers engaged."   —*The Virginian-Pilot*

"A terrific account of an unusually eventful voyage."
    —*Publishers Weekly*

"A sharp harpoon, a keen eye, an unerring throw."
    —*Kirkus Reviews*

"An informative and vividly re-created picture of America's maritime past."   —*Library Journal*

"A must read in maritime history. . . . Druett's prose, imagery and use of primary sources bring to life this lost American experience."
    —The Great Lakes Historical Society

"Though this is a work of history, it reads fast, like a novel. *In the Wake of Madness* is easily one of the best-written books of popular history I've ever read."   —JESSICA POWERS, *NewPages*

"In addition to its gripping narrative, Druett's book provides a virtual encyclopedia of life (and death) on whalers in the 1800s."
    —*The Dukes County Intelligencer*

"Anyone who enjoys maritime history, the works of Melville or a good yarn will love this literate, entertaining book."
    —*Pawling News Chronicle*

"Like a combination primer in nautical life in the 1800s and a slowly building drama, author Joan Druett's book is a powerful true historical account. . . . You need not have read *Moby-Dick*, or be partial to nautical history or fiction, to find *In the Wake of Madness* a captivating book."
    —*The Decatur Daily*

"Druett is a fine historian."   —*The Boston Globe*

IN THE WAKE OF MADNESS

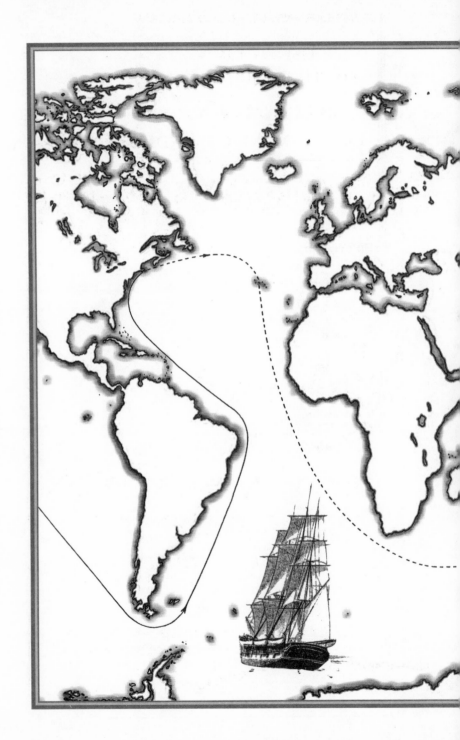

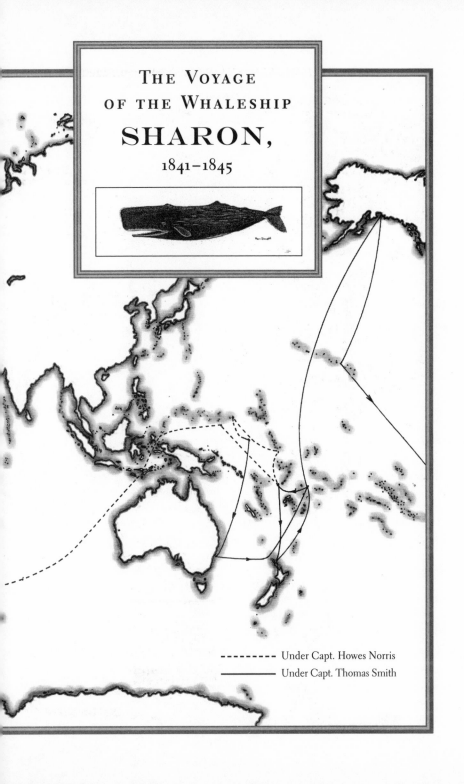

THE VOYAGE
OF THE WHALESHIP
SHARON,
1841–1845

- - - - - - - - Under Capt. Howes Norris
———— Under Capt. Thomas Smith

IN THE WAKE
OF MADNESS

THE
MURDEROUS VOYAGE
OF THE
WHALESHIP *SHARON*

BY

JOAN DRUETT

ALGONQUIN BOOKS OF CHAPEL HILL
2004

Published by

ALGONQUIN BOOKS OF CHAPEL HILL

Post Office Box 2225

Chapel Hill, North Carolina 27515-2225

a division of

Workman Publishing

708 Broadway

New York, New York 10003

Illustrations © by Ron Druett.

Map by Ron Druett and Laura Williams.

First paperback edition, April 2004. Originally published by
  Algonquin Books of Chapel Hill in 2003.

Printed in the United States of America.

Published simultaneously in Canada by Thomas Allen & Son Limited.

Design by Anne Winslow.

Library of Congress Cataloging-in-Publication Data
Druett, Joan.
     In the wake of madness : the murderous voyage of the whaleship
  Sharon / by Joan Druett.—1st ed.
       p. cm.
     Includes bibliographical references and index.
     ISBN 1-56512-347-6
        1. Sharon (Whaleship)   2. Norris, Howes, d. 1842.
     3. Whaling—North Pacific Ocean.   4. Mutiny—North Pacific
     Ocean.   5. Survival after airplane accidents, shipwrecks, etc.
     I. Title.
     G545.D78 2003
     909'.09645081—dc21   2003040403
     ISBN 1-56512-435-9 paper

10 9 8 7 6 5 4 3 2 1
First Paperback Edition

Human madness is oftentimes a cunning and most feline thing. When you think it fled, it may have become transfigured into still subtler form.

—HERMAN MELVILLE, *Moby-Dick*

Contents

Introduction

On May 25, 1841, the whaleship *Sharon* of Fairhaven, Massachusetts, set out on the first leg of what was to become one of the most notorious voyages of the nineteenth century—and yet one of its best-kept secrets. She was bound for the whaling grounds of the northwestern Pacific, where many small tropical islands lay scattered in an immensity of sea. In charge of the quarter deck were three men from the island of Martha's Vineyard—Captain Howes Norris and his first and second officers, both named Smith.

Earlier that year, on January 3, a sister whaleship, the *Acushnet*, had worked her way out of just the same bay. Her captain was another Vineyard man, Valentine Pease Jr., and among her crew was an aspiring writer, Herman Melville—a young man whose Pacific adventures, along with the stories he heard from other whalemen, would provide background and inspiration for his great novel, *Moby-Dick*.

Leaving Fairhaven in January, the *Acushnet* had steered south for Cape Horn, at the southernmost extremity of South America, to battle headwinds on the way to the eastern Pacific, where she would hunt whales off Chile and Peru and reprovision at the Marquesas Islands. These were waters that Melville came to know well—the same Cape Horn route and the same waters that were sailed by the Nantucket whaleship *Essex*, which was sunk by a whale in November 1820, providing the inspiration for the ultimate fate of Melville's fictional *Pequod*, though *not* for her course.

In *Moby-Dick*, Captain Ahab took the opposite route to Captain Pease of the *Acushnet*. He steered for the Cape of Good Hope, at the bottom of Africa, and then traversed the Indian Ocean to the East Indies, to negotiate the shoals and reefs there before breaking into the Western Pacific. Ahab's route was exactly the same as that followed by Norris of the *Sharon*, who hunted sperm whales in the same seas where Captain Ahab pursued the great white whale.

And Norris of the *Sharon*, like Ahab of the *Pequod*, was headed for disaster.

THE EARLIEST NOTICE of Norris's gruesome fate appeared in the "Shipping Intelligence" column of the *Sydney Morning Herald*, on December 23, 1842. "The *Sharon* has put in to obtain hands, and also on account of the murder of her late commander, Captain Norris," the announcement ran. Behind this bald statement lay a story so sensational that it raced across the world as fast as wind could fill sails, creating headlines wherever it went and gripping the imagination of the public.

The path to calamity had been laid on October 15, 1842, when the *Sharon* arrived at Ascension Island—now called Pohnpei—in the tropical northwest Pacific. Typical of the

Pacific paradises that young men dreamed of before they joined the crews of whalers, it was also a favorite spot for absconding from the ship—but not desertion on the scale experienced by the captain of the *Sharon*. Twelve men had escaped while the ship was anchored in the lagoon, an almost unprecedented number—a number that left the ship critically shorthanded. Captain Howes Norris had had no choice but to steer for the Bay of Islands, New Zealand, to try to recruit more men.

Ten days later, as the *Sydney Morning Herald* went on to describe, fate intervened. A school of sperm whales was raised. The swift flight to New Zealand was interrupted to lower two boats in the chase, leaving just four men and a boy on board. One of the men was Captain Norris. Three others were Pacific Islanders—who, once the boats were well away, seized their chance to slaughter the captain. "So craftily did the Islanders act," penned whaling writer Charles Boardman Hawes, "that neither captain nor boy had the slightest reason to suspect them of treachery." Without warning, the captain was felled—"The boy fled to the rigging and the savages ran amuck."

"About five p.m.," recorded the *Morning Herald*, "it was seen from the boats that the flag was hoisted half mast." At once, the oarsmen pulled for the ship. The three natives, naked, smeared with fresh blood, yelling war cries and brandishing weapons, were ready and waiting. The first mate, Thomas Smith, ordered a retreat, and a panic-stricken council of war was held. Prospects for survival were grim. The nearest land was seven hundred miles away, and there was no food and little fresh water stored on the boats.

However, as Hawes went on to relate, in their company was

a man "with the courage and presence of mind to meet the emergency." This was the third officer, a young man from Maine by the name of Benjamin Clough. After night had fallen, he swam to the ship—a remarkable act of courage, considering that the sea was shark-infested. Slithering through the cabin windows, he managed to overcome two of the natives and frighten the third into diving overboard. Single-handedly, Benjamin Clough had recaptured the *Sharon*.

It was an amazing exploit, sensational enough to sell many hundreds of the newspapers that reprinted the report as it filtered into American ports from the far side of the Pacific, and thousands of the books that recounted the rousing yarn later. But, because the single-handed recapture is such a capital tale in itself, only half of the story has been popularly told. The public imagination became so focused on Clough's remarkable feat that crucial questions were allowed to lurk unanswered, concealing important issues that dramatically alter the accepted version of events.

For instance, no one has looked for a good reason why so many of the crew ran away—or why Captain Norris was unable to recruit replacements from the pool of penniless seamen who hung about the beach. No one revealed, either, that these were not the first men to run away from the ship—nine had escaped at the island of Rotuma, in April 1842, six months before the ship had arrived at Pohnpei. No writer speculated about the motive for the murder. Instead, every newspaper reporter simply assumed that Norris's murder was committed by natives who needed no comprehensible reason to do it, their own blind "savagery" being reason enough to run "amuck." No one has publicly investigated the background of these so-called "savages," or explored their actions, in an attempt to discover the forces that drove this violent drama.

When the events took place, Herman Melville was in the Pacific and undoubtedly heard about the murder and the heroic recapture, as gossip ran round the fleet fast. He also would have read the official version in the papers. He was home in New York when the story hit the headlines again after the *Sharon* arrived back in February 1845. He heard more details from his old *Acushnet* shipmate Toby Greene, who in 1843, less than a year after the sensational events, had socialized with the *Sharon* sailors during several lengthy midsea visits. It is probably no coincidence that Captain Ahab found disaster in the same empty tropic seas where Captain Norris was killed.

Over the next 160 years, however, the dark tale that Melville and his shipmates heard was lost to history, because of a pact of silence. It is only now, because forgotten journals kept by participants in the grim drama have become available, that the other half of the story can be told.

ONE

MARTHA'S VINEYARD

ON A GALE-RACKED DAY in the hamlet of Holmes
Hole — now called Vineyard Haven — on the island of Martha's
Vineyard, Massachusetts, a whaling captain arrived at the front
door of a substantial house that commanded an unbroken view
of the storm-tossed waters of the harbor. His name was Howes
Norris; he was thirty-seven and had just seventeen months left
to live.

The date was May 14, 1841, a day set apart as a national holiday to commemorate the death of President Harrison, and so
Captain Norris would have been formally dressed, as befitted a
whaling master. He was an impressive figure. Strongly built and
tall for his time at five feet, nine inches, Norris had the thick,
sloping shoulders of a man who had spent much of his youth

pulling heavy oars. Pale-complexioned, with ears that protruded from thinning brown hair and a full-lipped mouth that appeared disdainful in repose, his face was dominated by large and heavy-lidded eyes, wide-set under arching brows. What would have made him most distinctive, however, was his bearing—that of an experienced and successful whaling master, which counted for a great deal in the social milieu of Martha's Vineyard.

It was little wonder that Howes Norris had chosen whaling for his career. As the Rev. Joseph Thaxter, minister of the Edgartown Congregational Church, remarked back in 1824, Vineyard boys could be relied on to "scorn to Hoe a field of Corn, but will row a Boat from morning till Night and never complain." Like his schoolmates, Howes Norris had been raised in the unmistakable island aura of whale oil, clams, smoked herring, and the ocean. As a boy he had swum naked in the lagoon; had taken out boats after codfish and halibut; had swaggered over the oil-soaked planks of Edgartown jetties; had swarmed illicitly through the rigging of anchored whalers.

Like his friends, Norris had regarded the sea as his playground, and his boyhood as a kind of apprenticeship. From childhood, he would have been well aware that he would have to seek his fortune on the ocean. "The Sea is the source from whence the People look for their Support," Thaxter noted, the island being only marginally fertile. Indian corn was raised in a few scattered clay patches, along with rye, potatoes, and turnips, but not enough to satisfy the local market, let alone export to the mainland. So, for young Howes Norris, farming had not been an option.

Born on September 19, 1803, the son of a humble Edgartown, Martha's Vineyard, pilot, Norris first went to sea at the age of sixteen, shipping on the brig *William Thacker* of Edgartown on June 2, 1820. Probably he managed this by pretending to be older than he actually was, because when he joined the *Ann Alexander* of New Bedford on August 1, 1825, he declared his age to be twenty-three. This obvious dedication was rewarded in July 1828, when he was given the command of the *Leonidas* of Fairhaven. It was a grave responsibility for such a young man: the *Leonidas* had been just eight years in the Fairhaven fleet, and had a history of making profitable cruises. Norris managed to fulfill the owners' expectations by bringing her back from the South Atlantic inside twelve months, with a cargo that was worth the creditable amount of thirteen thousand dollars. Norris would have looked back on this voyage with nostalgia, as a wonderful example of beginner's luck.

Single-minded, ambitious, and hardworking, Norris had stopped just one month at home before again taking charge of the *Leonidas*. This voyage, though, was not nearly as fortunate. Not only did the whales prove much more elusive, but Norris was forced to put into the port of Rio de Janiero, as four of his men were down with scurvy. Still worse, he had to linger there five weeks for expensive repairs, a rotten mast being in dire need of replacement. Then he steered south, back to the Brazil Banks, but it took another season to fill his holds with oil, with the result that they did not arrive home until mid-1831.

Perhaps because of this, the command of the *Leonidas* was passed on to a fellow Vineyarder, Captain John H. Pease. However, the owners still had enough confidence in Norris to entrust him with the maiden whaling voyage of the *London Packet*.

He left in November 1832, on a cruise to the Indian Ocean that took thirty-three months to complete—and came home tight-lipped about much of what had happened.

However, he was able to report nineteen hundred barrels—sixty thousand gallons—of oil, which meant a reasonable profit for the merchants who had invested in the ship; reasonable enough to encourage them to give him the command of the *London Packet* again. And this time his luck held. This voyage was an excellent one, with the spectacular report of well over twenty-five hundred barrels. Because of this, and because secrets had been kept, Norris now had the enviable reputation of a man with luck on his side.

Was he still lucky? It would take another voyage like that one to prove it. Down in the anchorage an assortment of sloops and schooners lay huddled under the cold southwest gusts, waiting for the wind to swing east and moderate, so they could sail down Vineyard Sound on the first fair tide. Until then, the shipping was trapped. Captain Howes Norris watched the scud of the waves, and the way the craft pulled at their anchors, clutching his tall hat and the flapping skirts of his frockcoat as he studied the gale-whipped scene. His next command, the *Sharon*, was waiting for her captain in Fairhaven, in mainland Massachusetts, and he had to cross that water to get to her—to once more look for good fortune on the whaling grounds.

Two days before, the whaleship *Champion* had blown into Edgartown harbor on the breast of this cold southwest storm, at the end of a sperm-whaling voyage to New Zealand that had lasted three years. She had an excellent report—more than three thousand barrels full of sperm oil from spermaceti whales, the best and most valuable kind. Hearty congratulations were due to her master, Captain George Lawrence. With sperm oil fetching the price of ninety-four cents per gallon, a gross profit of $90,000 was likely—cause for celebration, particularly considering that it had cost only about $10,000 to outfit the ship in the first place. Once that oil was gauged and put onto the market in New Bedford, Lawrence and his officers could expect to take home a very good sum, and even the lowliest crew members would be relatively pleased.

As Norris understood well, it was good voyages like this one that encouraged the merchants of New England to keep up their investment in the whaling trade. Every now and then some legendary skipper would bring in a huge cargo after a remarkably short time away, giving renewed hope to the citizens who sank their money into the ventures. One such was the fabled Captain Obed Starbuck of Nantucket, who had made two record-breaking voyages on the *Loper*. In 1829 he had sailed home with every one of his barrels full of sperm oil after a voyage of just seventeen months. No sooner had he exchanged his full casks for empty ones than he had turned round and gone out again, returning fourteen months later full of oil again. In just thirty-one months he had harvested 140,000 gallons, grossing more than a hundred thousand dollars, an enormous sum at the time.

What would have nagged at Norris's mind, however, was the knowledge that every one of those gallons had been rendered out of what had once been a live whale—that every good report meant fewer whales for him to hunt. Voyages were lengthening as the ships had to cruise farther in search for prey, and reports were worsening with each season that passed by. The Nantucket ship *Obed Mitchell* was still at sea thirty-two months after departing on her maiden voyage, and, like everyone else, Howes Norris would have heard the rumor that she had taken only eight hundred barrels in all that time. If true, this meant financial disaster for her owners and a crippling loss of prestige for her captain.

It didn't bear thinking about. His mind edged away. All those who speculated in whaleships—and especially those who commanded them—were gamblers at heart. Optimism was essential, because a man who did not secretly believe that his next cruise was going to be a record breaker would never be able to force himself to embark on a voyage that was increasingly doomed to last three or more years. And, as in all other kinds of gambling, superstition played a large part, too.

The whaleship *Sharon* did look as if she would be lucky. She had been out on just one previous voyage, to the Pacific Ocean under the command of Captain John Church, and it had been a very good one. Departing in June 1837, she had returned on December 10, 1840, a voyage of forty-two months, which was longer than most men liked to be away. Her holds, though, had been crammed with oil worth $80,000, a sum that made the protracted voyage seem worthwhile.

Naturally, then, Norris was anxious to take over his new and promising command. It is likely that he had already made arrangements with a young man by the name of Holmes Luce —who called himself "Captain" and his humble sloop a "packet" because he made his living ferrying Vineyarders to the mainland—to take him to the Acushnet River. But sailing down the sound could not be done until the wind and tide set fair, which meant Howes Norris had time to take part in a family gathering.

INSTEAD OF KNOCKING and waiting, Norris would have opened the door and walked in unannounced. That he was able to do this would have given him great satisfaction. Set south of Owen Park and on the harborside of Main Street, the house he was visiting was in one of the most prestigious locations in town. Eastville, where Norris had been born and raised, had a very different reputation from Main Street, Holmes Hole. In the years since he had first gone to sea, Norris had risen mightily in social status.

Now known as East Chop, Eastville is a respectable part of Oak Bluffs today, but back then it was nicknamed "Barbary Coast," because it was considered nothing better than a hangout for transient sailors. As well as being despised by the gentry, Eastville was off the beaten track. Howes's mother, Lucy Shaw Norris, would have found it difficult to go shopping, let alone enjoy any social life. To get to Holmes Hole she either had to go by small boat across the harbor—extremely uncomfortable in the northerly winds of winter—or else get in a wagon and drive all the way around the lagoon, a bone-jolting trip of at least four miles each way. For an Eastville man to be accepted in Main Street, Holmes Hole, was a tall step up the ladder of gentility. Yet Norris had managed it, partly because of his success as a whaling master, but mostly because of an advantageous marriage. The fine house he stepped into on this blustery day was the property of his father-in-law, Captain Nathan Smith.

Nathan Smith, who, as host, would have stepped forward first to shake Norris's hand, was a stocky, middle-aged man with an affable smile, a pleasantly open expression, and a benevolent air. "Captain" was an honorary title. Nathan Smith had not made his fortune out of whaling, but out of the liquor trade, running one of the most prosperous and popular watering holes in town. Called Smith's Tavern, the establishment had been built around 1750, and was originally owned and operated by Captain David Smith, Nathan Smith's father. There, Captain David Smith had served Nevis rum at one dollar per gallon, along with "breadstuffs" that he brought in from New York by running the British blockade with the assistance of his son Nathan, who must have been a flamboyant character in his youth. Nathan had inherited Smith's Tavern after the death of his father in 1818, and had spent the next twenty-two years serving behind the bar. It is easy to picture the practiced hospitality of his demeanor as he entertained his guests in front of a roaring fire in the "keeping-room"—or "keeping-company room" —of this fine house, which had been bought with the proceeds of selling the tavern, after his retirement in April the previous year.

Because of the holiday, it is probably safe to assume that Nathan Smith's fifty-six-year-old brother, Captain Thomas Harlock Smith, was in the room as well. Another prosperous man, Thomas had established the foundations of his fortune by sailing in the foreign trade as an "adventurer," speculating in cargoes, and investing his profits in Martha's Vineyard property. In a typical transaction just the previous month, Thomas had sold a lot for $200 that he had bought for $135 in July. Considering the short time of ownership, this was no small return, and the revenue from several transactions like this would have quickly added up to a sizable sum. Quite apart from an energetic program of buying and selling, he owned and operated a chandlery store, which he kept in a boat shed on the beach below his house, on Main Street and south of Owen Park, a couple of lots to the north of his brother's place.

Both brothers had done well when they had married, too. Captain Nathan Smith's wife, Polly Jenkins Dunham Smith, was wealthy in her own right, being a member of a family that had become rich from taverns, stores, and profits made in foreign trade. Captain Thomas Smith's wife, Deborah West Smith —familiarly known as Depza—had brought him both property and the expectation of a substantial legacy from her father, Jeruel West. Both women had given them sons. Two of these would also have been present, having a great deal in common with Captain Howes Norris. Both were whalemen, and both were due to sail with him on the *Sharon*.

The younger of the two, Nathan Skiff Smith, was the son of Captain Nathan Smith, and therefore Norris's brother-in-law. A brown-haired, narrow-eyed twenty-five-year-old, Nathan Jr. looked a lot like his father, though his expression was not nearly as jovial. One eyelid was markedly lower than the other, so that he looked both alert and suspicious, an impression emphasized by a down-turned mouth. The other whaleman was Nathan Skiff Smith's first cousin, Thomas Harlock Smith Jr., a light-complexioned, sandy-haired, tough and nuggety little fellow, just four feet, nine inches tall. Though a mere five feet, four inches, Nathan Skiff Smith had quite an advantage in height.

Norris was going to rely on these men a lot: Thomas Harlock Smith Jr. would be his first mate on the *Sharon*, while Nathan Skiff Smith would be the second officer. Both would play a vital part in the daily running of the ship. They would transmit the captain's orders and be in charge of discipline, functioning as intermediaries between Captain Norris and the crew.

The fact that they were in-laws must have been a factor when the two Smiths were offered the prized jobs, but nevertheless Norris would have been acutely aware that the performance of these two fellow Vineyarders could make or break the voyage. He had never sailed with his brother-in-law Nathan before, and probably knew little of his reputation at sea. Since shipping first at the age of seventeen on the *Albion*, Nathan Skiff Smith had shifted from vessel to vessel, never staying longer than one voyage with each captain. However, Howes Norris knew his first officer, Thomas Harlock Smith Jr., very well. Thomas Smith had signed up with Norris on the *Leonidas* in 1829, as a fifteen-year-old greenhand, and had sailed with him again as a harpooner on the 1832 voyage of the *London Packet*. Thomas was tight-lipped, a trait Captain Norris would have valued highly. That he could be relied upon to keep secrets would have been another reason Thomas Harlock Smith Jr. had landed the plum job of first mate.

It is likely that the wives of Nathan Jr. and Thomas Jr. were present, too—though they may have found the company of their confident, prosperous mothers-in-law somewhat intimidating, as their own circumstances were unusual. Nathan Skiff Smith and his wife, Jane Bousiron de Neuville Smith, had been married on April 26, 1835, when Nathan was not quite nineteen years old and Jane was twenty-eight. That he should have wed so young and chosen someone nine years his senior was unusual. Thomas Harlock Smith Jr. had married much more recently, on March 21, just a few weeks earlier. In contrast to Nathan's choice of a bride, his wife, Elizabeth West Dunham Smith, was only thirteen years old.

Nathan Skiff Smith's sister was also in the room. This was Elwina, the wife of Captain Howes Norris, who no doubt had gone to stand possessively beside her. A small, slim, brown-haired woman with deep-set eyes and the same down-turned mouth as her brother, Elwina was quiet and submissive, her entire attention on the baby she nursed and the two children playing by her skirts.

Once he had taken off his coat and relaxed, in fact, Norris would have dominated the company. A natty dresser with a penchant for frilled shirts and fancy cravats, today he would have been wearing a black band about his left upper arm, in remembrance of his eldest sister, Lucy, who had died on April 20 at the age of fifty-three, after a fever that lasted just one week and one day. Despite this sad loss, however, he would have been smiling and talkative, the most glib and charming man in the room. Captain Norris was at his best in the company of substantial, well-to-do men like the senior Smiths, and a quiet, demure wife would have been an excellent foil.

When he had proposed marriage to Elwina, the family must have discussed it deeply, with reservations about the suitability of the match. If he had not had the reputation of a successful whaling master, Norris probably would not have been considered an acceptable suitor. He would have been disqualified by his social origins. However, on August 5, 1832, he triumphantly made eighteen-year-old Elwina his wife. He had not had long to enjoy the enhanced status of being married to a daughter of one of the most prosperous and influential families in town, however. Sixteen weeks after the ceremony, he had sailed off on the *London Packet*, taking Elwina's cousin Thomas with him, and he had not returned until nearly three years later, on the last day of August 1835.

Those three years were tough for Elwina. On May 18, 1833, she gave birth to a daughter, Octavia Ann Yale Norris. Now, the eight-year-old was a healthy round-faced child, the apple of her father's eye. However her birth had been followed by painful and dangerous complications. In those days it was considered necessary for a new mother to lie flat on her back for two or more weeks after the confinement, and obedient Elwina had developed a blood clot in her upper thigh, leading to a condition called "milk-leg." According to the diary kept by her physician, Dr. LeRoy Yale, the afflicted leg swelled to such an agonizing extent that she could not bear to put any weight on it. When Howes Norris had returned from that first *London Packet* voyage, he had been fortunate to find his wife alive.

The emotional, physical, and financial strain on the wives was immense, but the husbands were deprived domestically, too. The first time Howes Norris had seen his daughter, Octavia was two years old. Norris never saw her as a baby. By the time he accepted the command of the *London Packet* for the second Indian Ocean voyage, another infant had been conceived, a son named Albert Howes Norris, familiarly known as Alonzo. When his father arrived home on August 16, 1839, Alonzo was a walking, talking toddler of three. It was a deprivation Howes Norris felt acutely, and which played an important part in his actions later.

Because this second *London Packet* voyage had been so profitable, Captain Norris had been able to afford a two-year break, during which time a second daughter, Mary Shaw Norris, was born. His family was growing fast—and Captain Norris had celebrated, by buying Smith's Tavern. He had shut down the business and turned the building into a fine family home, a grand gesture he was able to afford only because of his luck with whaling. He also owned a sailboat and had invested in several woodlots.

The house alone cost Norris $1,500—a very expensive purchase by the standards of the era. Because of his extravagance, the nest egg was gone, and so Norris had been forced to seek another command. If he was lucky, it would work out well. Another voyage like the last *London Packet's*, and he could afford to retire. It was a stake that made the gamble of going back to sea seem worthwhile—but now, on the eve of the departure on the *Sharon*, Howes Norris had just learned that Elwina was once more with child. Again, she would be facing pregnancy and childbirth without her husband's support.

There could be worse in store than a few years of loneliness. As a native of Martha's Vineyard, Elwina was well aware of the dangers of the whaling trade. Lines kinked, and whales fought back. Dropping anchor at foreign shores involved exotic diseases. If a ship lingered too long on the whaling ground, men fell ill and died of scurvy. There was always the grim possibility that Elwina Smith Norris would never see her husband again. But even she could not have expected his end to be quite so brutal.

Two

FAIRHAVEN

ON MAY 17, 1841, frozen snow still lay on the ground in Martha's Vineyard, but the farmers were beginning to plant their corn. The wind settled, and Captain Holmes Luce's packet sloop tacked out of Holmes Hole and steered for the Woods Hole passage, Buzzard's Bay, and the Acushnet River, with Captain Howes Norris, Thomas Harlock Smith Jr., and Nathan Skiff Smith on board.

Even for seasoned whalemen, the approach to New Bedford would have been spectacular. With a population of twenty thousand, New Bedford was proclaimed to be the most prosperous city of its size in the world—prosperous on whale oil and whalebone that Massachusetts ships had harvested. The traffic was heavy in both the bay and the river, with sloops, schooners, and fishing smacks all bent on urgent trade. Palmer's Island would have come into view, then the towns of Fairhaven and New Bedford, facing each other from opposite banks of the Acushnet River. There was the smoke of industry in the blue spring sky, but the scene was dominated by whaleships — whaleships at anchor, moored to wharves, hove down in the disarray of repair, or loading or discharging cargo, or, in the distance, nestling half-built in cradles of struts.

On the New Bedford side, Union Street and Centre Street and Water Street were laid out to view in a welter of buildings and flags and chimneys. Light would have glinted off the glassed cupolas of fine shipowners' mansions in County Street, on a rise beyond the downtown streets. As Herman Melville wrote, nowhere else in America were there "more patrician-like houses, parks and gardens more opulent, than in New Bedford." On the opposite bank of the Acushnet River, Fairhaven was much less industrial, its flat skyline dominated not by candlework chimneys but by the lovely spires typical of New England churches. It was to the Fairhaven shore that the three Vineyard men focused their attention, where the whaleship *Sharon* was moored, and where the *Acushnet* had been fitted out before sailing off for the Pacific. For four weeks, in fact, the two ships had lain together. Then the *Acushnet* had sailed off with a Vineyard man in command, just as the *Sharon* would.

In some ways it was apt for Vineyarders to command Fairhaven vessels, as both the island and the port were overshadowed by more forceful neighbors. First, Nantucket — neighboring island to Martha's Vineyard — dominated the whaling trade, and then, as the average whaling vessel became too big to negotiate Nantucket's shallow, sandy harbor, New Bedford—just across the river from Fairhaven—took over. Though they certainly played their part in the colorful story of American whaling, at no stage did the island of Martha's Vineyard or the town of Fairhaven successfully compete with their much more powerful rivals.

Yet it was the Indians of Long Island—not Nantucket—who had taught the pioneers how to whale. According to contemporary accounts, the Indians set out from the beaches of the Hamptons to pursue their prey in dugout canoes, attacking passing whales with bone harpoons that were attached by thongs to "drags" made of wooden floats or inflated deerskins, and then killing them with bows and arrows. Each canoe was crewed by six men—four oarsmen, a steersman, and a harpooner—and the procedure of the chase was the same as that followed by thousands of American whalemen for the next three hundred years.

In the beginning, the European settlers had been satisfied with cutting up carcasses that drifted ashore during storms. The arrival of one of these "drift" whales heralded a village bonanza, because whale oil burned with a much cleaner, brighter flame than tallow, even if the blubber from which the oil was rendered had been rotten. Not only did the pioneers use it themselves, but it could be sold in New York for a gratifying sum. Then, as the Long Islanders noticed the yearly migrations of right whales just a few miles offshore, and learned that the Indians had a tradition of taking their canoes out after them, they took a more entrepreneurial stance. Instead of waiting for the whales to die of natural causes, they hired Indians to go out and kill them, supplying the crews with cedar boats, iron harpoons, and lances, all of which were much more efficient than the dugout canoes, bone harpoons, and bows and arrows that had been the old tools of the trade. The carcasses were towed up to the beach, where the Indians' employers waited with knives and cutting spades to flense the blubber and then boil—or "try out"—the oil in "try-pot" cauldrons that had been set up on the sand. This was known as shore whaling. As time went by, the Indians realized they were in a strong negotiating position. Not only did they become much more expensive to hire, but there were too few of them to meet the growing demand. So the settlers were forced to take a more active role, going out in the boats themselves.

This enterprise proved so successful that in 1672 James Loper of East Hampton was invited to Nantucket to teach the Nantucketers how to whale. Other shore settlements, including Edgartown in Martha's Vineyard, also followed the Long Islanders' lead. Then, in 1712, the Nantucket whaling industry suddenly overtook the rest, after a whaleboat was blown offshore in a gale, and came up with a pod of sperm whales. The headsman, Christopher Hussey, harpooned one, and then the boat outlasted the storm by taking shelter in the smooth waters at the lee of the oily carcass. Once the tempest was over the prize was towed home, to the amazement of all, and with instant enthusiasm a fleet of single-masted craft called "sloops" was assembled and sent out.

The sloops were only about thirty tons in size and were outfitted for voyages that lasted no more than about six weeks, but it was the world's first attempt at a sperm whale fishery. As the whales were hunted farther and farther out to sea, the vessels became bigger, reaching about sixty tons, some of them schooner-rigged. Indians made up part of the crews, the Nantucket shore-fishery having developed in a similar pattern to the Long Island enterprise, and Nantucketers commanded them. Then, as available men became scarce, the Nantucket owners lobbied for Vineyard mariners to make up their crews. And so men from Martha's Vineyard could be found in increasing numbers serving on Nantucket ships. Some even reached the rank of captain.

It was not until around 1738 that the Vineyard commenced its own sperm-whaling operation, and then it was a whaleman from Nantucket, Joseph Chase, who led the way, after he moved to Edgartown and took his sloop *Diamond* with him. Even then it was hard for him to stimulate much local interest. This was partly because Vineyard whalemen were already sailing on Nantucket ships, and partly because of the differing physical terrain of the two islands. While Martha's Vineyard was only marginally fertile, Nantucket was not fertile at all. Nantucketers were forced to find the whole of their living at sea. By the year 1775 Nantucket listed a fleet of 150 vessels with an average burthen of one hundred tons, while the Vineyard could claim just twelve.

Being overshadowed by a much more prominent neighbor applied to Fairhaven as well. Around 1760, when Elnathan Eldredge of Dartmouth bought a tract of land within the present town of Fairhaven, it was recorded that a shed fitted out with try-pots was part of the property. However, Fairhaven's prospects as a great whaling center were doomed as early as 1765, when the entrepreneur Joseph Rotch arrived from Nantucket with the intention of establishing a whaling business in Fairhaven but was unable to obtain suitable shore privileges. Instead he purchased ten acres on the opposite side of the river, in New Bedford, and the great whaling port was born. By the time the *Sharon* was to set sail, New Bedford owned 179 whaling vessels, while Fairhaven boasted just forty-five.

Many Fairhaven merchants, captains, and bankers were nonetheless involved in the New Bedford enterprise. They used the same harbor and employed the same builders, riggers, and shipwrights—men who had built the *Acushnet* and the *Sharon.*

Both ships had been built on the Acushnet River, in the town of Rochester, now called Mattapoisett. The *Sharon* was completed in 1837 and the *Acushnet* three years later. Identical in every detail, both were 105 feet long, 28 feet broad, and 14 feet deep, and were tubby enough to hold three thousand barrels of oil. Technically, the *Sharon* displaced 354 tons, slightly less than the *Acushnet*'s 358, an optimum size for a whaler.

Both were ship-rigged, with square yards on all three masts. Because as much deck space as possible had to be kept free for cutting up huge slabs of blubber, all the living quarters were below decks, so that the only structures above were the cook's galley (on the foredeck so that the smoke from the fire would not get into the eyes of the man at the wheel) and a framework called "the skids," sternward of the middle, or "main," mast, on top of which the spare boats were stowed. Usually whalers were flush-decked, so that there was a clear run from stem to stern, but both the *Acushnet* and the *Sharon* were double-decked, the aftermost deck a foot or so higher than the rest, providing a quarterdeck for the captain.

Two other important features distinguished whalers from ordinary sail-driven freighters. Four whaleboats hung from sturdy davits, three along the port, or larboard, side, and one at the stern quarter of the starboard side. Unlike lifeboats, they swung on the outside of the ship, so that they were ready to drop into the water the instant whales were sighted. In addition, there was a stout brickwork furnace on the after side of the front, or "fore," mast, which held two or three great iron try-pots where blubber was melted into oil. Sturdy and thick-hulled, both the *Acushnet* and the *Sharon* were instantly recognizable as whalers, admirably suited for braving the far-off deeps in search of the elusive whale.

Captain Howes Norris would have made it a priority to inspect the *Sharon* personally, going over her bit by bit, from stem to stern. Like an airline pilot today, he would have been very conscious that his life, and the safety of all those who traveled with him, depended on the structural soundness of the vehicle. However, he would also have been driven by unpleasant memories of a ship that had let him down badly in the past. And, because Thomas Harlock Smith had been one of his crew on that problem voyage, it is likely that the man who would be first mate of the *Sharon* was with him every moment of the careful examination.

While Norris's first command, of the *Leonidas*, had been both swift and lucky, his second voyage on the same ship had been cursed with constant problems, including rotten timbers. In June 1830 Norris had been forced to put into the port of Rio de Janiero for expensive repairs, including the replacement of a mast, which had played a crucial part in keeping him out a year longer than the owners of the ship had anticipated. This had led to the command of the *Leonidas* being taken away from him, a humiliation Norris would have preferred to forget.

Once satisfied that the *Sharon* was seaworthy, Norris would have given the crewmen who had arrived on board an equally careful inspection. A ship this size demanded a total of thirty men, including a carpenter, cooper, steward, and cook. Eighteen of the complement would be foremast hands—men before the mast, who were supposed to be physically powerful, strong-stomached, brave, and sharp-eyed. They were the brute muscles of the ship, trained to steer, furl, heave, and haul. They would be expected to work high in the vertiginous rigging and pull oars in the whaleboats for hours upon end. They could be ordered to attack huge whales with flimsy weapons that they would throw by hand. Even if the sea was rough and the vessel tumbling, they would have to be strong enough to flense the thick, heavy fat, chop it into fragments, boil the pieces into oil, and stow the great casks of cooled oil in the holds.

However, as Norris had found out to his cost in the past, good foremast hands were increasingly hard to find. The numbers had to be made up with greenhands—young men with dreams of adventure in their heads, who had signed up for the whaling life without a notion of what lay in store. This was a fundamental change from the way the ocean-bound ships had originally been manned. Then, the new hands had been young men who fully intended to make whaling their lifetime careers —boys from Nantucket, Martha's Vineyard, and the ports of mainland Massachusetts and Connecticut, boys who knew exactly what whaling involved. Entire crews might hail from the same village, many related by blood or marriage. This close family and village network had been both emotionally satisfying and very efficient; in fact, it was one good reason for the tremendous success of American whaling. New England had grown to dominate the business worldwide because New England villagers were prepared to devote the necessary resources to the trade. They provided the ships, the money, the whaling craft and gear, and, until the second decade of the nineteenth century, had provided all the crews, too. This had worked outstandingly well, as a greenhand who had absorbed the vernacular from early childhood—had "nursed at the maternal sea," as Melville phrased it—was never a greenhand for very long.

Back then, however, numbers had been manageable. In the year 1832, when Captain Norris, newly married to Elwina, had taken over command of the *London Packet*, the American whaling fleet had come to total more than seven hundred vessels, requiring upwards of twenty thousand men. The need was so critical that boys from most inappropriate walks of life were welcomed with open arms by the agents—a major reason the 1832 voyage of the *London Packet* had turned into a nightmare.

Norris had had trouble with the crew right from the day of departure. Thomas Harlock Smith, promoted to the rank of boatsteerer, had been one of the few loyal hands. The foremast men had been lazy and disobedient. On the rich whaling grounds of the Indian Ocean, harpooners had deliberately missed their targets, or had cut whalelines rather than risk battle with angry whales. The men had not been afraid to battle each other, however. Knives had been drawn during quarrels. Worst of all, however, had been the conflict over the provisions.

It had been another Vineyard whaling master, Captain Charles Downs, who had pointed out to Norris during a mid-sea encounter that his men were deliberately throwing their rations overboard, in order to shorten the voyage. Both the *London Packet* and Downs's ship, *Oscar*, had been out ten months, having left home on exactly the same day, and yet Norris's men had used up much more meat and bread than the crew of the *Oscar*. After the two ships parted, Norris, angry and humiliated, reduced the men's allowance — a disastrous move that had led to open mutiny. Fearing for his life, pursued by foul and abusive language, he had been forced to flee to his cabin, leaving the ship in the possession of the foremast hands. He did not regain control until the ship dropped anchor in Zanzibar, and a local warship came to the rescue.

The shameful story, however, had not followed him to the Vineyard. Norris had not publicly revealed the details of the mutiny, and Thomas Harlock Smith had kept his mouth shut; he had sailed home with a good report of 1,900 barrels of sperm oil, and so Norris had retained his reputation as a successful whaling master. It was inevitable, however, that his expression should be grim and his demeanor guarded as he inspected the men who had already taken up berths on the *Sharon*.

ON THAT CHILLY spring afternoon in 1841, only seventeen men had reported on board so far, two of them boatsteerers — harpooners, who were supposed to know how to steer a whaleboat and pitch a harpoon. As the *Sharon* was a four-boat ship, two more boatsteerers were yet to be found. Three other early arrivals were so-called idlers, or tradesmen: the carpenter, Frederick Turner, the cooper, Andrew White, and George Babcock, the eighteen-year-old steward, who had the job of housekeeping in the after cabins, where the captain and three mates would live.

The rest of those standing for Norris's inspection were foremast hands. Their living space was the forecastle, a miserable hole set in the bows directly below the foredeck, measuring about sixteen feet both ways and lined with tiers of wooden berths. The ceiling was so low that it was impossible for the average man to stand upright—not that there was very much standing room, the massive foot of the foremast taking up much of the free area at the bottom of the ladder. At sea, in this cramped and dingy space, nineteen men would sleep, gamble, sing, gossip, and read during off-duty hours. There, in bad weather, they would attack their food with their fingers and a jackknife, each man seated on his sea chest, which was set at the foot of the tier where he had his berth. Here, even breathing would be a struggle, since there was no ventilation other than the air that eddied down from the hatch. Though the *Sharon* had been lying in the river for five months, overpowering smells of rancid oil, old sweat and urine, stale food, tobacco gobs, and smoking lamps would have clung to its planks. In summer this cramped space would be a sweaty oven, while now, in the chill of early spring, it was undoubtedly and most unpleasantly dank. With twelve in residence, it would have seemed unbearably crowded, but seven more were yet to arrive.

Only two of the twelve who had already taken berths in the

forecastle were experienced seamen—twenty-year-old William Smith, who hailed from Newburyport, Massachusetts, and a twenty-three-year-old black New Yorker by the name of Samuel Leods. Neither, though, had shipped on a whaler before. Like Herman Melville, who had sailed a voyage as cabin boy before signing onto the crew list of the *Acushnet*, they were novices to whaling.

The other ten were totally new to any kind of seafaring. Only three of them came from seaside towns—Portland, Maine; Baltimore, Maryland; and Hartford, Connecticut. The rest, mostly New Yorkers, were from inland farms or city streets. Of these men, only one, an eighteen-year-old who signed up under the name of William Sweeny, left a personal record of his voyaging. However, this was not until after he had left the *Sharon*. William was one of the twelve who would later jump ship in Pohnpei in October 1842, leaving behind whatever kind of journal he might have kept, along with his other personal possessions.

The diary he kept on his next ship, the *Wilmington & Liverpool Packet*, conveys only a hint of his reasons for going on voyage. "Oh! If I had only staid at home," he wrote on April 10, 1843, "but it is too late to repent. Patience William Patience Patience," he counseled himself. "Forty months more." So it seems that William had made some enigmatic vow to give sixty-three months of his life to the sea. Perhaps he was filling in the time until he turned the magic age of twenty-four—but it is impossible to tell for sure. Running away from home might have been part of it, as he shipped under an alias. His real name—as he candidly confessed on the *Wilmington & Liver-*

pool Packet—was William Wallace Weeks. "William W. Weeks," he wrote on the flyleaf, "son of Caleb and Abigail Weeks. Born at Kensington Penn. January 17th 1823. Left the United States of America May 25th 1841 in the Whale Ship *Sharon* Norris master."

Whatever his motives, he certainly had no idea that in seventeen months' time he would be in hiding on the far-off island of Pohnpei, in company with eleven other desperate men who had managed to escape from the ship. In those days, running away to sea had a certain romance. In the public imagination every voyage was an odyssey, every ship was sailed by a crew of bold Vikings, and every cargo was worth untold riches. Nautical books of discovery and adventure were read with breathless interest by a fascinated public, and every newspaper and journal printed colorful and dramatic descriptions penned by traders, captains, and castaways.

Whaling was considered particularly adventurous. Two books written by British whaling surgeons—Thomas Beale and Frederick Debell Bennett—were best-sellers, partly because of the drama of the whale chase, and partly because it was well understood that whalers penetrated unknown corners of the ocean in search of their prey. More than four hundred islands had already been "discovered" by whaling captains, who had named them after their ships, their ships' owners, and themselves, adding to the aura of adventure that glamorized the brutal business. Popular interest in Pacific discovery was so intense that Congress had been moved to raise money for a U.S. Exploring Expedition, which was headed by Charles Wilkes and had sailed in 1838.

That so many of the whaling yarns were spun by those who had actually been there contributed to the myth, as the listener had no way of knowing that a great deal of tedium and nastiness had been edited out. Vineyarder Fred Tilton stowed away on a whaler at the age of fourteen because he had heard so many exciting anecdotes related by two older seafaring brothers, "and every time I heard of the life a whaler led and of the money to be made by whaling I longed for the day when I could go to sea." It did not take long at all to regret his credulity and his rashness, but by then it was far too late.

WHILE A GREENHAND might ship on a whaler in search of adventure, he certainly did not do it for the money. When William Wallace Weeks had first arrived on board the *Sharon*, on May 3, 1841, he had stood with six others to listen to an owners' agent read the shipping agreement—the Whalemen's Shipping Paper, familiarly called the Articles—aloud. This closely printed page commenced with the resounding phrase, "It is agreed between the Owner and Master, Seamen and Mariners of the ship *Sharon* of Fairhaven, Howes Norris Master, now bound from the Port of Fairhaven on a Sperm Whaling Voyage to the Indian & Pacific Oceans," and then plodded on through ten paragraphs of legal information, before arriving at the columns where the men's names were written, along with a fraction, which indicated a previously negotiated rate of payment.

A whaleman was not paid a wage but a "lay," which was a share of the outcome of the voyage, calculated after the ship had arrived home. First, the oil was gauged, and then it was valued, according to the prevailing market. After that, the costs of the voyage, plus the owners' half of the profits, were subtracted from the gross amount, and the remainder shared out according to the whalemen's lays.

Captain Norris, as the most important man on board, would get 1/16, meaning that the net profits from one barrel of oil in every sixteen belonged entirely to him. The first mate, Thomas Harlock Smith, would get 1/28, the second mate, Nathan Smith, 1/48, and the third mate, yet to arrive, would be allotted 1/60. The cooper, Andrew White, had already bargained for a 1/50 share, which was a better deal than anyone else's save those of the captain and first and second mates. Not only was this evidence of his shrewdness, but an indication of the high status of the cooper in a whaleship, where there was such a vital need for watertight casks. The carpenter, Frederick Turner, by contrast, was getting only a 1/175 share.

It is a testament to William Wallace Weeks's innocence that when it was his turn to sign the shipping paper, he did not question the fraction he had been allotted—1/210, the meanest lay of any of the crew. Enough whale oil to fill 210 barrels—6,615 gallons—would have to be collected before he could profit from even a drop. The other greenhands, even those who were illiterate, signing with a cross, were allotted 1/185 each, which was right at the bottom of the usual scale.

Some ignorant city boys were fooled into believing the bigger the fraction, the bigger the share, but William was a well-educated lad who should not have been so easily cheated. Perhaps he was distracted by his *own* duplicity; perhaps, just for a moment, he regretted running away from home and shipping under an alias. But then he signed the paper and presumably thought the deed was done.

With the arrival of Captain Norris, however, William found out that things were not quite so simple. He was informed that he had to go to the Customs House and apply for a Seaman's Protection Paper. This, a legal document, was, as the name implies, necessary for his own protection. It certified that he was a citizen of the United States, and ensured that if he was cast adrift, sick or penniless, on some foreign shore, he could apply to the local U.S. consul for help. In many ways it was like a modern passport, and all American seamen were supposed to carry one. The problem was that he had to produce some kind of testimony that he was, in fact, William Sweeny. Another greenhand, twenty-five-year-old Alexander Yellott of Baltimore, Maryland, went with him to the Customs House. Yellott, who had strolled on board on May 10, had presumably been ordered to get a Protection, too. Somehow William managed to convince the officer that Sweeny was his real name, because he, like Yellott, walked away with his Protection safely stamped and signed.

In the eyes of the law he was now William Sweeny, American greenhand seaman.

FIVE MORE HANDS were shipped on May 20, including a third boatsteerer—Jacob Hathaway—a cook, and three more greenhands, all from New York. Another novice from that state, John M. Bacon, was signed up the next day. It must have been a relief to Captain Norris when some experienced seamen reported for duty—John ("Jack") Baker, Thomas Williams, and

Manuel José des Reis. Baker, age eighteen, and Williams, nineteen, were both from New York, while des Reis hailed from Fayal, in the Portuguese Azores. Manuel's age is unknown, but later events indicate that he was very young, probably just a boy.

The fourth boatsteerer, twenty-one-year-old Leonard H. Wing, signed up on May 21, while Benjamin Clough, who joined the ship as third mate on the same day, was just twenty-two. It was a very young crew altogether. Apart from Norris himself, the cook, Henry Mills, was the only man over the age of thirty. Mills, who gave his birthplace as Richmond, Virginia, was the third black man of the complement. As cook, he would work closely with the eighteen-year-old steward, Babcock.

George Babcock, a young man who gave his residence as Newport, Rhode Island, and who was described in his Protection as yellow-skinned, with woolly hair and black eyes, was called "mulatto" by other members of the crew. Interestingly, the crosses made on the Articles by both Mills and Babcock (neither of whom could read or write) were witnessed by E. R. Johnson—a sign that they were fugitive slaves. Ezra Rothschild Johnson was one of a family of black activists who helped runaway slaves find refuge on the whalers of Fairhaven and New Bedford.

If Mills and Babcock were indeed fugitives, a whaling voyage could have looked very attractive to them, as whaleships offered better concealment than other vessels. While calling at American ports was dangerous, their wharves trawled by bounty hunters, whalers were bound for the Indian and Pacific Oceans, where there were no slave masters' agents, and where desertion to the wider world was an option. So men like Johnson encouraged fugitive slaves to seek berths on the whalers of Fairhaven and New Bedford and were actively assisted by the antislavery Quaker shipowners, who had quickly established a tradition of employing black runaways as crew. In fact, through the efforts of men like Ezra Johnson, it became commonplace for the jobs of cook and steward to be reserved for men of color —just as on the whaleship *Sharon* in 1841.

As far as Captain Norris was concerned, though, the important factor was that with the cook in the galley and the steward in the cabin, the crew list was complete—except, boatsteerer Jacob Hathaway failed to turn up. There is no record why he did not report on board. Perhaps, like Melville's Ishmael, he had heard mumbled warnings—"ambiguous, half-hinting, half-revealing, shrouded sort of talk"—from someone who had sailed with the captain on the *London Packet*. Or it could have been an overpowering hunch that this voyage was going to go disastrously wrong.

Whatever the answer to the mystery, Hathaway's absence was an unwelcome snag for Captain Norris. A replacement was not found until May 24, the day before sailing, and then it was yet another teenager, eighteen-year-old Nathaniel Shearman of Bridgeport, Connecticut. A young man who did not take very long at all to regret filling Hathaway's place.

THREE

INTO THE ATLANTIC OCEAN

PRECISELY AT NOON on Tuesday, May 25, 1841, Captain Howes Norris seated himself at his big chart desk and took out a ledger with pale blue, unlined pages and stiff marbled covers. After squaring the book on the blotter in front of him, he placed a sheet of paper that he had ruled with black lines behind the second right-hand page, to serve as a guide that would keep his small, neat script as straight as it would have been in an exercise book at school. Heading the page, "The *Sharon* of Fair Haven on a Whaleing Voyage," he wrote the date in the margin, followed by his first entry: "Fresh breezes from S.W. all these 24 hours at 6 A.M. took our anchor and worked out the river & Bay in company with ship *Mercury*."And, with that, he closed the book, without bothering to describe the chaos and commotion of weighing anchor and setting sail.

Norris was in the transom or "after" cabin, the sternmost room in the ship; the desk was set against the forward partition that divided this cabin from the next. On the wall in front of him hung a barometer and a thermometer, and above his head, in the caged skylight set into the deck, was the compass in its binnacle box. In this cabin, too, the ship's cutlasses and muskets were stored. Behind him a row of salt-smeared windows in the square stern threw more light over a massive settee that was built into the transom, with a wide shelf above and behind it. As this cabin measured just fourteen feet across by six deep, the large desk and big settee left very little floor space to spare, but nonetheless the tiny room was a cherished prerogative of the captain. No one could enter without knocking first and then getting an invitation, which meant that Captain Norris was the only man on the ship with a sitting room to himself.

However, this did not mean that he was insulated from the rest; there was very little privacy on a whaler. Now, echoing through the skylight overhead, he would have been able to hear Benjamin Clough and Nathan Smith hassling the crew into some kind of order. He would have known, too, that on the *Mercury*, which was sailing in company down the Acushnet River, there would be the same queer mixture of ferocity, frustration, and despair in the officers' voices. Captain Dennis Fordyce Haskell of the *Mercury* had a preponderance of greenhands in the forecastle, just as Norris did, and a crew that was as much an unknown quantity as his own.

On the *Mercury*, a greenhand, twenty-year-old Stephen Curtis of Boston, described exactly the kind of day that William Weeks and the other novices on the *Sharon* were experiencing. "On the morning of the 25th," he wrote, "we were roused from our slumbers by a stentorian voice at the gangway of the fore-castle, *All hands!*" Though it was the first time he had heard the preemptory summons, the meaning was obvious enough to set him scuttling obediently up to deck. And there, without even a pause for breakfast, Curtis and his shipmates were set to "*loosing* the sails, and weighing anchor."

Neither of these jobs was easy. The first involved clambering up the tall masts and sidling along ropes that were slung beneath the yards to release furled canvas, while at the same time men on the deck hauled at lines and braces to secure the corners of the sails and spread them out. "Weighing anchor" involved heaving at the windlass, a huge horizontal spindle in the bows that was turned with wooden handspikes. These spikes were thrust into slots and yanked down rhythmically by eight men who worked in pairs.

Not only was it backbreaking labor, but it required coordination. And, while raw novices could manage the first, the second was quite beyond them. On the *Mercury*, only "five were able to perform ordinary seaman's duty, the remaining being *greenhands* not understanding the use of one rope from another, entirely unskilled in nautical affairs of any description," Stephen Curtis noted wryly, and left the rest to his reader's imagination.

On both ships, heaving the anchor had been interrupted by the arrival of a sloop alongside. This was the pilot boat, with the captains of both ships on board, as well as two pilots. Captain

Haskell of the *Mercury*, like Captain Norris, was returning from the Customs House, where he had been clearing up the last of the paperwork. One pilot boarded the *Sharon* while the other went onto the *Mercury*, their job to get the ships safely out to the verge of the open sea. Then both would return to the wharf in the pilot boat, which would follow them out of the river.

"After taking them on board, we again *manned* the windlass," wrote Curtis. The ship was slowly "walked" up to the anchor as chain was wound in, inch by inch, until the lookout posted in the bows who was peering down into the muddy water was able to shout, "Anchor's a-peak!"—which meant that the bow was right above the anchor, and the last of the chain was straight up and down. All that was necessary then was to set the sails so that the ship surged forward, plucking up the anchor as she went— though in the case of the *Mercury* even this was not easy, as "the anchor somewhat reluctantly loosed its hold from Yankee bottom," as Curtis commented. But at last the hook was up, dripping rust and mud. The yards and sails were braced, and off the two ships glided, down the river and into Buzzard's Bay.

IN THE SMALL CABIN that he shared with Nathan Smith, the third mate, Benjamin Clough, used his first free moments to rummage a ledger of his own from his sea chest. While it was not legally required for him to keep a logbook of the voyage, Clough, an ambitious young man with his eye on a brilliant whaling career, intended to keep one as a testimonial to his keenness. Because he was writing on his knee, his book was not as tidy as Captain Norris's, but his entry was just as professional. "At Sunrise this morning took our Anchor and commenced to beat out of the harbour," he wrote. "About 2 PM discharged our pilot."

Twenty-two-year old Clough was remarkably well seasoned for his age. Born on March 19, 1819, in the rural town of Monmouth, Maine, he had known what he wanted very early. In September 1835, at the age of sixteen, he had joined the crew of the *Jasper* of Fairhaven by convincing Captain Stephen Raymond that he was three years older than that. Being solidly built and tall for his age at five feet, eight inches would have helped. On the other hand, Ben Clough was a handsome lad, with a direct gaze, level eyebrows, thick brown hair, and a dimple in one cheek, which should have counted against him in the rough and tumble of the forecastle. However, he had proved hardy and determined enough to survive.

The *Jasper* headed for Cloudy Bay in New Zealand, where whalemen battled each other with fists and weapons for the best places to get at the whales—"coming Cloudy Bay fashion" was an eloquent slang phrase of the time. Once the anchor had been dropped in a chosen inlet of the sparsely inhabited, thickly forested bay, the ship was securely moored, and the sails and yards were taken down, turning the deck into a factory platform. Then, at four each morning, the boats were manned. Instead of the whaleship doing the hunting, as happened in the open ocean, whaleboats were sent out to find the quarry.

As a method of whaling, it was much closer to the shore whaling that the early settlers of Long Island had known than it was to the deep-sea whaling that Nantucketers had pioneered. The boats headed out to the entrance of the bay, where they jockeyed with the other boats for the best position to lie in wait for the "cows" — female right whales — that were migrating into the bay to give birth. Once a capture was made, the boat's crew towed it back to the ship to be flensed. Not only did the gigantic size and weight — generally about eighty tons, but often more — of the carcass mean a long, hard haul, but the weather was usually shocking. It was the southern winter, and the climate of Cloudy Bay was notorious.

Seventeen ships lay in Cloudy Bay that season, each one sending out four boats. Shore parties sent out many more, so that the slaughter was immense. The skies were stained with sooty smoke from the tryworks furnaces, and the stench of burning fat and rotting flesh was appalling. Once flensed, the huge carcasses were set adrift, to be pulled apart by dogs, wild pigs, and scavenger birds as they bobbed about in the ebbing and rising tides. On the beaches, huge bones piled up in ghastly cairns.

It was a revolting life as well as a rough one, but young Ben Clough stayed undiscouraged, signing onto the crew of the *Friendship* less than two months after getting home. This ship steered for New Zealand, too — to Otago in the far south, where it was even colder, and the whaling equally arduous. Still, young Clough was determined to make whaling his profession. No sooner was he home in 1839 than he shipped out again, this time as a boatsteerer on the *Rajah* of New Bedford — headed, coincidentally, to the same Pacific seas that the *Sharon* was bound for now.

The berth on the *Rajah* had not suited him at all though. There had been arguments over the rations, and after less than eight months, tired of being starved, Clough had run away from the ship. To get back to New England, he had been forced to sign onto the crew of the *General Pike* as an ordinary foremast hand. Being offered the job of third mate on the *Sharon* had been a marvelous stroke of luck; he must have been very relieved that Captain West of the *Rajah* had not got home in time to put a word to the wise in Captain Norris's ear.

This time, he was determined to do well. The position of third mate was a big step up the ladder to a future command of his own. If he came back with a favorable report, he could hope for the job of second mate—or even first officer—in his next ship. Keeping a formal logbook would improve his chances even further, he would have reasoned, because he would be able to produce it as evidence of his aptitude and enthusiasm.

As he penned his carefully formal entry on that day of departure, Benjamin Clough did not have an inkling of the ghastly secrets he was fated to record in that book.

At six in the afternoon the *Sharon* was off Cuttyhunk, the last of the Elizabeth Islands, a string of low-lying islets that stretched out from the elbow of Cape Cod. Every outgoing captain used Cuttyhunk as his point of departure, despite the fact that it was so remarkably inconsequential in appearance, a sand heap scarcely scooped out of the waves. Against this backdrop of gray sand and gray ocean, the *Mercury* was setting the last of her square sails in a series of uncertain jerks. Like the *Sharon*, she was on the verge of entering the open sea.

"The greater part of the first day of our departure was spent in stowing away the cables, lashing the anchors, securing loose spars, clearing decks &c.," wrote Stephen Curtis, "after which all hands were summoned aft for the purpose of dividing them into two watches, the starboard and larboard, the former commanded by the second mate, the latter by the chief mate."

On the *Sharon*, too, the foremast hands were being divided into two groups, eight of them in the starboard watch and eight in the port, or larboard, watch. This was because the twenty-four hours of each day were split into six four-hour periods, taken by each watch in turn. When one watch was on deck, the other was below, except for "dog-watch" in the early evening, when all hands were on deck. Sleeping was allowed only in the watch below—if sleeping was possible, with the noises of the ship and the sea, and the shouting of the watch on deck, the whining of the cooper's grindstone, the clatter and crunch as the cook chopped wood for the galley, and regular screams, as livestock were sacrificed for the cabin dinner. For greenhand William Weeks, eight hours' uninterrupted sleep would be a dim memory until his voyaging was over.

After that, the captain and three officers took turns choosing oarsmen for the four whaleboats, each of which had a total crew of six. The headsman was the officer in charge of the boat, and the second in command was the boatsteerer. Four foremast hands were assigned as oarsmen for each boat, so that sixteen in all left the ship. The remaining three would stay on board to help the cooper and carpenter, steering and trimming the sails while the boats were off in the chase.

That done, all hands were called to attention to listen the captain's first speech, traditionally a diatribe about obedience, fighting, cursing, and food. No one recorded the words of Captain Norris's address to the crew of the *Sharon*. On the *Mercury*, Captain Haskell "delivered a speech which in point of eloquence stands unrivalled in the annals of the world," Stephen Curtis wrote dryly.

> Now men! You are bound on a long voyage, and you must have no quarrelling and striking each other. If there is any striking to be done, I am the one to do it. When you are called to do anything, come as soon as you are called. I want to see no hanging back, no sogering, no waiting for one and another. And as long as you behave yourselves like *men* you will get treated as such, but if you don't (*assuming a sort of theatrical frown, and shaking his fist at us*) by *God* you will smell trouble; now you can go forward.

The tirade had the required effect, Stephen recording that he and the other foremast hands "scampered forward as fast as our legs would carry us, not caring for a smell of the cloven-footed gentleman's trouble." It was not to be the last time that he likened Captain Haskell to the devil, or that Haskell accused the men of being "sogers," meaning as lazy and undisciplined as soldiers were reputed to be.

Discipline. The safety of the ship depended on it, or so Captain Howes Norris would have reminded his crew. Orders were to be obeyed at once, with no questions asked. Unless ordered to go aft—to work the sails on the mizzen mast, for instance, or take a turn at steering the ship—the foremast men had to stay forward of the waist. For them, the after part of the ship was out of bounds unless they were specifically instructed to come. Then, if they were ordered to the quarter deck, they had to walk on the lee side, or the larboard side if the ship was before the wind.

After that, Captain Norris would have described what they could expect in the way of food—and perhaps his men would have noticed the tense, angry way he emphasized what he said. He would have assured them that the *Sharon*, like most American whalers, was well provisioned with salted meat, dried peas and beans, flour, and ship's biscuit. There would be nothing for the crew to grumble about, and so he did not expect to hear complaints. The crew could rely on three meals a day—breakfast at six, dinner at noon, and supper at six—which would arrive from the galley in a large wooden trencher called a kid, to be dished out by the men themselves.

The tin plate from which each man ate was his own property, as was the tin mug—"pot"—which he held out to the cook for his share of tea or coffee. If he did not own a plate and a pot when he came on board, then they were supplied from the ship's store, called the "slop chest," and charged against his account. Few men had forks. Instead, they managed with a jackknife and their fingers. Coffee was traditionally served with the breakfast ration of biscuit and meat, while tea would be ladled out with the baked or boiled midday dinner. Tea also accompanied supper, which would be either a concoction of leftovers or a repetition of the breakfast provender.

And anyone found throwing food overboard would be punished severely. With that sharp warning about the penalty for wasting provisions, the men would have been dismissed. Those on watch were sent to their duty, while those off duty would have a four-hour watch below, when they could relax in the forecastle, unless summoned on deck by some emergency.

It was the first taste of a routine that was marked by bells, and which would rule their lives every day they were at sea—

a psychological entry into an entirely new world. As Stephen Curtis phrased it, he and his fellow greenhands "were leaving a home with all its quiet enjoyments, and beloved scenes for the wild and daring life of a sailor" — a huge adjustment to make.

Old habits had to be forgotten and new skills learned. Captains and officers, even if they were contemptible, must be obeyed without question, and the most corrupt and ignorant forecastle mates must be regarded as equals. Every intelligent greenhand understood instinctively that the experience ahead was going to change him forever, that even after the voyage was over he would never be quite the same person again.

NEITHER CAPTAIN NORRIS nor Captain Haskell was in a hurry to leave the North Atlantic, simply because seafaring was such a new experience for so many of the hands on board. This was the time for working up the crew into a state of discipline and practicing "the different evolutions required while in pursuit of, and when fast to, a whale," as Stephen Curtis phrased it. Over weeks of intensive tuition, novices were relentlessly turned into what whaling officers called "fishy men," who would respond to orders as naturally as the *Pequod* hands did to Captain Ahab's catechism:

"What do ye do when ye see a whale, men?"
"Sing out for him!" . . .
"And what do ye next, men?"
"Lower away, and after him!"
"And what tune is it ye pull to, men?"
"A dead whale, or a stove boat!"

The sooner they lowered boats for sperm whales the better, experience being the best teacher, and this is exactly what Norris and Haskell were hoping for. If sperm whales did not present themselves for the slaughter, blackfish—a small toothed species like miniature sperm whales, more properly known as pilot whales—would do. "Saw Blackfish," wrote Captain Norris in his entry for May 29, just four days after leaving Fairhaven.

The lookout place was a small platform at the top of the topmast, in the topgallant crosstrees. There, a double iron hoop was secured at the height of the average man's waist, to stop him from pitching overboard. It looked like a giant pair of spectacles. A greenhand perched inside one half, and a boatsteerer stood in the other, so he could point out to the lad what a spout looked like. And with the sight of blackfish, for the first time William Weeks would have heard the traditional cry, "She blows!"

This would have led to much commotion about decks, as confused and overexcited greenhands were harried into fetching whaling craft and gear, and then assembling in proper order by the davits where their boats were dangling. With the order to lower away, the davit falls were released, letting the boats down with a rattle. An officer and a boatsteerer went down in each one, handling the ropes so that the boats landed evenly. Once the light, graceful craft were settled in the water, the other men jumped down the side of the ship, to be hassled into their proper places, where they would take up the heavy oars, which could be as much as twenty feet long.

Greenhands were naturally clumsy and would have been

particularly so just days out from port. To an experienced whaleman like Benjamin Clough, it must have seemed a miracle that this unhandy bunch managed to harpoon and kill two blackfish—but somehow they did, and "took them to the ship and hoisted them in—saw many more, but wild," wrote Norris, meaning that the whales were too jumpy and skittish to track down and harpoon.

Being only about fifteen feet long and weighing less than three tons, and therefore small enough to be hoisted up with the windlass and butchered on deck, these two blackfish would have produced very little oil—just two barrels altogether, as Clough recorded. However, it would have given the greenhands a chance to learn a fraction of the flensing business. Then, once the stripped carcasses were thrown overboard, the *Sharon* set to searching again—"cruising for Whales under easy sail," wrote Clough on June 2—but the result was nil. "Ground dull, no sperm whales," wrote Norris two days later.

Day followed day with the same monotonous report. "No sperm whales," Norris wrote on June 18. By the end of the month they were off the Azores, so he was able to check his chronometer and found—no doubt to his relief, as an accurate instrument was necessary for calculating longitude—that the shipboard clock was correct. It was also a chance to take on a stock of fresh provisions. The farmers of the fertile Azores—called the Western Islands by the whalemen—made a good living by supplying the fleet with fruit and vegetables. A boat was sent into the main settlement of Fayal to collect potatoes, onions, cabbages, and pumpkins. Then, after loading these, the ship made sail again.

Next day, however, Clough went on to record that "the Captain discovered that his Pocket had been Picked of his Wallet." Back to the island they tacked, "and the Captain went on shore found the Man that stole his Pocket Book but could not get it." Determined to regain his property, Norris reported the theft to the U.S. consul, who agreed to set a signal if the wallet was recovered. Then Norris returned to the ship, and everyone waited to see what would happen.

Keeping close to the island involved standing off and on, an irritating maneuver in which the ship sailed back and forth on short tacks to keep more or less in the same position. At last, however, the agreed signal was seen fluttering in the air, and a boat was sent on shore to recover the contents of the pilfered wallet, "finding them stowed under the Consuls gate." Three days had been wasted, though—a delay that Captain Norris did not want to be publicly known, it seems, as he made no mention of the loss in his logbook. Instead, he simply noted, "working out from Fayal having been in and sent the Boat onshore for some things"—an early indication that he was secretive and self-protective by nature.

Another American whaler, *Gratitude*, was also at the Azores. On board was a seaman, Joseph Eayres, who in future months was to become very curious about the situation on board the *Sharon*. "The ship *Sharon* of Fairhaven is near lying off and on," he noted, but knew nothing more to add at the time, since there was no communication between the two ships.

Four days later Norris set a course for the Cape de Verdes Islands and the equator. There were still no whales to be seen, but his logbook reveals that he was pleased to find that the

Sharon had a good turn of speed. "The ship has gone at the rate of 8 miles an hour for the past 5 days," he penned on July 17, three days before pausing at the island of Brava for fresh meat. It was impossible to buy any hogs, so he gave up on the Cape Verdes Islands, too, and after this most inauspicious start, squared yards and set all sail for the Cape of Good Hope.

It had already become plain to all on board the *Sharon* that their captain was a natural-born competitor, a man who liked to keep every inch of canvas flying. On July 28, just as the sun was setting, Norris noted that they had come up with a ship with all her sails set. At once, he ordered the *Sharon* put on the same course, to see how easily they could overhaul her. At noon the next day the other vessel was lagging eight miles astern. "That is the way to beat them," he wrote with rare satisfaction, and from then on "Carried all sail" appears in entry after entry.

The problem was that a hard-driven ship meant frayed ropes and torn canvas. Day after day, the men were kept setting up and fixing rigging. This for Norris was a constant aggravation, as squalls and constant repairs slowed down their headlong flight. "Wet, rainy, uncomfortable, disagreeable and lonesome weather," he griped. Sperm whales were raised on August 17, when they "lowered and chased them untill sunset." But the whales, like the blackfish earlier, were too wary and fast for their pursuers to catch up with them. On September 10, off the Cape of Good Hope, more blackfish were raised and two more taken, but it was a paltry celebration of their entry into the Indian Ocean.

Meantime the *Mercury*, which had taken the opposite route

toward the Pacific, following in the wake of the *Acushnet,* was making hard work of getting around Cape Horn, "which place is the dread of every mariner," as Stephen Curtis observed. "Here we were beating about, with contrary gales, the weather intensely cold, with terrible squalls of wind, hail, and snow."

All was not awful, however. The seascape could be breathtaking. "No words can exaggerate, or imagination enhance the beauty of the surrounding scenery as the sun slowly sank in the west," Curtis rhapsodized once. At the horizon the sky was "tinged with rich vermillion, blended with a deep orange yellow, and at last as the fiery orb disappeared, seemed burning with deep, fiery crimson." And then there was the camaraderie of the forecastle, when on calm evenings "the foremast hands gather upon the *sailors' sofa* (windlass)," and "spin yarns" and "sing ballads." It was just so on the *Acushnet*: Melville's shipmate Toby Greene remembered "the many pleasant moonlight watches we passed together on the deck of the *Acushnet* as we whiled away the hours with yarn and song."

There was also the whalemen's traditional social pursuit—the gam. Originally a Nantucket word which meant a group of whales, *gam* became applied to a group of whaleships that had gathered together to exchange gossip and news. It was a legacy from the time when all the crews hailed from the whaling villages of New England, and relatives and neighbors could be expected to be found on the other ships.

First, the two ships signaled each other with flags. The downwind ship would heave to, bracing about her yards so that the sails pulled against each other and the vessel lay relatively still. Then the upwind ship sailed past the stilled ship's stern, while the captains roared out greetings. One would invite the other to come on board with his boat's crew, and so commenced the gam. It might last hours, or it might last days, with boats in constant motion between the two ships and the two sets of foremast hands entertaining each other "in relating their grievances, spinning yarns, singing sea songs and ballads," as Stephen Curtis described.

Despite the "grievances," it was bound to be fun. It was a time when books, papers, and keepsakes were exchanged; it was during a gam that Melville was given the published account of the sinking of the *Essex* by a whale. But to have a gam—as Melville pointed out—it was necessary for the captain to be sociable. Which his fictional Captain Ahab was not—"he cared not to consort, even for five minutes, with any stranger captain."

And Norris was another Ahab. While the *Sharon* was spoken by other ships—the *Clifford Wayne* of Fairhaven on July 2, and the *Elizabeth* of New Bedford and the *Heroine* of Fairhaven on July Fourth, for instance—Captain Norris never issued an invitation to come on board, or visited another ship himself.

FOUR

TOWARD THE PACIFIC

WHILE THE MERCURY was beating slowly about Cape
Horn, the *Sharon* was storming her way through the Indian
Ocean, still under imprudent canvas. Like Melville's *Pequod*,
the *Sharon* "day after day tore on through all the swift madness
and gladness of the demoniac waves." As the third mate, Benjamin Clough, noted, "We shaped our course for St. Paul's Island where we arrived making a quick passage." It was the
twenty-fourth. The *Sharon* had traveled from the longitude of
the Cape of Good Hope to the remote island of St. Paul's in
just thirteen days.

St. Paul's is a lonely outpost on the last leg to the western
coast of Australia, called New Holland then. While uninhabited, it was a favorite provisioning place for whaleships, because

the fish and crayfish were so plentiful. "We stopped here a few hours and I went ashore in the boat," wrote Clough in a letter to his father, Asa Clough, and went on to describe a desolate, rocky little island that was once the crater of a volcano, where nothing but rough grass grew. The men amused themselves by catching fish and cooking them in one of the boiling springs on the beach. Then they rowed back to the ship, passing through a great pod of right whales as they went. "Saw many Right Whales laying just outside the Surf," Captain Norris recorded.

These whales belonged to the same species that Benjamin Clough had hunted when he was in Cloudy Bay, New Zealand, as a member of the crew of the *Jasper*. Norris, however, did not see this as an opportunity to fill up his oil casks. Instead of the valuable spermaceti that was used to make the most expensive candles, the huge right whale heads contained baleen, useful for making corset stays and buggy whips, but not nearly as marketable as the waxy stuff from sperm whale heads. And, while right whale blubber would render into oil just like sperm whale blubber, the oil from right whales was worth less than half the price of sperm. Only the most desperate sperm whaler captain would fill his barrels with right whale oil. If he did, the unkind fates would be bound to send shoals of sperm whales just when there was no room for more—and it was far too early in the voyage for Captain Norris to take that risk. Instead, he kept his course for the Timor Straits, and the sperm whaling grounds of the Pacific.

On October 1, it looked for a little while as if the ship's luck would change, the dandelion-like spouts of sperm whales being glimpsed in silhouette against the lowering sun. "At 5 PM raised Sperm Whales and lowered 4 Boats for them," wrote Clough. However, Norris's logbook recorded another disappointment: when one of the boatsteerers managed to plant his harpoon in a great glistening flank, he did it so feebly that it drew out with the first hard tug, and then, after managing to row alongside another whale, the harpooner somehow missed his huge target.

The one who missed was Nathaniel Shearman, the man who had been shipped in a hurry because Hathaway had not turned up. Since the boat was headed by Captain Norris himself, Shearman would have kept a low profile as he clambered back on board the ship after the fruitless, frustrating chase. Night was coming on, so the *Sharon* resumed her course to the East Indies.

TWO DAYS LATER, the cooper, Andrew White, went to the sea chest that was stowed beneath his wooden bunk in the steerage quarters and rummaged out a book of his own. He had packed it to use as a journal but had so far neglected to write. Then he laboriously penned his first entry, which was a simple notation of the weather, and shut the book with no explanation for the late start. He gave no reason for keeping a diary, either. Indeed, he seems an unlikely man to be the author of one of the most revealing accounts of the fateful events on the *Sharon*. Only semiliterate, White had no idea of punctuation and spelled words the way he heard them. Probably he had gotten into the habit of writing a daily record during his apprenticeship as a barrelmaker, when he would have been taught to keep an artisan's daybook, a brief accounting of jobs done and payment received.

White's journal reveals him to be a fiercely independent character who got away with his bravado because he was physically impressive. A native of Tiverton, Rhode Island, the twenty-six-year-old was five feet, seven inches tall, brown-haired, and fair-skinned. Because of his occupation, his strongly muscled lower arms would have been deeply tanned; his face would have been reddened and weather-beaten with a life spent mainly outdoors. Andrew White had worked on the family farm until he was seventeen, when he had left home to learn his trade. Then, at the age of twenty-two, he had gone to sea, taking out his Protection in July 1837.

Being physically strong—he once lifted a 135-pound anvil with a rope gripped in his teeth—he managed the rough existence of a seaman well. However, in the census he always described himself as a farmer. Like many hundreds of the sons of rural New England, Andrew White was filling in his time at sea until he could inherit the family farm. At the end of his first voyage, he had married a local girl, Louisa Tripp. The union, which took place on September 17, 1839, was swiftly blessed with a son, named Charles, but, because his father was still capable of managing the property, Andrew White was forced to ship out again, despite his new status as a family man. And so October 1841 found him on board of the *Sharon*, taking out his book and commencing it at last, with no idea that he was on the brink of describing events that were a great deal more momentous than details of wind, work, and weather.

On October 26, however, he simply noted that the ship was "steering on the wind" to the East Indies island of Timor, where he would be kept busy setting up barrels and supervising the collection of fresh water at the local stream. And at six that evening the *Sharon* arrived at Kupang, dropping her anchor for the first time since leaving Fairhaven.

According to a description penned by an observer of the time, Kupang—also known as Fort Concordia—was a fine sight from a distance. The buildings that fronted the anchorage were faced with white stucco, which showed up boldly against the lush tropical vegetation. Lofty trees shaded the streets, and brilliantly colored birds flickered through the hot, humid air. The shops, which were owned and run by Chinese, were embellished with fancy giltwork and silken banners, while the substantial stone houses of the Dutch administrators were lavishly lit with oil lamps at night.

Going on shore, however, was a disillusioning experience. The local natives lived in a shantytown of thatched huts that was not picturesque at all. The Chinese shopkeepers stocked little to tempt an American sailor to dig into his pockets, specializing in ingredients for the local vice of betel-nut chewing instead. "A few Dutch here, and a thing by the name of Fort, but not much more," wrote Benjamin Clough in a letter home to his father. "Some Chinese and the rest Malays. The Chinese have a Temple here and the Malays a Mosque, which are of not much account."

Despite his dismissive opinion of the place, being here in Timor would have given Clough much food for thought. First, he must have felt surprised that Captain Norris had chosen to come straight to this poor anchorage instead of cruising for whales in the equatorial Indian Ocean, where he could have bargained for provisions and fresh water at familiar ports like Johanna.

Clough would have known that Norris had taken the *London Packet* to the Indian Ocean on his last two voyages and had done well there, so the captain's decision must have puzzled him. When he had signed the crewlist of the *Sharon*, he must have noticed that Norris's instructions were to take the *Sharon* "on a Sperm Whaling Voyage to the Indian & Pacific Oceans" —yet Norris had made no attempt to deviate from his headlong course to the Timor Straits. It was as if he had deliberately avoided returning to the ocean that he knew so well.

That was intriguing enough. More thought-provoking was that these were the waters where Ben Clough had blotted his copybook by running away from the *Rajah* just eighteen months before and had had the incriminating word *deserter* noted by his name in the ship's logbook.

It was probably typical of Benjamin Clough that it should have been one of the best-organized desertions on record. While the *Rajah* had cruised off the beautiful island of Bali in the company of the *General Pike*, Clough, accompanied by the third mate, a fellow boatsteerer, the ship's cooper, and the cook, plus two daring foremast hands, had stealthily lowered the waist boat, which they had already stocked with sails, kegs of provisions and water, oars, a compass, a telescope, and a whaling lance. The seven runaways even had their personal possessions, in Clough's case including his journal.

Once safely down in the water, they had rowed off into the night without raising the alarm. When the sun rose the ship was well out of sight, so they set a sail, "and had every prospect of A pleasant passage." Their plan was to get to Java. Then all at once they realized that they were being pursued by seven of the large local craft called *perahu*.

It was a horrible shock. These spectacular, vicious-looking vessels were propelled by lateen sails and banks of oars, their fighting platforms packed with native warriors. Clough, the first of the runaways to gather his wits, grabbed the steering oar. While the rest frantically pulled at the oars, he aimed the boat at a nearby beach.

No sooner had the hull hit sand than all seven jumped out and dashed headlong for the trees, hotly pursued by "Hundreds of half Naked Malay Pirates." Clough was soon separated from the rest. Doubling back in the undergrowth, he hid behind a rock until the stampede had passed. Then, summoning all his courage, he ventured back to the beached boat, having re-membered that a "large brass Horse Pistol" was hidden on board. After locating and loading the pistol, he glimpsed two of the pirates heading in his direction, "with the intention of mak-ing me a prisoner." Without hesitation, Clough shot one dead, threw the heavy pistol at the other's head, and sprinted for the trees.

And there his account finishes. The rest of the book is filled with meaningless scribbles, mostly in another hand. It is as if young Clough deliberately left his reader in suspense; it is like reading the first episode of a serial. Furthermore, it seems evi-dent that he enjoyed picturing himself as the boy-hero of dash-ing adventures.

Despite the highly colored tone, it seems that the details of the mass desertion are true. The ship's logbook confirms that seven men stole a boat and ran away that night, and lists the ar-ticles they stole. It also supplies a motive for running away: The previous December all hands went aft to lodge a formal complaint that they had not "a Nuff to eat," but received no satisfaction, Captain West simply informing them that on the contrary "they had a Nuff." The *General Pike* was at Bali at the time, and Benjamin Clough arrived home as one of her crew. Presumably he, with some or all of his companions, managed to launch the boat, elude the warriors, and get to the safety of the other American ship.

NONE OF THE *Sharon* hands tried to run away from the ship while at anchor in Kupang. They certainly had the chance, each watch being given "liberty"—or a day's holiday— while they were there, but all of them returned obediently to the ship at dusk. Clough himself certainly had no intention of leaving the ship. Being here would have reminded him how extraordinarily lucky he had been to land the job of third mate of the *Sharon*. It would have reinforced his determination to do well on this voyage and repair his image after his lapse on the *Rajah*.

Meanwhile, the water casks were being filled under Andrew White's supervision, and Captain Norris was trying to negotiate with the locals for fresh fruit and vegetables. Both tasks were frustrating ones. While there was a fine stream of fresh water to the east of the town, it was very difficult to tow the filled barrels, which were lashed together to form a raft, through the heavy surf. Many were damaged on the way by bashing on the rocks, and Andrew White had to carry out instant repairs on the beach.

Norris had his own problems. The Dutch administrators were hostile to Americans, and probably because of this he was only able to procure a couple of pigs and three paltry bushels of yams. Finally, on Saturday, October 30, 1841, he issued the order for the anchor to be raised.

And the most nerve-wracking leg of the passage to the Pacific began.

For a greenhand like William Weeks, this leg of the voyage would have been marked with glorious moments, especially when he was on masthead lookout. No one could help but marvel at the eerie sense of privilege and power that being a hundred feet above the swaying sea bestowed, and here the tropical water would have been translucent, a rich indigo in the depths, taking on the colors of a peacock's tail where it shallowed. All about the ship forested peaks and vividly white, palm-fringed beaches marked the shoreline, and ineffable fragrances of cloves and nutmegs wafted about the star-clung rigging at night.

For the captain of a sail-driven ship, however, negotiating the tortuous route from Timor to the Pacific could be a nightmare —and particularly so for an impatient one. Charts were unreliable, because the depths kept on changing as silt washed into the sea. Everywhere there were high peaks that stole the wind, and in the narrow seas between the islands, strong, capricious currents dragged the ship toward rocks and reefs. "Sum of it is inhabited by savages," Andrew White observed as the *Sharon* beat slowly along the northwest coast of Timor. Many of these "savages" were reputed to be cannibals, while it was a well-known fact—as Ben Clough could have reminded them—that the local fishermen augmented their living with piracy.

It took five days of nail-biting navigation to cover three degrees of latitude. Finally, on Thursday, November 4, Norris was able to write, "At 1 P.M. took a light breeze from N.E. and for the first time since we passed the N.W. Cape of New Holland took a fair current." For a little while it looked as if they could celebrate by capturing more blackfish. The boats were lowered, but they came back with nothing—"found them very wild, could not strike."

It was yet another disappointment. There were whales of a kind—"Saw a humpback," Andrew White wrote several times —but they were not the sort that Norris wanted. Only sperm whales would do. With the help of a favorable current the *Sharon* passed into the Banda Sea, so that only the Gilolo Passage, to the eastward of the sprawling island of Halmahera, was yet to be negotiated before they plunged into the open Pacific. A major obstacle had been conquered, but still the sea seemed barren of prey.

Then, on November 12, almost six months after leaving Fairhaven, the lookouts on the *Sharon* finally spied the jets of sperm whales for the second time.

IT WAS FOUR in the afternoon, the drowsy time of day. With all those false sightings, it was little wonder if the cry "She blows" from the masthead of the *Sharon* was uncertain. Captain Norris would have been quicker on the uptake, crying, "Clear away the boats! Luff!" But it would not have been surprising, either, if some men worked clumsily as the boats were swung out and lowered. It was quite an art to scramble down the side of a rolling ship and jump into a boat that was dancing up and down on the waves.

Traditionally, the officer in charge of each boat stood in the stern, gripping the great twenty-foot steering oar, the only man who faced forward. He would have exhorted his oarsmen to pull harder, harder, toward a quarry they could not see, because they had their backs to the breaching whales. They were not allowed to turn their heads, because the sight of the massive prey was so terrifying that novices might freeze into immobility or even jump overboard in panic. Instead, the boat's crew rowed blindly, the only hint that they had reached their target being the sound of water washing thunderously down gigantic sides and the rhythmic suck and gasp of spouts.

This was the climax of the chase, when the boatsteerer, who had been working the oar at the bow of the boat, was ordered to drop his oar and "stand and face," while the four other oarsmen sculled to keep the boat steady. Up until the instant that order was given, he had been setting the pace for the rest of the crew. Now, without a chance to recover from what could be hours of frantic rowing, he was supposed to drop his oar, stand up, turn to face the whale, grab his heavy harpoon, and pitch it so hard into the gargantuan gleaming side that it would stick fast during the following struggle.

Three of the *Sharon* boats reached the whales, and so three boatsteerers—Nathaniel Shearman, Leonard Wing, and Isaac Place—were ordered to stand and face. Trembling with exertion as they balanced in the tossing boats, they lifted the heavy ash handles of the harpoons in palms that were blistered and bleeding, their eyes fixed desperately on the great backs that were wallowing deep, almost entirely immersed in the greasy sea. In that state, and being woefully out of practice, it was almost impossible not to fail.

"Shearman, Wing, & Place were all three carried up fair alongside of Whales and all three missed," Captain Norris penned in his neat, deliberate script. "Chased till dark but could not get up with them again. 150 Bbls lost by good for nothing Boatstearers."

It is impossible to tell exactly how Nathaniel Shearman, Leonard Wing, and Isaac Place felt about their leading roles in this fiasco. It is reasonable to guess that they slunk back on board. It is also likely they cringed away from angry blows. As Shearman had already learned to his cost, there was anger in abundance on the quarterdeck of the *Sharon*.

Norris was under great pressure. The ship had been at sea six months without taking a single whale. For a while there had been the exhilaration of sailing fast, but now the passage was nerve-rackingly difficult. Days dragged by while the ship's course inched tortuously across the chart of the Banda Sea. Nothing improved. The winds failed. The *Sharon* was gripped by a current that dragged her relentlessly west when Norris was desperate to sail east. Breaking into the Pacific was a short-lived relief, as there were adverse currents in that ocean, too. "Light variable airs from all points of the Compass and intervening Calms all these 24 hours," wrote Norris on December 7; "took the advantage of every shift to get Eastward but find by Observation that we have made but one mile."

The calm tone was deceptive. By the time the *Sharon* crested the expanse of sea known as the Groups, Captain Norris was laying the blame for the poor voyage on his unhappy crew—not himself, and not even on the vagaries of luck—setting in train a terrible string of events.

"I would here observe," wrote Benjamin Clough to his father, Asa Clough, "that Capt. Norris has been frequently beating the steward, Geo. Babcock, a mullato belonging at Newport, R.I., in the most barbarous manner." The situation exploded on the night of December 11.

FIVE

REBELLION

"On the Eleaventh day of December 1841 I was in the Ship Sharon Capt Howes Norris in the Lattitude of 1 Degree South and longitude of 150:33 East. The sun arose in great splendour and the day was most beautiful," wrote Benjamin Clough in his journal. "And passed away with the usual work on board of A Whale ship at sea. Such as looking out for whales steering the Ship at work in the rigging &c."

That idyllic late afternoon, Benjamin Clough was engaged in a domestic task. Having done his laundry, he was standing in the slung larboard boat at the stern quarter, hanging two pairs of pantaloons on a line he had stretched between the davits. Then, as he recorded, "I overheard the Capt. floging the Steward in the Cabbin."

There is no explanation for the whipping, though Captain Norris was shouting, "Will you lie to me?" Then Clough heard him yell, "Let go of that!" Evidently Babcock had grabbed the flailing end of the captain's rope, because Clough heard the steward's voice scream, "But you will kill me if I do!"

Then there were the sounds of a struggle.

Thomas Harlock Smith, the first mate, had overheard the shouting, too. Clough heard him go into the cabin and grapple the rope out of the steward's desperate clutch. Then Norris came up the stairs and ordered Nathan Smith and Benjamin Clough to "seize up"—secure—Babcock "in the larboard side of the Mizzen rigging," ready for a flogging.

"At 5 PM the Capton seased up the Steward in the riggen and flogged him," wrote Andrew White. Such scenes must have been highly unpleasant for greenhands like William Weeks. Norris had an unusual style of flogging, too. Usually the victim's shirt was removed, and he was lashed across the bare back, but according to Benjamin Clough's journal, once Babcock had been tied up in the rigging by the wrists and ankles, Norris "took down his pantaloons," exposing his naked buttocks. Then, as Clough recorded, Captain Norris "gave him 2 dozen" with a thick, doubled rope.

After letting him down, Norris ordered the steward to go back to his work in the pantry. Instead, the instant the officers and captain were safely out of sight, George Babcock fled to the forecastle—or, as the cooper phrased it, "went forid."

George Babcock did not belong in the forecastle: as a steward, he did not have a berth there. On most ships the men who did live there would have told him in no uncertain terms to take himself back where he belonged. Usually the steward was a despised member of the crew, the foremast hands considering him nothing better than the captain's lackey. On this occasion, however, the off-duty hands broke tradition by giving Babcock a refuge.

For a while, the officers in the after quarters did not realize what had happened. As Clough recorded, all seemed peaceful. He and first officer Thomas Harlock Smith were on duty on the quarterdeck, passing away the time by strolling up and down in the coolness of the descending night, telling each other yarns. Then, down in the cabin, the bell rang for the steward.

There was no reply. It rang again. Still no answer. Clough and Smith looked about the shadowy decks, but Babcock was nowhere to be found. So Thomas Harlock Smith "sung out" loudly, demanding to know if the steward was in the bows of the ship. He was answered by the seaman from Newburyport, William Smith, who called out from the forecastle, "Aye, he's here."

The defiance in William Smith's tone was a warning. With Benjamin Clough close beside him, Thomas Harlock Smith hurried forward. Arriving at the top of the ladder that led down into the forecastle, he called out for Babcock again, to be answered by a chorus of determined voices, saying that the steward "was not comeing up untill he was used better." The foremast hands had had enough of the captain's brutal treatment of the young black man and were determined to defend him.

This was open rebellion. Unless it was countered swiftly and decisively, control of the ship could be seized by the men.

Clough, instinctively understanding the danger, ran back to the quarterdeck. Meeting Norris, he "told him how things stood." Norris, white-lipped, his fists clenched, strode grimly forward, yelling the steward's name. Again, the men answered for Babcock. The steward had told them he feared for his life, and they believed him.

Captain Norris did not waste time in argument. Instead, he turned to Clough and Thomas Smith and ordered them to go down into the forecastle and fetch Babcock out by force.

Clough went first. It must have taken some courage to jump down the ladder into the dark confines of the forecastle, lit only by the smoky, wavering flame of a single tallow lamp. The first man Clough recognized when his sight adjusted was a tall fellow from New Hampshire by the name of John Witcher. The seaman was swinging a heavy tool called a top-maul, gripping its two-foot handle in both fists. He was a menacing form in the shadows. Clough cried out a warning to the captain, at the same time lunging forward. The sudden, decisive action worked. Witcher lost courage. Backing away, he whined that he did not mean to hit anyone.

The captain and both officers were now in the forecastle, which was a babel of noise. Captain Norris was yelling at the steward. A chorus of men was repeating their demand that the steward should be "used better." Clough recognized the voice of the mate, Thomas Harlock Smith, calling for assistance. "I looked around," he wrote, "and saw him trying to get the Steward away."

George Babcock was clinging desperately to the edge of one of the berths. As Clough helped Thomas Smith drag the steward away from the bunk, he could hear Captain Norris shouting out for Nathan Smith. No sooner had the second mate come down the ladder than one of the men hauled it away, trapping them all in the forecastle below.

Chaos reigned. Clough heard Babcock crying out, "They will kill me, they will kill me!"—while all the time the men were shouting, "They shan't hurt you!" William Smith, braver than the rest, was dancing in front of the captain, his fists up ready to fight. Tall and powerfully built, he was an intimidating figure, but again Clough did not hesitate, shouldering in front of Norris and facing up to the seaman.

William Smith shouted out something. It sounded like an attempt to persuade him to support the men in their protest, but Clough refused to listen. Instead, he put his palm on the front of the seaman's shirt and shoved. William Smith backed away, still calling Clough's name, still trying to make him understand. But, Clough claimed, because of all the noise, "I did not hear the rest of the sentence."

To add to the commotion, Captain Norris was shouting out for a rope. No one moved to obey him. Again, it was up to Clough to act. He vaulted up to the deck and looked around in the dark. Sighting Andrew White, he ordered him to get one. Instead of moving, the cooper stared at him levelly. Then, deliberately, he turned away.

So Benjamin Clough got the rope himself and made a noose of it. Jumping back into the forecastle, he flipped it about the steward's neck, then hauled him to the forecastle hatch like a runaway animal, while the men surged after him, crying out in protest.

Clough and Nathan Smith shoved the cringing, weeping steward to the quarterdeck. The captain and the first mate followed. The men crowded up behind, half-seen as they clustered in the shadows cast by the tryworks, masts, and boat skids. The light from the binnacle lamp glimmered as the ship rolled back and forth on the oily shine of the dark equatorial sea.

Captain Norris ordered Clough to hold Babcock's wrists while he punched him. After knocking the steward flat on his back on the deck, he jumped on his chest with both heavy sea boots—three times, according to Clough's reckoning. Then the captain stood back, waited until Babcock had crept upright, and ordered him to fetch the ship's cutlasses, to be used against the men who had tried so hard to protect him.

The hunched, wheezing young man painfully obeyed, helped by Clough. Two cutlasses were found, and then two muskets, which were charged and fitted with bayonets. Norris handed these to the boatsteerers, with a sharp order to use them if needed. Shuffling and unhappy, the boatsteerers muttered that they thought they had done enough, but took the weapons all the same. Having assembled this reluctant soldiery, Norris ordered them to seize hold of William Smith and bring him to the quarterdeck.

William Smith came of his own accord, his manner proud and defiant. Emboldened by his courage, the others pressed close behind him. Sharply, Norris ordered them back, instructing the boatsteerers to fire their muskets if necessary. Sobered by this threat, the crew retreated as far as the tryworks, where they hovered in an indecisive group. Then, as iron shackles were produced, William Smith roared, "If there are any *men* among you, come aft!" But the vital moment was lost. He, the ringleader, had been secured.

John Witcher, the man who had threatened Norris with the top-maul, was the next to be summoned. No sooner had he reached the mainmast than Captain Norris lunged forward, gripped him by the back of the neck, and shook him violently before shoving him the rest of the way to the quarterdeck. Then Witcher, like William Smith, was handcuffed. Next, eighteen-year-old Jack Baker, a seaman from New York, was ordered to present himself. He likewise was "assisted aft" by the captain and put in handcuffs. After that, it was the turn of Thomas Williams, another New Yorker, who, like Baker and William Smith, was a qualified seaman. At the sight of him Captain Norris flew into a paroxysm of rage, shrieking that he "could hardly keep his hands off him." Clough, horrified, saw Norris grab up a hammer, swing it, and smash it into the sailor's left cheek.

Dazed and bleeding, one hand cradling his crushed upper jaw, Tom Williams staggered the rest of the way to the quarterdeck, where he, like the others, was shackled. Then Sterling Taylor and John Allen, both twenty-one-year-old greenhands, were grappled. That done, Captain Norris commanded Clough to "fetch Sam A Negro." Though Samuel Leods denied having anything to do with the rebellion, he was handcuffed, too. John Moore, a nineteen-year-old greenhand from New York, was the last. They had run out of irons, so "the captain gave him A slap in the face and said tie him up with A piece of spunyarn."

Nine men were lined up by the mizzenmast, one spitting teeth and blood, another hunched over in dreadful pain:

Samuel Leods, John Witcher, John Allen, John Moore, Jack Baker, Sterling Taylor, William Smith, Thomas Williams, and George Babcock.

Behind his violent rage, Norris must have been thinking clearly and coldly. From his experience on the *London Packet,* he knew how swiftly control of the crew could be lost. Obviously, William Smith had headed the rebellion. He was the man who had confronted him with his fists raised; he had been the one with the loudest demands. If William Smith had been able to summon the crew with his cry of, "If there are any *men* among you, come aft!" Norris would have been forced to flee to the safety of his cabin. If he tied up William Smith and flogged him, though, it could trigger a rush to seize the quarterdeck, despite the leveled muskets. So Norris needed a scapegoat—a substitute for William Smith, who was not, like William Smith, a natural leader. Thinking he knew how to find one, he turned to the first mate and said, "Put the steward in the rigging."

George Babcock began to blubber. Despite his crying and pleading, he was seized up again—and cowardice proved his undoing. Cross-examined, he screamed out that it had been Jack Baker who had promised that the men would protect him if he took refuge in the forecastle—Jack Baker! "And," wrote Clough, "when he said he was advised by Baker the captain said let him go and Baker out of Ions." So Babcock was released, and Jack Baker was seized up in his place. The sailor's pantaloons were taken down, and his buttocks exposed, ready for a whipping.

Norris had yet another agenda. Judging by Clough's account, the only officer who had acted with resourcefulness in the face of rebellion had been Clough himself, the third mate. Both the first and second mates could have been much less resolute than Norris would have liked, a good reason for involving them in the brutal punishment to come. So Norris ordered Thomas Harlock Smith to carry out the flogging. "The captain told the mate to put it onto him where there was the most flesh," Clough recorded. Accordingly, Thomas Harlock Smith "gave him 2 dozen with 8 part of yarn," while Jack Baker shrieked and begged, "Ofering to take his Oath on the Bible that he did not start Mutiny, calling the lord to have mercy on his soul and promising to do better."

Norris then ordered the mates to put Witcher in the rigging. This time it was Nathan Smith's turn. Norris gave the order, "And the Secont Mate gave him A dozen," Clough wrote. Then, turning to Thomas Harlock Smith, Captain Norris inquired whether he would like to deliver the next half of the punishment, and the first officer took the doubled rope and dealt the moaning seaman yet another twelve lashes.

That done, Norris addressed the others, asking if they wanted to plea for pardon—"beg off." Utterly intimidated, prepared to go to any lengths to avoid the pain and indignity of a flogging, they all caved in and craved his forgiveness. Norris grudgingly consented—but not before they had signed a written promise that they would "do better for the future."

CLOUGH, PERHAPS BECAUSE he suspected that Captain Norris was not going to make the proper official notification of the failed mutiny, summarized the unpleasant incident in his logbook.

at 7 last Evening A parted [party] of the Crew got the Steward
down in the forecastle and refused to let him come on deck
when called by the captain and Oficers on account of the Captain Misusing the steward but after A short time we got him up
and put 8 of them in Ions and then gave 2 of the head ones 2
dozen apeice sent them to their duty after they had signed A
writen acknowledge that they would behave themselves on
board.

To make it legal, both he and Thomas Harlock Smith signed
with their initials. The two officers, alarmed at the ferocity of
the captain's retaliation, would have had good reason to suspect
that Norris would not report the incident. If the authorities—
having heard gossip, perhaps—started asking questions, this entry would serve as a lawful record of what had happened.

It was a wise precaution. There is no official affidavit with the
ship's papers, and Norris did not even mention it in his logbook. The entire entry for Saturday, December 11, 1841, reads,
"All these 24 hours light breezes from the N.Eastward and
pleasant—lay up from S.S.E. to E.S.E.—all sail set and trimed
to the best advantage—the Westerly current still continues but
not quite so strong—Lat. 1:00 South Long 152:35 East."

Captain Norris's silence, like his failure to record the loss of
his wallet, was self-serving. He had been adroit enough to keep
the uprising on the *London Packet* away from public knowledge, and he intended to do the same now. If word of his violent reprisal got back to New England, it would look bad on his
record, something he wanted to avoid at all costs. However,
he—unlike Benjamin Clough—was ignoring the fact that it

was an official requirement to make a full notation of any kind of rebellion in his crew.

The Act for the Government and Regulation of Seamen in the Merchant Service, passed by Congress in 1790 and amended in 1835, was specific. Where "any one or more of the crew of any American ship or vessel" should "unlawfully, willfully and with force, or by frauds, threats or other intimidations," try to wrest control of the ship "from the master or other lawful commander thereof," then "every such person so offending, his aiders and abettors, shall be deemed guilty of a revolt or mutiny and felony," and the crime, investigation, and punishment should be duly noted in the logbook. "And it shall be the duty of the Master to see that a proper record is kept therein," runs the pertinent clause in the Articles.

Despite his illicit silence, Norris should have been feeling deeply uneasy. He was steering for the Kingsmill Islands—a group of equatorial atolls widely scattered across longitude 160° to 170° East—where systematic whaling would commence. Like the aircraft that search today for lost ships, flying slowly back and forth, once a whaling vessel had arrived on a known whaling ground, it sailed to and fro in an endless search pattern, quartering the sea in a constant, wearying hunt for the prey. It was a tiresome, tedious procedure that went on for weeks, taxing ship, captain, officers, and crew to the limits of endurance. Yet before it had even started, the ship *Sharon* was an uneasy kettle of frustration and fear.

The crew had just cause for an official complaint, but it is unlikely they were aware of their legal rights. On the whaleship *Samuel Robertson*, also in the Pacific in that year of 1841, the hands certainly did not know the law as it applied to seamen. Greenhand William Allen, after recording that Captain William Warner had beaten a man for not repeating every word of one of the mate's orders, wrote, "it seems to me that if capts can abuse their men in this way and yet not go contrary to law," something should be done. Melville himself wrote that "the outrageous abuse to which seamen in our whaling marine" were subjected was "matter which demands legislation."

However, something had indeed been done. If they had known their law—and had had recourse to an official such as a U.S. consul—the crew of the *Sharon*, George Babcock in particular, could have invoked Section 3 of the Seamen's Act of March 3, 1835. This stated: "Every master or other officer of any American vessel on the high seas, or on any other waters within the admiralty and maritime jurisdiction of the United States, who, from malice, hatred, or revenge and without justifiable cause, beats, wounds, or imprisons any of the crew of such vessel, or withholds from them suitable food and nourishment, or inflicts upon them any cruel and unusual punishment, shall be punished by a fine of not more than one thousand dollars, or by imprisonment not exceeding five years, or by both, according to the nature and aggravation of the offence."

Despite this, however, even the most maltreated seamen often found they had no means of redress against sadistic captains or mates. If they had the persistence and eloquence to get the case heard before the judiciary, the men still had to prove that the actions had been motivated by "malice, hatred, or revenge," and that the punishment itself was "cruel and unusual." Just four years after the failed rebellion on the *Sharon*, the *Meteor* of Mystic, Connecticut, was discovered with the crew in control and the cooper in command. The hands had trapped Captain Francis Lester and his officers below decks by the simple process of nailing down the hatches and blocking the companionway door. Apparently the mutiny was justified, as the captain and officers were loading pistols at the time. The ringleaders hailed the next whaleship they raised, which proved to be the *Midas* of New Bedford, and asked Captain Jacob Davis of that ship to come on board to mediate. After hearing them state their case, Davis persuaded Captain Lester to write an affidavit promising "to discharge any number of his men that wish to be discharged at Oahu," without confiscating their belongings or punishing them in any way for standing up for their rights. "When the anchor is down and the sails furled," the document elaborated, "you are at liberty to take your things and go on shore."

Instances where authority figures like Captain Davis were prepared to recognize that the seamen were justified in taking such action were very rare, however, partly because of well-publicized bloody and apparently unjustified mutinies, such as that on the *Globe* of Nantucket.

On the night of January 25, 1824, four of the crew of the *Globe*, headed by a boatsteerer, Samuel B. Comstock, murdered Captain Thomas Worth as he lay asleep in his berth. They shot the third mate, Nathaniel Fisher, in cold blood, severely wounded the first and second mates, and threw all four bodies overboard, though two were still alive when they fell. Taking over control of the quarterdeck, the mutineers then steered the ship to Mili, in the Marshall Islands, intending to strip and destroy her. Six of the crew, most of whom had not taken part in the murders, managed to recapture the vessel there, and sailed her to Valparaiso, Chile, where they handed her over to the American consul. The ten left at Mili were all killed (by the natives or each other), save two, Cyrus Hussey and William Lay, who were rescued by USS *Dolphin*.

The recaptured *Globe* had to be sailed to Chile because there was no American consul in the waters where the mutiny was staged—incidentally the same part of the Pacific where Norris quashed the rebellion on the *Sharon* eighteen years later. There was still no American consul in the empty waters where the *Sharon* cruised, but even if there had been one, there was no guarantee that he would support Babcock or the men who had tried to protect him. In fact, it was much more likely that officialdom would affirm the captain's right to total authority.

On an unnamed ship sailing out of Long Island about this time, a journal-keeper noted that one of the men, "a coloured man or Darkie," ran away in Guam. This fellow was a slave who had worked for his freedom—"he formerly belong'd to East-hampton from there he was sold to a man in Oysterponds where he stayed his time out." The ship's captain went to the governor of the island to report the desertion, and the runaway was quickly recaptured. Instead of immediately returning him to the ship, the authorities "put him in the Calaboose the same as our prison and kept him there till we came away and every morning they gave him twenty-five lashes."

The end of the saga of the peaceable mutineers of the *Meteor* of Mystic was equally dismal. The ship arrived at Honolulu on June 6, 1846, and the crew found out the hard way that Captain Lester's affidavit was not worth the paper it was written on. The U.S. consul, informed of the case, immediately went on board, arrested the ringleaders, and threw them into jail. Over the next few days other shipmates shared their fate. But, as Melville grimly queried in *Typee*, where else but at the consular office could abused sailors apply for relief? Nowhere. The fact of the matter was that when they had arrived in the Pacific, American seamen "had left both law and equity on the other side of the Cape."

Though an extreme example, Norris was certainly not the only sadist in the whaling fleet. Dreadful acts did take place with a certain frequency on the empty seas. Dozens of captains who were apparently decent, righteous citizens in Nantucket, Martha's Vineyard, and New Bedford metamorphosed into feared tyrants once around Cape Horn or the Cape of Good Hope. After years of witnessing floggings on the *Samuel Robertson*, William Warner wrote with wry amusement on the day the ship moored in New Bedford at the end of the voyage, "Capt. Warner is an altered man!"

Before he shipped on the *Mercury*, Stephen Curtis had heard "very tough yarns" about Captain Dennis Fordyce Haskell's treatment of his crew on the previous voyage. On shore, though, his appearance did not "indicate a character so devoid of all sense of humanity and sympathy." In fact, when Curtis first saw Captain Haskell he was quite impressed, describing him as "a man of rather a good figure, quite tall and well proportioned. His features were coarse and irregular," he went on, but added that the total effect was, "to the eye of a stranger, somewhat pleasing." Within weeks he found that Haskell flogged for enjoyment. Even the hardened first mate used to plead with the captain to call it a day.

The problem of overzealous discipline seemed to become more marked around 1830, partly because there were so many unsuitable greenhands in the forecastles of the ships. In November 1841, Joseph Eayres of the *Gratitude* remembered the many chilling shipboard cruelties he had witnessed in his twelve years as a seaman, saying, "I sincerely believe that the captains of whaleships at the present day are the most cruel and unfeeling men (at sea) of any class of people on the face of the Earth." Eayres attributed it to the "very limited education" of most captains and officers in the whaling trade, though he also mentioned going to sea too young, visiting depraved places, hard drinking, and whoring.

He could have pointed out that the expansion of the whaling fleet meant that a lot of men who were unfit for the job were in charge of the quarterdeck. He certainly would have agreed with the seafaring wife who observed that these were men who "left their souls at home."

Six

THE GROUPS

On December 26, the lookouts raised the first islands of the Groups. This, a small cluster of islets surrounded by a single reef, was Nukuoro, in latitude 3.45 North, longitude 155.06 East. It was not laid down in Norris's charts, so he wrote an unusually long description.

> At daylight saw a Group of small Islands about 12 miles distant, bearing N.E. worked up towards them and at 10 A.M. they bore N.N.E. 8 miles distant—saw a reef & Breakers from the N.W. part streaching of in that direction 2 or 3 miles—as we could get no nearer to them could not examine them so closely as I had wished but there apeared to be about 8 or 10 in number surrounded by a reef . . . 18 canoes came off having in them from 1 to 12 men, in all about 100.

For Norris, this fleet of canoes created yet another problem. Andrew White recorded that Norris ordered guns, swords, and cutlasses to be broken out. On the *London Packet* almost exactly eight years earlier, Captain Norris had had a bad encounter at an equally isolated island. Standing in for an islet in the Comoros, he had set a flag, hoping to trade for provisions. Three canoes had paddled out, and though the natives had been too nervous to come alongside, they had indicated that they were willing to exchange foodstuffs for tobacco. Norris had then sent a boat in shore, but instead of trading as promised, the "savage and thievish" natives had made a sudden rush at the boat, and "it was with difficulty the crew could keep her." It was only by panic-stricken rowing that the boat's crew had gotten back to the ship and safety.

Because of incidents like this, caution had characterized encounters with the peoples of Oceania ever since whalemen had first ventured into the Indian Ocean and the Pacific. Clashes between two very different cultures had been unavoidable, and there had been some well-publicized atrocities. As the nineteenth-century whaling historian Alexander Starbuck solemnly wrote, "In the early days of Pacific whaling, not only did our sailors have to seek and encounter their gigantic antagonist amid the dangers of hidden reefs and an unexplored and unknown ocean, but frequently, when putting into some of the numerous islands for supplies, they were compelled to fight the wily and treacherous savages inhabiting some of those groups. Many a vessel had been 'cut out,' and not a man survived to tell the story of the massacre."

One such instance occurred in June 1834, when the New

Zealand–based whaling schooner *Victoria* dropped anchor off an unnamed island in the Groups. Crew member James McLaren noted that the natives seemed friendly enough; when Captain Dowsett invited them they clambered on board willingly, greatly astonished at the size and complexity of the ship. There was a problem with attempts to steal anything made of iron, such as files, nails, and tools, but the encounter went so peaceably that after the natives had left the ship a whaleboat was sent on shore to forage for provisions. In the boat were the captain, the trading master, the chief mate, a seaman by the name of George Brown, and a few other hands, some of them Polynesian. After they had been away awhile, McLaren was startled by a sudden cry, and turned to see George Brown swimming frantically for the ship, a native canoe in hot pursuit. Fending off the natives with musket fire, the shipkeepers picked up the swimmer, who told them that he had seen two natives killing the trading master and believed that all the others were dead.

The second mate immediately ordered the carpenter to cut the cable, and they got the ship underway. Sailing close to the shore, they saw some natives hauling the whaleboat up under the trees and fired seven rounds from the cannon, which sent them shrieking into the bush. Then, as they tacked away from the beach, one of the men sighted a corpse floating facedown in the bay. It was the first mate, easily recognized by a distinctive bald patch on the top of his head. When they hauled aback to take the corpse on board, they heard another frantic cry, this time from the water. This proved to be one of their Hawai'ian seamen, who had also escaped the slaughter.

It was impossible to guess what had set off the massacre. According to George Brown, when the men in the boat had reached the beach, they had straggled off in different directions, hunting for birds' eggs and other fresh provender. Brown's stroll was brought to a swift halt when he heard a distant cry of, "Oh my God!" Running back to the beach, he was just in time to witness the murder of the trading master. After that, self-preservation came first—he dropped to the ground, crawled to the lagoon, and saved himself by swimming underwater.

The Hawai'ian and George Brown were the only survivors. The remnants of the crew buried the first mate in the sea and then held a conference to decide whether to keep on with the cruise or flee for Honolulu. They chose Honolulu.

The case that really hit the headlines on the eastern seaboard of the United States took place the following year, when on October 5, 1835, the *Awashonks* of Falmouth, Massachusetts, touched at Namarik Island—also in the Groups—and Captain Prince Coffin allowed the natives on board. Just as on the *Victoria*, the visitors seemed so peaceable that the whalemen were taken off their guard. Suddenly there was a rush for the rack of whaling spades, and in short order the captain, the helmsman, and the first mate were butchered.

The second mate was clubbed to death as he tried to escape, but the third mate, Silas Jones, managed to make a bolt for it down the fore hatch. After some moments of consternation, the crew members who were aloft on lookout gathered their wits and cut the braces so that the ship fell off the wind, while Silas Jones and the seamen below decks worked their way to the cabin, where the ship's muskets were stored. A session of sharp-shooting, along with firing a keg of gunpowder at the top of the companionway, saved the day, and an hour later the ship was back in rightful hands. Jones took charge and sailed her home.

To what extent the whalemen had brought this upon themselves is difficult to determine. The natives of Oceania were proud and stalwart people, many of them valiant warriors. Their wars had been traditionally tribal, but they would not hesitate, if provoked, to give battle to white men. Indeed, it was common for the first white visitors to be referred to as "ghosts" — *'atua* in Rotuma, *eni* in Pohnpei. This was not because they were considered divine, but because they were believed to be potentially malevolent.

Having heard stories such as that of the *Awashonks*, wary captains regarded any flock of canoes as a threat to the safety of the vessel, a nervousness that was intensified when large and noisy groups of natives boarded. Such distrust inevitably led to occasional outbreaks of violence. Theft was a common trigger — particularly the theft of ironwork, as McLaren had described. To an islander, the ships would seem so rich in material goods that a few nails would not be missed, but captains, conscious that what they carried had to last them for three years or more, would often go to extreme lengths to regain property and punish offenders.

That the foreign sailors were so greatly outnumbered by the local inhabitants led to violence, too. In April 1841, a naval party from the U.S. Exploring Expedition, commanded by Lieutenant Charles Wilkes, burned a village at Tabiteuea Island as a payback for the unproven murder of a member of the crew.

Three islanders were killed in the fracas. "Good whaling-ground exists in the vicinity," Wilkes wrote in justification of this military overreaction, "and our whalemen are in the habit of cruising in this neighborhood: those who visit these wretches ought to keep a constant guard against treachery, for their numbers are large and they are prone to mischief."

Apart from these seesaw bouts of revenge and retaliation, however, the encounters were more likely to be friendly and peaceful, because both sides were eager that all should go smoothly. The whalemen needed water and fresh food—and women too, if they could get them—and the natives of the Groups valued access to tobacco, iron articles, and bric-a-brac, such as beads and mirrors, that could only be obtained from the European and American shipping. Elsewhere in the Pacific, trading was usually initiated by the ship captains, who steered for anchorages known to be safe and then, after mooring the ship, traded either with the natives directly or with white intermediaries.

Here in the Groups, where small islands were scattered widely across an immensity of ocean, the lead was often taken by the islanders themselves. Instead of waiting for the ships to come to them, they went out to the ships. Loading up their canoes with hogs, chickens, mats, lines, shells, and coconuts, they paddled out for miles, so eager to trade that the risks of their overloaded craft capsizing or being carried away by an unexpected storm seemed insignificant. The whaling captains liked this system a lot because it made it possible to load much-needed foodstuffs without interrupting the whale hunt.

So it was with the Nukuoro men in the canoes that clustered

about the *Sharon*, who were keen to trade coconuts, fish lines, and locally made sennit rope for tobacco—an article of no practical value, but which the islanders would eagerly take in exchange for artifacts that had taken hours to make and were often necessary for their survival. It was part of a shift throughout the Pacific from a self-sufficient economy to a market-based one, where the islanders were kept increasingly busy making curiosities such as shark's-teeth swords, mats, hats, and bark cloth, to trade for largely worthless goods. After three or four hours of this amicable bartering the islanders returned to shore, everyone pleased with the friendly exchange.

FROM NUKUORO THE *Sharon* steered east, heading for the Kingsmills. The weather turned squally, and the rigging, already overstrained from the driving passage through the Indian Ocean, was falling apart. Yet for three months the *Sharon* quartered the equatorial sea. Though whales were sighted and boats lowered and set in chase, for some considerable time none were captured and killed. "At 11 AM raised Sperm Whales and lowered the Boats for them and the Mate Gallied them and we got none," wrote Benjamin Clough on New Year's Day, 1842. "Gallied" meant that the whales had been scared off by a sudden noise or a misthrown harpoon—something that certainly should not have been committed by a boat's crew headed by someone as high in the ranking order of the ship as first mate Thomas Harlock Smith.

"It seems as though we were never to get any Whales," Norris griped. Five days after Harlock Smith's unforgivable blunder, however, they made their first catch, after an arduous six-hour chase. For everyone on board, it must have been quite a moment. The ship was eight months out from Fairhaven—eight months with the ignominious report "clean," meaning no sperm whale oil taken at all—but at least their first catch was multiple. Four sperm whales were killed, one by each boat.

Towing the carcasses to the ship was heavy work, with a great deal more work awaiting when they got there. Over the fruitless months the blubber room—an area between decks reserved for cutting up whale blubber—had become cluttered up with ship's gear, which had to be cleared out and stowed elsewhere. Men had to go aloft to fix the cutting falls—heavy ropes and tackle used for heaving the blubber up off the whales—because even that basic groundwork had been neglected. It was not until the next day that Clough was able to write, "Called all hands at daylight and commenced cutting our *Whales*," underlining the word as if to underscore the novelty.

The backbreaking labor that loomed was certainly a new experience for the greenhands like William Weeks. Unlike blackfish, these sperm whales were too big to hoist onto the deck, and accordingly had to be flensed in the water. The first corpse was secured alongside the starboard side of the ship, its blocklike head pointing to the stern and the tail to the bow, attached with ropes and chains in a special fashion so that it could revolve where it lay. Then a narrow stage was lowered over the carcass until it hung over the far side of it, parallel with the ship. The first and third officers—Thomas Harlock Smith and Benjamin Clough—sidled out onto this precarious platform, each armed with a blubber spade, a heavy oblong blade sharpened at the bottom edge and fastened to a twelve-foot wooden handle.

Braced only by a narrow rail, the two mates leaned down and jabbed at the whale, marking a spiral two or three feet wide into the thick fat so that it would come up off the whale in a great ribbon called the "blanket strip." When this scarfing was done, the heavy blubber hook that dangled from the end of the cutting falls was poked into a hole hacked into the end of the spiral, by the corner of the jaw. Once it was safely lodged, the second mate, Nathan Smith, called out the order to man the windlass. Then, with the cry of, "Heave!" the cutting falls straightened as the hook strained at the blubber.

Heaving up the blanket strip was quite a different business from weighing anchor, since there was no way of using the pull of the sails to help. The only force on their side was the current that urged the carcass away from the ship. The blubber, though scarfed, still stuck to the flesh beneath, and so the gang at the windlass had to heave mightily to get it started. At the same time the mates on the stage hacked at the junction of fat and flesh, slashing at the fibers that held the fat tight. Slowly, as the windlass was heaved, fibers tore with an audible snap, and the strip began to unreel from the carcass. With more heaving, the blubber strip rose high in the air, until it was as high as the top of the mast. After being severed from the rest, it was lowered through the hatch that led to the blubber room between decks, where other hands were waiting with boarding knives to chop it up into smaller blocks. And so the heavy labor progressed, until the four cadavers were completely flensed, and all the fat was in.

Trying out was the next job to learn. Chopped chunks of fat were thrown up from the blubber room onto the deck, where they were minced up further, ready to be boiled in the huge try-pot cauldrons in the tryworks. The fires were started with wood, but as the first oil was rendered the fibrous "scraps" that floated to the top were scooped out, shaken, tossed into the furnace, and burned. These made a thrifty and highly efficient fuel that blighted the air for five miles downwind with a slaughterhouse stench of burning fiber and fat, while above the bowed heads of the foremast hands eddies of dense black smoke soiled the glimmering white sails.

It was tedious and exhausting labor—and yet, by whalemen's standards, these were small whales. Clough noted that the total fare was seventy-four barrels, an average of under twenty barrels each, which would mean that they were all under twenty feet long, the rough whaling measurement being a foot for every barrel. "At 2 got them cut in and started the tryworks," he continued; "at 4 PM raised Sperm Whales and lowered 3 Boats the Waist Boat missed & got nothing.

"Lat. 00.30 Long 169.05."

ON JANUARY 26 they took four more small whales, which made just over seventy barrels in all. However, it was much more common for the boats to return to the ship with nothing to report. On February 5, "at 10 AM saw Sperm Whales," Norris wrote; "lowered the Boats—got up to one and the Boat-stearer missed him—the School went of to windward could not get up with them again—A Miserable set of Boatstearers."

Bad temper was general. Thomas Harlock Smith started laying into Jack Baker, Tom Williams, "and a good many more," as Andrew White recorded later. When his boatsteerer, Otis

Tripp, missed yet another whale, the first mate attacked him with a heaver—a heavy wooden spike, usually used for twisting strands of thick rope—and felled him with a blow to the head.

Though the casks in the echoing holds might be slowly filling with oil, morale was abysmally low. Even the stalwart cooper was not exempt from the general unpleasantness. In February he recorded that the captain asked him in sarcastic tones if he thought he had enough to eat. White would have been puzzled as well as angry, not knowing the source of Norris's obsession with provisions. On the *London Packet*, exactly seven years earlier, Norris had written furiously in his private logbook that the crew's excuse for refusing to work was that "they did not have enough to eat which was false and I can prove it." On the *London Packet* just over a pound of salted meat had been issued to each hand per day, "which is amply sufficient for any man"—or so he had declared, being convinced that the sailors were deliberately throwing their rations overboard with the intention of forcing him to turn back home.

Andrew White, unaware that he was treading on dangerous ground, chose to make a smart retort: He demanded to know whether the food he ate was begrudged. Norris, his savage temper flaring, lifted his fist and ordered the cooper to shut up, "and if I did not he would nock me to hell." White did not record his reply to this, but whatever it was, it further infuriated Norris, who gave the cooper a choice—take his things and go forward, "or go to hell, he did not care where." Stubborn White chose the forecastle and moved in with the foremast men.

Typically, Captain Norris made no mention in his logbook concerning his demotion of someone as important to a whaleship as the cooper, merely noting, "Saw Porpoises & blackfish but no Sperm Whales—a very strong Westerly current—nothing more worthy of remark."

By the beginning of April the state of the ship had become critical. The foretopgallant mast backstay—an important part of the standing rigging, because it kept the mast braced upright—had been carried away, and all the topgallant and royal yards needed urgent repairs. Supplies of fresh water were running short. Within days Norris was forced to give the order to steer south for the island of Rotuma.

SEVEN

DESERTION

EARLY VISITORS RHAPSODIZED about the beauty of Rotuma as viewed from the sea, describing an island made up of old volcanic peaks that were lush and green all the way from the glittering white beaches, thickly fringed with coconut palms, to the summits of the lofty hills. Thatched houses were scattered among the mango and breadfruit trees that clustered on the lowest slopes. As the *Sharon* approached the coral reef and turquoise lagoon, people would have run out of these to launch canoes and paddle out in welcome.

Usually, a white beachcomber was one of their number. Because of the attractions of the island, as well as the chance to escape from intolerable conditions on board, sailors had been jumping ship at Rotuma since 1824, when six men had deserted from the London whaler *Rochester* after robbing her of whaling tackle, guns, cutlasses, and other weapons. Therefore, it is likely that Captain Norris was accosted by a man who had been on the island a number of years, had taken a Rotuman wife, raised a family, and made himself indispensable to the village in some way. He may have been tattooed from the knees to the waist in a pattern of fine blue curves and coils; he could have been circumcized in the native fashion, and he was probably coated with reddish oil. Norris, like the great majority of his fellow whaling masters, would have considered him nothing better than a white renegade, a traitor to his society and his race. However, despite their unsavory reputation, the English-speaking beachcombers were useful to the visiting captains. They acted as middlemen for the chiefs, negotiated on the captain's behalf for water and provisions, would pilot the ship to a safe anchorage for a fee, and were an excellent source of local knowledge.

Because of the inherent profit, the man who came on board the *Sharon* would have been anxious to inform Captain Norris of the advantages of dropping anchor at Rotuma. Though there were no rivers or streams, every village had a deep well, so an abundance of water was available. Coconuts were very plentiful, and yams, sweet potatoes, bananas, sugarcane, a large starchy root called taro, and common fowls were readily obtainable, along with hogs, which had been bred from stock that earlier whalers had given to the islanders. Sperm whale teeth, tobacco, and glass beads were the favorite currency. As long as the wind did not come from the north, the ship could safely find an anchorage in about seventeen to twenty-five fathoms of good holding ground.

As evidence that this was an excellent place to refit and re-provision, the men on the *Sharon* would have been able to glimpse the furled sails of the London whaler *Onyx* as she lay at anchor in a northwest bay. However, there was little or no communication between the two ships. Instead, the crew of the *Sharon* spent the first day getting off a raft of water, and taking on "about 300 yams." Two hogs were bought and killed. "Samuel A. Nichols Deserted," Clough added in his journal. Greenhand Nichols must have been one of the watering party, and seized a chance to run while the officer in charge was not looking in his direction, as the men were not allowed any liberty until April 10, when the starboard watch had a twelve-hour vacation.

On that first day of liberty, three of the watch failed to return to the ship at sunset, one being Lyman Bligh. The day after that, the larboard watch had a day on shore. "And 9 of them deserted," wrote Clough laconically. There were eight foremast hands in the larboard watch, so all the men who had taken part in the failed rebellion had seized the opportunity to disappear into the bush. The ninth man was the cook, Henry Mills. His motive for running away is obvious. Being black and illiterate like the steward, Mills had good reason to fear the same brutal treatment, even if he had not been beaten already. If he was indeed a fugitive slave, his instincts for self-preservation would have been very well honed. It seems likely that he would have run off with Samuel Leods, the black seaman of the crew, who would have felt a grudge because the captain had punished him even though he denied taking part in the rebellion. However, George Babcock, who had the best reason of all to desert, was not able to join them. Benjamin Clough wrote to his father that the steward was kept in confinement while the ship lay at anchor, which indicates he was put in irons and imprisoned in the run, a small hold beneath the captain's cabin.

Of the larboard watch, John Moore and Jack Baker were unlucky enough to be recaptured after Captain Norris set up a bounty. On April 12, Clough noted that "the natives brought off 1 of our men for which they received A piece of cloth," and three days later, "the Natives brought off Another of our men and received A piece of cloth." One of the three starboard watch runaways changed his mind and swam back to the ship at night. All the rest got away.

The nine successful absconders would have found a pleasant refuge. Early visitors remarked on the hospitality and friendliness of the islanders. Captain Peter Dillon, who called at Rotuma in 1827, stated unreservedly that the Rotumans were "remarkably kind to Europeans, as well as to all other strangers, nor have they ever been known to molest any of their foreign visitors." Their only failing, he claimed, was the widespread Pacific Islander vice of stealing anything made of iron. Indeed, that only two deserters had been delivered back to the ship, despite the very tempting bribe of a piece of cloth, would have been because of the natural kindliness of the Rotumans.

The islanders were attractive in appearance, too, the English whaleman Robert Jarman commenting in 1832 on the generally "mild and pleasing cast of features, with a light copper color complexion, fine black eyes, and long black hair, hanging about their shoulders." The men were stalwart and handsome, and the women pretty. The runaway whalemen from the *Sharon* would have been amazed, like Jarman, to find that maidens advertised their virginity by cutting their hair short and plastering it thickly with lime, so that they looked as if they were wearing white helmets. These they maintained, along with their purity, until the day they married. However, the deserters would have soon found lovers. According to the trader Edward Lucett, who visited Rotuma just a few months before the *Sharon* called, while both maidens and married women were inviolate, a kind of divorce based on mutual consent was common, and divorced women were free to "act as libertinely as they please without their character being affected." When Captain Peter Dillon called, he recorded that a number of Rotuman women "volunteered to join us in the expedition," but his crew had their Maori wives on board, and so he did not have the room, at which the Rotuman ladies "seemed much disappointed." There was one strange disadvantage to this generous friendliness, though. All the natives, both male and female, coated their bodies with a mixture of turmeric and coconut oil, which gave a pretty appearance and was said to deter insect stings and bites, but did rub off onto others very readily with contact, and once on the skin was very hard to wash away.

Despite the generosity and friendliness, it is unlikely that any of the ex-*Sharon* hands sought a long-term home on the island. While many men jumped ship in Rotuma, drawn by the attractions of the place and the people as well as the prospect of escape from unpleasant conditions on board, very few remained on a permanent basis. In 1827, Captain Dillon noted that two of the deserters from the *Rochester* "came alongside in a canoe and begged leave to come on board; which I refused, asking them how they could presume to desire such a favour, having deserted their own ship in this remote part of the globe." However, other shipmasters were not so righteous, having empty berths in their forecastles to fill. At one stage in the late 1820s the pool of beachcombers had risen to about seventy, but by 1842, when the *Sharon* men joined them, only about twenty-five foreigners were in residence, including some native Hawai'ians and New Zealand Maori. Intemperance and in-fighting had played a part in the reduction of numbers, but mostly it was because so many had given up the overromanticized existence and begged places on other vessels.

The plain fact of the matter was that island life was not quite as easy as expected, despite the fact that the natives were so friendly and helpful. Many early observers remarked how gentle they were; today, violence is still extremely rare on the island, and serious crime almost unknown. This is because of the strong emphasis placed by Rotuman society on self-control. To betray anger, according to Rotuman belief, was shameful, while being able to contain anger was a sign of strength; anger in others was perceived as potentially destructive, something to be deflected with kidding around. To the *Sharon* runaways the playfulness would have looked like simple high spirits at first, but then the prospective beachcombers would have found that ridicule had to be absorbed with good humor, not easy for men who placed much less value on self-control than the Rotumans and were used to the constant skirmish of the forecastle.

In the Rotuman village, mockery was one way of controlling the behavior of others, and gossip was another. However, the most powerful deterrent to wrongdoing was an abiding belief in the retribution of the fates—an unquestioning knowledge that ancestral spirits would punish offenders. While sailors were traditionally superstitious, the ex-*Sharon* hands would have found the ramifications of this rather daunting. Rotumans believed that spirits of the dead took over the bodies of animals or plants, becoming *'aitu*. Each village had its own *'aitu*, a kind of totem god. Still more intimidatingly, other ghosts were bodiless *'atua*, malevolent vampirelike spirits that sought to torment living humans by taking them over, mind, body, and soul. In self-defense, Rotumans tried to appease both *'aitu* and *'atua* by setting out food offerings, often including pork. With the malicious *'atua*, however, the best policy was to avoid them altogether, by steering clear of places they were known to frequent, which was part of the reason why outsiders had to learn where not to blunder. In certain circumstances, evil *'atua* wandered from their haunts to hunt unwary humans. Then—or so the sailor would have been informed—it was necessary to scare the *'atua* away by making loud chaotic noises, such as the banging of drums and the rattling of shells.

For a sailor who had left his ship with no possessions save his wits and nothing to stake his future on save whatever seamanship he might have learned, starting anew in such an exotic society was a challenge. All in all, it was easier as well as safer to move on. One of the greenhands, Lyman Bligh, came out of hiding as soon as the *Sharon* had disappeared over the horizon and shipped on the whaler *LaGrange*. John Allen signed onto the crew list of the whaleship *Addison*. Seaman Thomas Williams, his face forever misshapen where Captain Norris had broken his cheekbone with a hammer, was recorded next in the port of Talcahuano, Chile, signing on for short cruises at the rate of $14 per month and plying the same Pacific waters where Herman Melville sailed. William Smith, the ringleader of the failed rebellion, also left the island, making his way to the eastern Pacific, where he sailed on the *Houqua*.

Because the great majority of deserters were keen to sail away again, it was easy for shipmasters to find replacements. Norris was able to fill six of the empty places in his forecastle from the pool of drifters on the beach who wanted to get clear of the island. "We shipped 2 White men, 4 Kanakas, 2 Rotumah men, 1 Ocean and 1 Hope Islander, the last two being left here by other ships," Clough wrote in his letter to his father.

One of the white men, according to Clough's logbook, was named John Brown, while Andrew White mentioned a man named Paddy, who may have been the other. "Kanaka" was a catchall term for the people of Oceania in general, so the two Rotumans, plus the Ocean Islander and the Hope Islander, made up the total of "4 Kanakas."

The Rotumans would have volunteered to join the *Sharon* in the same spirit of adventure that had inspired the women to beg Captain Dillon to take them along. A seafaring people, the Rotumans built huge double canoes, some as long as ninety feet and capable of carrying two hundred men and women. In these, many of the islanders had ventured as far as the Fiji Islands and Samoa, while others had headed for the distant horizon, never to be seen again. Puzzled by this recklessness, whaleman Robert Jarman wrote that the "expeditions seem to have been undertaken more from a restless desire of seeing and visiting other lands, than from any other motive," and concluded that the Rotumans, being inquisitive by nature, simply wanted to gratify their curiosity. It seems very likely, then, that the two young Rotuman men would have eagerly signed onto Norris's crew list, anticipating an exciting escapade that would take them to distant parts of the globe.

The Ocean Islander and the Hope Islander shipped by Norris had been left on the beach by other captains, so they could be considered experienced seamen. Ocean Island—known to the native inhabitants as Banaba ("the Rock")—and Hope Island—more properly called Arorae—were two of the Kingsmill Group, nowadays part of Kiribati. Both atolls were several days' sail from Rotuma, but in different directions, Banaba to the northwest, and Arorae to the northeast. Since the year 1821, when Captain George Barrett of the *Independence* had pioneered whaling along the equator, Banaba and Arorae had been visited frequently by American whaling captains who were following the December-to-March sperm whale migrations. There was no anchorage at either island, so the ships merely paused to lay off and on, but the trade for fresh provisions and the favors of local women was an important facet of Kingsmill Island life. At the same time, just as on Rotuma, natives could be shipped to fill empty berths in the forecastle, the Kingsmill Islanders being as keen as Rotuman men to try out the experience. Naked when they arrived on board, they quickly metamorphosed into ordinary foremast hands once issued a pair of pants and a shirt.

When the captains recruited these men, they were supposed to return them to their home islands once the whaling cruise was finished, but many, like the Ocean Islander and the Hope Islander who were shipped by Norris from the Rotuman beach, were dropped off in the handiest place. This was not always the captain's fault. The Ocean Islander and the Hope Islander might have jumped ship. Indeed, they could have considered taking up residence, as not all beachcombers were white. There was a lot about Rotuma that was compatible with the other islands of the Pacific, including a belief in the power of the spirits of the dead and the need to fend off malevolent 'atua by creating chaotic noises, or by beating the ground in an outward arc from the recently dead; and these shared beliefs often meant that Kanakas could feel comfortable in foreign Pacific Island societies. In 1814 a Hawai'ian named Babahey had settled in Rotuma after many years of sailing out of Sydney and interpreting for captains in the Hawai'ian Islands, Tahiti, the Fijian Islands, and the northwest coast of America. For five years, until he passed away, he had happily regaled his Rotuman friends with marvelous tales of the wonders he had seen—though it is impossible not to wonder how he described ice and snow to people who had never left the equator.

But if the two Kingsmill Islanders had tried the beachcombing life on Rotuma, they had since changed their minds, just like the great majority of the white sailors who jumped ship there.

TYPICALLY, NORRIS WAS as silent in his logbook about events in Rotuma as he had been about the rebellion and floggings. In the log entry beginning Thursday, April 7, 1842, he simply noted:

First part light breezes from E.S.E.— heading N.E.. Middle and Latter parts pleasant worked up to the Island [of Rotuma] and 9 A.M. came to anchor at the N.W. Bay—wooded and watered, got our refreshments—painted the Ship &c. and Sailed again Wednesday April 20th on a cruise—

His next entry was dated April 21, the day after departure. Then it was the usual seamanlike notation of the direction of the breezes and the set of the sails, ending: "unbent the chains and stowed the anchors." There is absolutely nothing regarding events while the ship was in port. And yet the captain was specifically instructed by both the Articles and the law to make note of any changes in the crew list—the U.S. State Department was adamant that it should be informed of the whereabouts of Americans on the deep and wanted a check on foreigners who shipped on American vessels, too.

Arriving at Arorae—Hope Island—twelve days after leaving Rotuma, Captain Norris did note, though only casually, that he "shipped two natives." Recruiting native labor usually involved sending a boat on shore with either the captain or the first mate, who would dicker with the head man of the village for a couple of volunteers. It was also possible that two of the men in the canoes that came out to trade shipped of their own accord. According to whaler gossip, the two Hope Islanders were kidnapped—when he first heard of the murder, seaman Joseph Eayres of the *Gratitude* noted that Norris had been killed "by some of the natives that he had forced out to sea with him." If they were indeed abducted, it went unmentioned in both Clough's and White's journals.

There is no mention, though, of the Hope Islander Norris had taken on at Rotuma being given a chance to return to his home village; so he, like George Babcock, might have been confined to prevent his escape. Kidnapping was certainly not unknown. Early in the century, unfortunate islanders were snatched from beaches and carried to Europe or America to be paraded like biological specimens. Twenty years after the *Sharon* voyage, "blackbirding," where whole village populations were seized and carried off to be sold for plantation labor, reached plague proportions in the Kingsmills.

However, it is likely that when the *Sharon* sailed away from the island all three Hope Islanders were on board of their own free will, just like the two Rotumans and the Ocean Islander. The fashion for joining the crews of American vessels had started with the Hawai'ians—then called Sandwich Islanders— who had happily shipped on board the fur traders that sailed between the northwest coast of America and Canton. Not only was there the prospect of romance and adventure, but the wealth they made could not be levied away from them by the chiefs at home. Joining whalers was a natural progression, one enthusiastically copied by other men of Oceania as the whaleships touched their island shores. It was because of this early Hawai'ian involvement that all islanders were known to the whalemen as *Kanaka*, the Hawai'ian word for person.

For an adventurous Kanaka, taking up shipboard life was like stepping over an invisible threshold into an entirely different world, just as it had been for William Wallace Weeks. Like any American greenhand, the islander would be changed forever by the experience. However, a ship—and particularly a whaleship, where small-boat skills were greatly valued—was not quite the challenge for a Kanaka that it was for a Yankee boy from the farm or a kid from the streets of New York. From antiquity, the people of Oceania had used the sea as their playground, their pasture, and their highway. All of them, like the Rotumans, had set out on long deep-sea voyages in their well-made canoes. They had also welcomed or repelled other islanders who had landed on their shores. Curious as well as daring by nature, they were eager to experience the far reaches of the Pacific, which they knew about but had not seen for themselves.

Many of these venturesome natives did not return. Tuberculosis, to which they had no immunity, took a dreadful toll. On the whaleship *Samuel Robertson*, which was cruising the Pacific at the same time as the *Sharon*, foremast hand William Allen noted that one of their Kanakas was very ill. "He is very intelligent has been to America and England, and it is 20 years since he left his home," he wrote. Their next port of call, Honolulu, was the sick man's home, and he had been eagerly anticipating his return, "but in all human probability he will never see it again," wrote Allen. Sadly, he was right, as the Hawai'ian, "George Worth" (a name bestowed by his first captain), passed away the next day.

However, those who did return home enjoyed higher prestige, partly because of the skills they brought back to the village and partly because of their intriguing worldliness. The glamour made the risks worthwhile. So, while the two white men Norris had recruited in Rotuma probably came on board with a cynical air of expecting the worst, it seems very likely that when the Kanaka greenhands arrived in the forecastle, they were excitedly anticipating something marvelous. They would not have minded the prospect of hard work, or even the strange and often insulting names that they were given by men who could not spell or pronounce their proud and proper titles—names such as "Spun Yarn," or "Bloody Scoundrel," which reflected a rough sense of humor. The Ocean Islander shipped by Norris had been dubbed "George Black" by his previous captain, because of the color of his skin.

Whether these accommodating Kanakas were socially and temperamentally capable of coping with Captain Norris's uncontrollable rages, though, would never have occurred to them until it was far too late.

EIGHT

REIGN OF TERROR

APRIL TURNED INTO May while Norris brooded over his charts and his lists of provisions used, obsessed with the bad luck of the voyage. "One year out this day and only 250 bbls Oil," he wrote. On May 31 they encountered the London whaler *Samuel Enderby*, a ship that was to be immortalized in the pages of *Moby-Dick*. For Norris, it was nothing more than a small event in another profitless day: "Saw the *Samuel Enderby* but no whales."

Sailing from London in June 1840, the *Samuel Enderby* had whaled off the coast of Chile until April 1841 and had then crossed the Pacific *en route* for the same whaling ground where the *Sharon* was cruising so unsuccessfully. Benjamin Clough recorded that the two ships sailed in sight of each other for three days. There is nothing to indicate that Norris broke his own rule of never stepping on board another ship, but the report the English shipmaster shouted as the two ships passed would have added to his frustration.

It was 1,200 barrels, almost a thousand more than his own.

Since the *Sharon* had left Rotuma not a single drop of oil had been taken on board. The psychological pressure was mounting. It was not until the next month, June, that sperm whales were raised, and then it was as late as the tenth. Four boats were lowered, but Clough recorded that Thomas Harlock Smith's boat frightened the pod away. Five days later, Nathan Smith redeemed the family name by taking three whales, one of them a large one, rendering seventy barrels. It was just a passing stroke of luck, though. Two weeks later, when the next whale was harpooned, the iron drew out as soon as the line went taut. The whale escaped, and the rest of the pod was alarmed into flight. "It seems to me that bad luck attends us and has attended us from the day we Sailed," Norris agonized.

The day after that defeat, the *Sharon* was hailed by the captain of the *LaGrange*, whose report was seven hundred barrels—more than double Norris's report, though the *LaGrange* had left Fairhaven a month later than the *Sharon*. As usual, Captain Norris did not gam—surely to the relief of Lyman Bligh, who was undoubtedly lurking out of sight. Perhaps it would have been better for him if he had been spied and recaptured by Norris, though: a note by his name in the Port Register reads, "Died on board the Legrange by a fall from the topgallant yard."

• • •

BUT AT LEAST he had avoided the living hell on board the *Sharon*. "This season the Devil appears to have entered our Captain with double force," wrote Benjamin Clough to his father. Again, Babcock was the chosen target. According to Clough, after they left Rotuma Babcock had been "turned out of the cabin and put in cook" in place of runaway Henry Mills. Manuel José des Reis, the young seaman from Fayal, had been given Babcock's old job of steward—a hazardous assignment, in view of Norris's history. As ship's cook, though, Babcock was more vulnerable than ever. The job involved measuring out the day's ration of meat, flour, and vegetables from the ship's stock of provisions, before cooking them up and serving them out to the men. Any hint of wastage and brutal punishment followed.

As cook, Babcock was also responsible for feeding the live-stock. This on Pacific whalers always included a number of hogs, which were allowed to run free on the decks, foraging for what they could find to supplement the table scraps and spoiled food—such as sprouted potatoes or mildewed rice and peas—that they were fed. When filling the pigfeed tub, Babcock would have been constantly forced to distinguish between what was good enough for men to eat and what was only fit for animals. If Norris spied anything fit for humans in the swill, he made Babcock crouch on all fours on the deck and eat with the animals. Worse still, in June even that humiliating means of getting something to eat was denied to Babcock, as Norris turned him out of the galley and gave the job of cook to the Ocean Islander.

By the middle of that month, George Babcock "was reduced to almost a Skeleton. Sometimes his eyes swelled so that he could not see, and the blood and corruption running from all parts of his body," wrote Clough to his father. Clough was describing symptoms of advanced scurvy, indicating that it had been many weeks since Babcock had eaten fresh fruits or vegetables. Because vitamin C is necessary for the body to produce collagen, which glues scar tissue together, the wounds from the constant beatings would have opened up and festered.

Given lemon juice to drink, or fresh fruit and vegetables to eat, Babcock could have made a miraculous recovery. Instead, the beatings continued. July Fourth was a particular torment: "The 4th of July he gave him 7 dozen on his back, one [dozen] on his head and one [dozen] on his feet," wrote Clough; "he being made what is called Spread Eagle." Babcock was lashed by his wrists and ankles to the rigging, his legs widespread so that his toes could not touch the deck to take his weight; then he was flogged eighty-four times on his bare back, twelve times on the crown of his head, and twelve times on the soles of his feet. "The rope used was hemp whale line," Clough continued. "From the first of July to the first of September he beat him almost every day, using any weapon that came to hand." Between whippings, Babcock was kept at grueling jobs such as sanding down the deck planks, "until his Knees were worn nearly to the bone and his foot a mass of corruption."

Before Babcock had left the galley, a kettle had tipped over, and "burnt his foot to blister all over," and since then the raw wound had festered. Like the great majority of American whaling captains, Norris was in charge of the medical chest, and, judging by his logbook, generally made a good job of it. However, each time he dressed Babcock's injury another bout of rage would boil up, and he would stamp on the scalded foot. While his victim was crouched before him on the planks, he would "kick him in the face until the blood would stream from his mouth and nose." Then he would make Babcock stuff his nostrils with bits of rope oakum, before ordering him to scrub up the mess he had made on the deck.

IT IS AN APPALLING LITANY, and yet, while there must have been some who felt horror and outrage at the captain's daily torture of the unfortunate young man, there is nothing to indicate that anyone made any kind of protest. The bravest of the original crew had all run away at Rotuma. The hands who had been with the ship since leaving Fairhaven, such as William Wallace Weeks, might have become so inured to Norris's brutality that it seemed a ghastly part of the normal routine. There is a great deal of evidence that the constant sight of evil is hardening, as if the viewer needs to grow a protective shell to avoid being driven mad by the repeated experience.

The occasional man might even have felt a sick kind of relief that it was Babcock and not himself being tortured. That Babcock was a black man must have been a factor. William Allen of the *Samuel Robertson*, who was so horrified at Captain William Warner's treatment of his crew that he kept a list of "men flogged" in his journal, meditated in December 1841 that most of his forecastle mates had never seen "their fellow creatures striped to the skin and the flesh quivering and lacerated by the cat-o-nine-tails like a southern slave—yes, worse than a slave for a slave is brought up where it is the practice."

Ironically, William P. Powell, the black activist and keeper of seamen's temperance boarding houses, believed that whalers promised a better refuge for a fugitive slave than any other branch of the maritime trade, writing in the *National Anti-Slavery Standard* that in the whaling service "there is no barrier, no dividing line, no complexional distinction, to hedge up the cabin gangway or the quarter-deck, to prevent the intrepid, enterprising, and skillful coloured sailor from filling the same station as the white sailor." It is a romantic view that makes Babcock's situation seem especially tragic. While harmonious ethnic relationships did occur on board many whalers—Ishmael's close friendship with Queequeg being a famous fictional example—racism certainly did exist and could well have been an element in Norris's appalling mistreatment of Babcock. If Babcock was indeed an escaped slave, as Ezra Johnson's signature on the Articles tends to indicate, some shipmates could have reasoned that he was accustomed to that kind of treatment. Maybe, in their abysmal ignorance, they even believed that beating did not hurt a black man as much as it did a white one.

Those who had been newly taken on would have not had the confidence to take the lead, as horrified as they must have been at the state of affairs on the ship they had unwittingly joined. Undoubtedly the Rotumans, who respected restraint and self-control, were appalled. With tribal invasions as part of their history, the men from Ocean Island and Hope Island were more accustomed to bloodshed, but they had even more reason to be afraid: Norris summoned Babcock every morning by shouting out, "Where are you, you damned nigger you?" Could one of the darker skinned Kingsmill Islanders be the next target of his sadistic rage? It must have seemed horribly possible.

All the hands were treading very carefully. Ever since the failed December mutiny, Norris had been waging a war of terror, and Babcock was by no means the only victim. On August 9 it was the turn of Nathaniel Shearman, the nineteen-year-old boatsteerer who had filled in for Jacob Hathaway and was the harpooner in Captain Norris's whaleboat. At dawn the cooper recorded all hands being called to make sail and begin washing down the deck. "The Mate spoke to Sherman and told him to wash off the Railing," Andrew White went on, "but Sherman misunderstood him." Thinking that Harlock Smith had told him to haul up another tub of seawater, Nathaniel Shearman set off toward the bows. The first mate pursued him, grabbed him, and gave him a beating. Then he ordered him back to the quarterdeck. The boatsteerer scurried aft, while Thomas Harlock Smith pursued him closely, still shouting curses. Captain Norris, hearing the commotion, came out on deck and grappled the unfortunate harpooner himself, to deliver a few hard blows of his own. Then he demoted Nathaniel to the rank of foremast hand. As Benjamin Clough put it, "the first Oficer and Captains boatsteerer Nathaniel Sherman had A few words when the Captain broke and turned him forward and put in Alexander Yellott boatsteerer." So, like Andrew White earlier, Nathaniel Shearman moved his sea chest into the forecastle.

Another unfortunate was John Brown, one of the white men shipped at Rotuma. While the *Sharon* was cruising off Pleasant Island—more properly known by its native name, Nauru— canoes came alongside with a few goods to trade. Nauru was notorious for the particularly vicious set of beachcombers that had settled there under the bloody-handed leadership of two

Irish runaway convicts. These men, Patrick Burke and John Jones, had reputedly seized the whaleship *John Bull* and then tried to throw the blame on the natives for the piracy and wrecking. Now, they made a living by smuggling grog to the seamen on the visiting whalers, and John Brown got hold of some of this. Half-drunk, he seized what he saw as an opportunity to run away from the ship by hiding in one of the canoes.

Unfortunately, as Ben Clough related in the letter to his father, Brown's disappearance was noticed. Ordered back on deck, he clambered up the side, his manner defiant. When Norris reached over the rail and grabbed him by the throat, Brown defended himself by clutching Norris's shirt. Norris "instantly sung out for help." After the mates had tied the sailor hand and foot, Captain Norris threw him to the deck and kicked him in the face. Brown swore to take the captain's life if he ever got loose, but he never got the chance.

Norris ordered him slung into an empty canoe. Then Brown was set adrift. The terrified Nauru natives had all fled back to the island. Setting a tied man adrift was a local method of execution, so it would not have occurred to them to try to rescue him. In 1851 a passenger on the trading yacht *Wanderer* noted that thieves and other criminals were "punished with the extreme penalty of the law"—placed in a canoe, they were "sent adrift to perish unheeded, far away on the wide ocean."

"We afterwards learned that he never reached the shore," wrote Benjamin Clough to his father. So Brown had been condemned to a protracted, solitary, horrible death.

On the same day Andrew White noted that Captain Norris "sent a man ashore by the name of Paddy." Unless "Paddy" was

John Brown's nickname, then it seems that the second white man shipped at Rotuma was so horrified at the fate of his shipmate that he demanded his discharge. But there is no official record of that, either.

"FRESH BREEZES FROM the Eastward and fair weather," penned Norris on Friday, August 26, 1842—

first part stood Southward—middle part Northward—Latter part Southward, the westerly current still continues—no whales to be found—hard luck—15 Months out and only 360 bbls. oil, the Lord have mercy on me—
  Lat. 0:26 South. Long. 164:21 East

Five days later, at six-thirty in the morning, Andrew White was working near the after mast. The watch had just finished washing the decks, and the planks steamed in the early sun. The northeast breeze was light, and so the ship rolled as she moved slowly along the glittering surface of the equatorial sea. Pleasant Island lay over the horizon, unseen; there was no sign of life on the water. High above the cooper's head two boat-steerers and two foremast hands were perched in the lookout hoops, their faces shaded by weatherbeaten straw hats as they fruitlessly searched for spouts. Another man was on duty at the ship's wheel, watching the wind's ripple along the edges of the sails to gauge its direction as he steered. Smoke drifted from the chimney of the galley on the foredeck, as the Ocean Islander who was the new cook boiled water to make coffee. It was the first mate's watch—Thomas Harlock Smith was in charge of the deck. Andrew White was at the carpenter's bench, but apart from the sounds of his hammering and the creaking noises of the ship, all was quiet as the crew waited for breakfast.

Captain Norris strode onto deck, yelling, "Where are you, you damned nigger?"

The cooper watched Babcock cringe up to his tormentor. Then he heard Norris order him to oil a brass cannon "that stood aft of the Mizenmast." No sooner had Babcock started to obey than fate intervened, in the shape of Jack Baker.

Baker was holding George Babcock's tea mug. Andrew White was close enough to see what was inside it: two small pieces of pork — "about 4 mouthfuls." He felt puzzled. Babcock had not eaten meat for months, because the captain had forbidden it, so how had it gotten there? White then heard Baker tell Captain Norris that he had found the pot on the deck where George Babcock had eaten his supper the night before. In effect, he was accusing Babcock of stealing meat and then wasting it.

It was hard to know Jack Baker's motive for telling such a blatant lie. Maybe he wanted to ingratiate himself with a boss who terrified him, and at the same time get some revenge on Babcock for the betrayal back in December. Yet it seemed unlikely that Norris would believe him. The mug might be Babcock's, but that hardly proved anything. The Ocean Islander, who was the new cook, might have tried to slip the meat to Babcock out of pity. Then again, if one of the islanders believed that the captain was possessed by a malevolent spirit, he could well have determined to try to placate the demon with a ritual offering of food. Lacking something in which to set it out, Babcock's mug could have seemed a good substitute. Whatever the background, if Babcock had found the meat, surely he would have eaten it. Not only was it dangerous to save it for a later occasion, there was no point in doing so.

Norris was not interested in solving the puzzle or even asking questions. White heard him tell Baker to put the mug on the hen coop, close to where he was working. For a few minutes it seemed as if the meat had been forgotten. Then White saw the captain go to the pot and pick it up for another look. Flying into one of his rages, Norris dropped it, and "commenced cursing and swearing at Babcock." Then he went over to the skylight and shouted down it to Manuel des Reis, the new steward, to "pass up his Piece of Rope."

The five-foot length of rope that Manuel handed up had one end bound with twine to make a handle, in imitation of the dreaded cat-o'-nine-tails used for floggings on men-of-war. A knot at the working end gave it weight and extra hitting power. Ordering Babcock to keep on working at the gun, Norris began to swing this weapon, swishing it down on his bent head and shoulders, and across the small of his back. He hit him many times: After three dozen blows, the cooper lost count. Then, at last, the bell rang for breakfast. Norris threw down the lash and stamped down the stairs.

Benjamin Clough was at the cabin table, along with Thomas Harlock Smith, who had handed over the deck to his cousin, the second mate. Norris ate his food, threw down his fork, picked up the ship's medical chest, and strode back up the companionway. Clough followed. Then Norris ordered Babcock "to take the bandages off of his foot which was scalded some months ago."

As Clough watched, Babcock meekly obeyed, sitting down and pulling off the stained rags to expose the raw wound. Opening the chest, the Captain made a plaster by spreading a piece of cloth with a lead monoxide mixture. This, a standard ingredient in medical chests of the time, turned the cloth into an equivalent of a modern adhesive plaster, by making it sticky. Clough heard Norris order Babcock to press it onto the open sore. Then the captain told the young man to "haul" it back and forth across the wound. The pain as the adhesive surface was dragged about the raw flesh must have been excruciating. Worse still, Norris, yelling "horrid oaths and Imprecations," was adding to the agony by "kicking of him in the head temples mouth nose." At last Norris wearied of putting the boot into his victim's face. Clough saw him step back, allowing Babcock to crawl to his feet. Then he heard Norris order Babcock "to go and draw water" to fill up a large tub amidships.

This was a tub that—as cooper Andrew White knew well—held one hundred gallons. Filling it up was heavy work, one of the hardest jobs on board ship. In fact, it was usually done by two men working as a team. It involved dropping a bucket into the sea with a line, scooping it full, and then heaving it up the side of the ship and over the rail. A major health hazard, it was the most common cause of hernia. And yet, as Andrew White went on to describe, the captain "stood over him with his Piece of Whaleline" thrashing his bent back, "and telling him to hurry which he did hurry as fast as he could."

Somehow the embattled Babcock managed the feat over and over again, dragging the bucket up, hauling it to the tub, and tipping it in, then going back to the rail to haul up another bucketful, and so on and on, while all the time the knotted rope whipped. At last the tub was full. Norris then ordered him to fetch sand to scour the decks. Again, Babcock meekly obeyed, but because his strength was almost gone he did not move quickly enough to satisfy Norris, who yelled at him to move, move, and urged him along with the lash.

Drawn by the terrible noises, members of the crew were standing motionless in corners of the deck. No one spoke; no one moved. Like Benjamin Clough and Andrew White, they watched in a paralysis of horror. Twice Babcock crashed to the deck and crawled upright again. The third time he fell was the last. He had fallen full length. Captain Norris ordered him to his feet, emphasizing the order with the whip. George Babcock struggled to obey, groaning helplessly as he pawed for hand-holds. Clough saw him get partway up several times, only to collapse again. Every effort was in vain: George Babcock had fallen *"to rise no more,"* as Clough bleakly recorded; "Capt. Norris beating him all the time and he saying *Oh Capt—I am dying."*

At that, the lash stilled. The creaking of the ship and the slow slide of the sea against the hull were the only sounds. After a long moment Norris bent, gripped Babcock's arm, and hauled him up. When he let go, his victim collapsed again.

Still, no one spoke or moved. The second mate, Nathan Skiff Smith, was watching, too. He was on duty—in charge of the deck—but had not interfered. Captain Norris turned to him. "Mr. Smith," he observed, "I do believe the nigger is dying."

At that, Nathan Smith reluctantly stepped up. "Lift him up," said Norris. Nathan heaved at the limp body, and Norris shouted into George Babcock's face. No response. Wrote Andrew White, "He was so far gone he could not speak." So Nathan Smith fetched smelling salts, but still to no avail. The young man was dead. As Clough grimly recorded, Babcock's "spirit had departed to the God who gave it, floged and beat as long as A breath remained in his body By Captain Howes Norris of Marthas Vineyard."

Captain Norris turned to the silent foremast men and asked if Babcock had a blanket. When one man nodded, Norris ordered him to fetch it and told the others to sew the corpse into it. Then Babcock's battered remains were laid on a plank on the hen coop.

For nine hours the shrouded body lay there, mute and still in the tropical heat. "There he laid till 6 PM," wrote Andrew White.

"He was sewed up in a blanket with his bloody clothes on and at sunset hove overboard," Clough somberly wrote. "So ends as cold-blooded a murder as was ever recorded, being about eight months taking his life."

"Babcock a colored Man was taken to the waste and launched overboard without a word of ceremony or a tear shed to my noledge," Andrew White wrote, adding, "He has gone I hope to rest." Over the months of torture and beating, Babcock had often told the cooper that he would have jumped overboard or cut his throat if he wasn't so frightened of going to hell. "I hope that he has gone home to Glory may God bless him," prayed the cooper. "And I hope this will be a warning to Capton Norris and all the rest of his officers on board."

"He was launched into the deep without being read over

him or a tear shed to his memory," Benjamin Clough concluded; "there to remain untill the last trump shall sound and
wake the whole earth and may God in his infinite goodness
have mercy on his Soul and may all who hear of this A warning
take."

"First part steared East," neatly penned Captain Norris in his
log. "Wind from N.N.E.. Middle and Latter parts calm—at
9 A.M. George Babcock died very suddenly—he complained
of having the cramp—

"Lat. 1:11 South. Long. 167:00 East."

NINE

THAT DIREFUL MADNESS

MEN HAD DIED on the *London Packet*, too.

In April 1835, three months after the mutiny, one of the few hands who had supported Norris passed away. His name was William Hennessey. One day he was reported sick, and the next day "hove the Ship to and burried Wm. Hennessey," wrote Norris, without bothering to elaborate any further. While he did not give the cause of death, it was possibly of scurvy, as several of the crew were off-duty with scurvy at the time, because of the scanty provisions.

Two men expired on the second *London Packet* voyage. Both died in the year 1838, but the circumstances were markedly different. The first, William Bullfinch by name, breathed his last while the ship was at anchor in Zanzibar. Again, Norris did not give the cause of death, merely noting that they "burried him on French Island." While not necessarily the result of ill-treatment, Bullfinch's demise is as mysterious as Babcock's would have been if Clough and White had not been on board to write down the ghastly details.

When the second man ailed and died, however, Norris went to great pains to describe it himself. The deceased was Silas W. Smith, the younger brother of Thomas Harlock Smith, and therefore first cousin of Norris's wife, Elwina.

Silas was just sixteen years old. It was his first voyage. The Smith family had entrusted him to Norris's care. On June 4, 1838, he was "very sick with a fever" that he had developed three days before: "Silas W. Smith very low," wrote Norris next day. "I fear he will not recover." Two days after that, Captain Norris was sitting by the boy's deathbed: "I asked him if there was anything he wished me to say to his Parents and Brothers." Weakly, Silas asked to be remembered to his family, and to tell them "that he thanked them for their kindness to him."

Norris then asked if he had thoughts of the next world, and "if he thought he was prepared for death." Silas, sinking fast, husked an affirmative, and late the next afternoon they hove the ship to and ceremoniously slipped his corpse into the sea. "It was my intention to have kept him untill tomorrow," wrote Norris, "but the weather being very warm I found it would not be prudent to keep him overnight as it might endanger the health of the Ship's company."

This detailed and solicitous account could not be in greater contrast to the disposal of young George Babcock's corpse. "At 6 P.M. buried the above named person," Norris wrote, concluding, "Saw some finbacks but no sperm whales."

It was as if nothing about the cruise had changed. The atmosphere about decks must have been grim, though. This was a time for sober reflection, as well as horror at what had happened. That no one had interfered in the brutal murder would be a guilt they would all carry around for the rest of their lives—"the secret part of the tragedy," as Melville called it, "this darker thread."

Perhaps in some sailors' boardinghouse or ship's forecastle, men who later ran away from the *Sharon* would confide the horrid story to outsiders, just like the *Pequod*'s Gayhead Indian boatsteerer, Tashtego, who "rambled in his sleep, and revealed so much that when he was wakened he could not well withhold the rest." However, they were only likely to put their trust in fellow foremast hands—men like Melville, who would understand exactly how subject they were to the captain's authority, no matter how demented his behavior might be. Like the sailors on the allegorical *Pequod*, too, those who had been on the *Sharon* that dreadful day would have been reluctant to communicate their shameful secret to officialdom, either at sea or on land.

Now that Babcock's corpse had sunk into the sea, most hands would have realized that something should have been done to forestall the murder. Something as simple as calling out, "There she blows!" would have distracted Norris, but no one had thought of it at the time. Or, if they had, were too scared.

The sturdy, independent-minded cooper, Andrew White, was obviously shocked by the brutal killing. At the time of the December mutiny, he had taken some sort of stand by refusing to have anything to do with it when asked by Clough to fetch a rope. But murder was a very different matter, one that demanded direct action—action he had felt unable to take. The whole of his seafaring experience would have drummed in the lesson that the quarterdeck was sacrosanct, and for White personally, there was too much at stake. He was a farmer at heart, and he would do nothing that would risk his inheritance.

Clough was in much the same situation. He had been very lucky to be offered the job of third mate, and now that he had made the first step onto the quarterdeck, he did not want to endanger his prospects of promotion. Moreover, while his letter and his logbook betray his obvious agitation, he knew very well that he did not have the authority to stop Captain Norris. The third mate's job was actually a lowly one, with a lay that was less than the cooper's, and a ranking only slightly above that of boatsteerer. In fact, the only reason there was a third mate at all was that an extra officer was needed to take charge of one of the boats. His job otherwise was to look after the ship's craft and gear, and help keep the crew in order. If Clough had tried to restrain the captain, he, like Andrew White, or any foremast hand, would have been branded a mutineer.

What was different for Benjamin Clough was that he lived in the after quarters of the ship, eating and sleeping in close proximity with the captain and the first and second mates. And, horrifyingly, Captain Norris was not stricken with guilt or shame at the dreadful act he had committed. He was *jubilant*.

According to Clough's letter to his father, Norris had known for some time that he would end up killing Babcock. Over the months of beating and kicking, Norris had raved that "he expected to go to Hell for him." While the captain was flogging the young black man to death, however, he had boasted that "he need not be afraid of going to Hell" any more. Instead, "they would kick him out," presumably because he was too evil even for that place.

By this twisted logic, Norris reckoned he was ensured a happy hereafter.

BEFORE SHIPPING ON the fictional *Pequod*, the narrator, Ishmael, was warned that Ahab "was a little out of his mind for a spell" on the passage home from his last voyage. "He's sick, they say," Ishmael admitted in reply, "but is getting better, and will be all right again before long"—at which the prophet who had delivered the advice snorted derisively, "All right again before long!"

Captain Ahab had a brilliant mind and was extremely brave, but was also clearly crazy. Captain Norris of the *Sharon* was all of these, too—he was sharp-witted, courageous in the boats, and patently deranged. On a whaleship, just as on a southern plantation, a brutal master might whip those under him, but only an insane master would whip any of his hands to death, because he was depriving himself of labor.

The character of Captain Ahab is popularly assumed to be based at least in part on the real-life commander of the *Acushnet*, Captain Valentine Pease. The novelist noted later that Pease ended up "in asylum at the Vineyard"—and this, it seems, was not all that uncommon. The Rev. Joseph Thaxter, minister of the Edgartown Congregational Church from 1780 to 1827, flatly declared, "Insanity prevails much." Strangely, he attributed it to "the Purity of the air and Water." Whatever the

cause, it does indicate that mental instability was not at all unknown in the clannish communities of New England—which
also infers that the shipowners might have had an inkling that
some of the men they entrusted with their ships were a danger
to their own crews. Perhaps, as Melville suggested, they even
believed that a half-mad captain "was all the better qualified
and set on edge, for a pursuit so full of rage and wildness as the
bloody hunt of whales."

However, this is hard to credit where the managing owners
of the *Sharon*, Gibbs & Jenney, were concerned—Jenney in
particular. The family featured prominently in Fairhaven whaling, the Jenney name cropping up repeatedly in whaling crew
lists. While the Gibbs & Jenney–owned *Sharon* cruised unhappily about the western Pacific in 1842, no less than nineteen
family members were at sea in whaleships. They ranged in rank
from greenhand upward: six were boatsteerers, five were either
first or second mates, and three were captains. Hardheaded as
shipowners were reputed to be, it is scarcely likely that Jenney
would knowingly appoint a potential murderer to the quarterdeck of one of his vessels.

The two other Jenney-owned ships that departed from Fairhaven in 1841—*Hesper* and *Columbus*—had men of good reputation in command. Captain Ichabod Handy of the *Hesper*
was well thought of by the missionaries, later on playing a crucial part in the establishment of a mission in the Caroline
Islands. He had a very good relationship with the Pacific Islanders he dealt with, going down in history as one of the pioneers of the coconut oil trade. Captain Frederick Fish of the
Columbus, as well as being famous for short voyages and good

cargoes, was considered "free-hearted" by a whaling wife who gammed with him, Mary Brewster of the Connecticut whaleship *Tiger*—a woman who was not known for her charitable opinions of her husband's fellow skippers.

If the firm had known what Norris was doing, they would have wanted him stopped. However, the only man on board with the authority to restrain the captain was the first officer— Thomas Harlock Smith. In fact, it was his obligation. The brutality was bad enough, but the murder was the last straw. According to Section Three of the Seamen's Act, it was Thomas Harlock Smith's duty to arrest Captain Norris, confine him to his quarters, sail to the nearest port with a U.S. consul—Guam —and hand him over for commitment for trial. But he did nothing, and neither did his cousin, Nathan Smith.

THERE IS NO record of what Thomas Smith was up to while Norris was flogging Babcock to death, so it is likely he was down in his cabin. Nathan Smith, on the other hand, had definitely been on deck, but had made no attempt to rouse up his cousin, the first mate, and persuade him to do something about Norris's extreme violence. Yet later accounts of Nathan Smith portray him as a warm and humane character. Twenty-three years after the murder, when he was in command of the *Java*, the fourth mate of the *Gazelle* went on board of his ship during a gam, later writing in his journal that Captain Nathan Smith was very kind—"as soon as I got on board he offered me tobacco, shoes, and as many clothes, thick or thin, as I stood in need of," he wrote. "I shall remember him as long as I live not for the gift exactly, but for the friendly feelings shown me."

But if Nathan Smith was indeed a kind and humane character, he seemed to find a good excuse for not extending a compassionate hand to the suffering Babcock—an omission that could have caused him a great deal of inner torment over the years ahead. So what was it that compelled him to stand by and watch a man be beaten to death?

If it was possible to find out just who offered the cousins the plum jobs of first and second mates, the answer might lie in that. If it was Norris himself who proposed they should come along as his officers—which seems plausible—then it would have been very hard for the Smiths to oppose his rule. Having sailed on two voyages with Norris, Thomas Harlock Smith owed him a special kind of loyalty. Nathan Smith had a different reason for allegiance. Howes Norris was his brother-in-law —which left the second mate with the awful prospect of trying to defend the family reputation if the news of the murder of Babcock ever got back to Martha's Vineyard.

Because they left no record, it is impossible to tell how the Smiths felt about their kinsman's mad violence. However, a clue lies in that fact that while the Smiths did nothing to thwart Norris, they did not actively support him, either. As the December rebellion demonstrates, they were slow to move until badgered by Norris, and diffident even when pushed. At best, they were halfhearted. Then, when Norris was beating George Babcock, their participation ranged from nil to minimal. It was as if they deliberately chose a stance of noninterference.

Now, however, their failure to intervene had led them into a most unenviable position. The thought of what would happen when—or if—the word of Norris's behavior got out must have haunted them a great deal. Brutality, like their own failure to restrain Norris's rages, could be talked away. Everyone was aware that the large whaling crews needed stern discipline, and everyone knew how the quality of the hands had deteriorated of late. Norris was certainly not alone in the harsh treatment of his men.

Beating one of those men to death, however, was quite another matter. *If* charges were laid at home, and *if* the men testified, it was very likely that Norris was ruined, and the reputation of the Smith family would suffer badly, too. Something had to be done—should have been done long ago. Perhaps they secretly hoped that Norris would die an honorable death in the jaws of a fighting whale. Because now, as in the past, they failed to make any attempt to restrain his actions.

"MODERATE BREEZES FROM the Eastward and fair weather all these 24 hours," Norris began in his logbook entry for Sunday, September 11, ten days after the murder. Then, after the usual notation of "no Sperm Whales," he added a thought that was deceptively philosophical and sane: "It is trying to ones patience to come here for a voyage and be so very unfortunate as we have been, but there is no whales here this season and we cannot make them, so it is no use to grieve."

The following Saturday, sperm whale spouts were spied at last, "but it being so near dark there was no chance," he wrote. As on many other pages in the book, the neatly penned names "Elwina M. Norris—Octavia A. Y. Norris—Alonzo Norris—Mary S. Norris" fill the bottom margin, as a testament to his homesickness. On the slip of card he used as a bookmark other names are more untidily scrawled—Harris Howes, Howes Morris, Nathan Howes—evidently names he was considering for the new baby, now just weeks away from his first birthday, which would be celebrated on November 2, 1842. The largest scrawl is "Howes Norris," which is what the baby had in fact been christened, far across the other side of the world, in frustratingly remote Martha's Vineyard, in a rite the father could not possibly attend.

About this time Clough noted two changes in the captain's behavior. First, Norris took to the bottle, being "half drunk" a lot. Second, he was no longer going down in the chase. Many captains did not go in the whaleboats, shipping a fourth mate to head the fourth boat instead. "Among whale-wise people it has often been argued whether, considering the paramount importance of his life to the success of the voyage, it is right for a whaling captain to jeopardise that life in the active perils of the chase," Melville mused in *Moby-Dick*. This was sensible enough. On the *London Packet* Norris had not gone down in the whaleboats at all. For some unexplained reason he had adopted a different policy on the *Sharon*. Now he changed his mind again and resumed his old habit of staying on board when the boats were lowered.

Because he was drunk? Or because he was suddenly afraid of the whales?

Whatever his reasoning, it was to prove fatal.

THE FARTHER NORTH Norris sailed into the waters around the Groups, the more he was tormented by the same adverse currents that had tried him so on entering the Pacific.

Stress was mounting. Charts were unreliable. The ship was badly in need of reprovisioning, but he did not know which islands could be safely visited. During the first week of October he passed inviting islets such as Strong's Island—properly called Kosrae—and Wellington's Island—Mokil—but did not dare land a boat. "There is no trusting them," he decided, and sailed on. And so, by degrees, more by accident than design, the *Sharon* arrived at Pohnpei.

It was Saturday, October 15, 1842. "First and middle parts light breezes and rainy working towards the harbour," wrote Norris. "Latter part pleasant with light breezes from the South at 10 A.M. came to anchor in the west harbour of the Island of Ascension—" At that point, just as at Rotuma back in April, Norris dropped his pen, and did not pick it up again until the ship was beating out of the harbor. "After the season was out we went to Ascension in Lat. 6.20 North, Long. 158.30 E," Clough wrote to his father. "Whilst we lay there recruiting the Captain kept drunk."

Drunk or not, Norris was still cunning enough to take measures to prevent desertion. The anchor was dropped half a mile from the beach, so that men could only escape by swimming or by stealing a boat—unless he allowed them liberty on shore, something he planned to avoid. When Norris traded with the canoes that came off to the ship for vegetables, fruit, pigs, and fowls, he also negotiated for women. "Came to anchor to Sention [Ascension] half a mile from the shore bought 1 hog some fish and plenty of Girls for tobacker," wrote the cooper on that first night.

True to form, Norris was manipulating the situation. He

hoped the hands would be so preoccupied with lust they would forget their grievances until they were safely back at sea.

This was a favorite option for captains with a jumpy crew. Cruising off the eastern coast of the North Island of New Zealand in February 1838, Captain Barney Rhodes of the Sydney whaler *Australian* noted in his log that he had sent a boat on shore to fetch "three ladies," knowing he would lose most of his men if he allowed them on shore. On the *Mercury* Captain Dennis Fordyce Haskell resorted to the same device while at the Marquesas in July 1842.

"Every night at sunset," Stephen Curtis recorded, the captain sent a boat ashore "for the laudable purpose of fetching off girls on board of the ship." It was not appreciated by all the men, Curtis writing that "scenes which ought to make a man blush were constantly before the eyes of the more virtuous part of the crew"—of which there were some, as he emphatically added. The consequences, too, were nasty. William Allen on the *Samuel Robertson* noted later, after a meeting with the *Mercury*, that seven of Haskell's crew were down with the pox. Of the seven hundred men on board a French man-of-war in port at the same time, he was told, all but seventy had fallen to this "loathsome disease." Evidently, Haskell had judged that the risk was worth it. However, the day he took his departure from Nukuhiva he was minus two men, as two of the Kanakas had swum ashore in the night.

Norris took the added precaution of feeding his crew well, trading freely for hogs, fruit, and vegetables. This, to him, would have been a huge concession. The Kanakas, like George Babcock earlier, were confined to prevent their escape. Otherwise, being adept swimmers, the natives could have slipped over the side at the first opportunity. As it happened, this is exactly what four white shipmates did—"4 Men runaway in the Night," wrote Andrew White.

"Caught our men that run away," wrote Benjamin Clough just twenty-four hours later. So the first attempt at desertion was a failure, probably because of the dense and spiky mangrove thickets that rimmed the harbor. Their proximity to land, however, emboldened the crew. Next day two of them openly defied Captain Norris. One of the foremast hands had been ordered to take over the job of ship's cook, evidently because the Ocean Islander had been confined. The sailor flatly refused to do it and was put in irons for disobedience, and the other was slapped into handcuffs for the crime of "taking up for him."

This did not subdue their newly acquired spirit. Two days later Norris faced another rebellion. It had become obvious to the men that he was not going to allow them on shore, except when they went in under the close supervision of the officers to collect firewood and fresh water. So the foremast hands of the *Sharon* put down their tools and refused to work—"because the capton said that he would not give them any liberty," wrote Andrew White.

After a great deal of fuss, in which the men remained obdurate, Norris, most uncharacteristically, caved in. In exchange for a promise to go back to duty, he told them, he would allow holidays on shore. As a precaution, though, he confiscated their Protection Papers. If they ran away they would have no evidence of their nationality and would forfeit the legal rights of American seamen.

That tactic did not work, either. For men as desperate to get away as the crew of the *Sharon*, the loss of their certificates seemed supremely unimportant. The next day—Sunday—the starboard watch was allowed on shore, and "at sunset they all came off but 8," wrote Clough. He was being sarcastic: eight was a huge number to lose all at once. On Monday the larboard watch was given leave, and "all came off but 2." So ten men were missing. Eleven days after dropping anchor the deck planks were echoing. Two more had absconded the day before, including "1 boatsteerer."

Three boatsteerers ran away in Pohnpei, so it is difficult to tell just which one this deserter happened to be. It could have been Otis Tripp, the harpooner who had been hammered over the head with a heaver; or Alexander Yellott, the greenhand who had been promoted to the nerve-racking position of harpooner; or Leonard Wing. Months earlier, Leonard Wing had missed what Captain Norris called two "good chances" at harpooning whales. "And so it has been all the voyage," Norris had added grimly. So it seems very likely that he was one of the deserters. If correct, the one boatsteerer left in the crew would have been the illiterate young New Bedforder, Isaac H. Place.

One of the foremast hands who ran away was Nathaniel Shearman. Having left his Protection on the *Sharon*, he had to apply for a replacement certificate when he got back to New Bedford, which he did on December 6, 1848. His reasons are plain—he was the boatsteerer who had misunderstood a command to wash the rail and had been beaten and cursed and demoted to the forecastle. Considering that he had been shipped at the last moment to serve in the place of a man who had failed to turn up, Shearman had been most unfortunate.

Thomas Davis, a fair-haired young greenhand from New York, was another to abscond; he shipped on board the *Emily Morgan*, a very bad choice, as Captain Prince William Ewer ran a very unhappy ship. In April 1843 Davis tried to desert at Samoa, but was recaptured and flogged. The following month he was one of a desperate gang who tried to escape by setting fire to the ship, but he did not succeed in that attempt, either.

Three other runaways from the *Sharon*—carpenter Frederick Turner and greenhands John M. Bacon and William Weeks—can be identified because of queries posted at the New Bedford Customs House when they did not arrive home. John Moore and Jack Baker, both of whom had tried to desert at Rotuma but had been recaptured, managed to get away this time. Later, Andrew White informed Thomas Harlock Smith that Baker had jumped ship because he was tired of being punched and beaten. However, his part in the Babcock tragedy could have been a factor.

The twelve deserters got away because they were sheltered by the locals. The first four had been less lucky, but since then the people on shore had heard the details of Babcock's murder and were more than willing to give the ex-*Sharon* hands refuge. As Benjamin Clough wrote to his father, "12 men left us here, saying they would not sail with a murderer." Worse still for Norris, because of the ghastly story the twelve runaways told, he was unable to ship any Pohnpei hands to replace them. Like most men of Oceania, Pohnpei natives had a healthy curiosity about the world and were keen to learn the skills that shipboard life offered—but not at the cost of shipping with a killer.

Captain Norris formulated a different theory for his problems. "Took in our wood and water, vegetables, fruit, some pigs, fowls &c and sailed again the 27th having lost   men by desertion which we could not get back again," he wrote on that date. The number of men he had lost was left blank. "Ascension would be a good place for a ship to recruit," he added, "were it not for the white men that lives there but they are the greatest pack of Rouges [rogues] I ever met with which causes a great deal of trouble and even makes it dangerous for a Ship to anchor." Thomas Harlock Smith agreed, stating to the newspapers after the ship's arrival in Sydney that the deserters could not be retaken because "the white people on the island" had "used their influence with the natives to protect them." Babcock's protracted ordeal had been dismissed by both as a possible motive.

When the *Sharon* weighed anchor, Norris was so short-handed that he had to pay some natives to help get the ship out of the lagoon. "At 10 A.M. of Thursday got outside the reef," he wrote; "at 11 discharged the Pilot or person that called himself one and once more found ourselves at sea—and clear of the vagabonds that lives on the Island—"at 12 noon 4 miles outside the Reef."

ONCE THE *SHARON* was safely hull-down on the horizon, William Weeks and his eleven fellow runaways emerged from hiding to find themselves in a place that was even more remarkable than Rotuma. Where there might be a few haunted houses in their home places back in America, and some of the superstitions of Rotuma might have seemed dauntingly alien, here on Pohnpei there was an entire haunted city.

Nan Madol is an ancient and deserted metropolis, measuring as much as eleven miles across, and so crisscrossed with canals that a boat is needed to explore the ruins of huge temples and palaces. Enduring legends say it was built by buccaneers—a story so old that William Weeks undoubtedly heard it—but in fact it was built by thirteenth-century ancestors of the Pohnpeians, who in ambition and mystery rivaled the pharaohs of Egypt. (The mystery is how, out of a population estimated at forty thousand at the time, they managed to find a large enough workforce to build such an enormous complex.) Because of the malevolent ancestor ghosts that prowled there, it was—and still is—not considered a wise place to spend the night.

Studded with curious stone structures even outside the Nan Madol area, Pohnpei is both intriguing and beautiful. Damp, luxuriant, and fertile, the island is surrounded by a glassy lagoon walled in by coral reefs dotted with wooded islets. Travelers found the people delicate, temperate, and clean, with flashing white teeth and masses of lovely black hair. The ranking system was complex, made up of kings, princes, and nobles; magic was part of everyday life, particularly in the practice of medicine. Homicide was embarked on rather lightly—as a visitor remarked in the late nineteenth century, "They don't think much of killing a man." However, what was probably the most remarkable feature of Pohnpeian society of the time was the surprisingly large role the beachcombers played.

Pohnpei had been the hub of beachcombing since the beginning of whaling in the Groups, and by 1842 there were about forty beachcombers who were long-standing residents. Some came from vessels that had been wrecked locally or in the Kingsmills, and a few were fugitives from the Australian penal colonies. Most, however, were runaway seamen. They congregated on Pohnpei because life was easier there than on the atolls, where lack of fresh water meant a monotonous diet of coconuts and fish. Not all of them were white—the beaches of Pohnpei were host to Oceanic drifters, too, including Hawai'ians, islanders from the Kingsmills, and New Zealand Maori. Just about all of them were rowdy, some were corrupt, and not a few were murderers. But, while they would kill each other without a qualm, they were all careful not to harm Pohnpeians.

Contrary to Norris's impression, they were not undisciplined. Like beachcombers anywhere in Oceania, they had worked hard to adapt to the local way of doing things, which here included being heavily tattooed with thorns or sharpened bird bones and semi-castrated, one testicle having been crushed with a rock. The complicated stratifications of the local caste system had to be thoroughly understood, because these renegades from other societies survived by the grace of the chiefs, who, luckily, found them useful. Traditionally, everything in Pohnpeian space belonged to the ruling class—including any ships that passed through the reef into local territory. Experience had taught the chiefs that the men on the visiting craft had different views of this, and so, in order to preserve order and save face, they needed intermediaries who would tackle the captains on their behalf and negotiate for the trade goods they greatly desired.

The beachcombers filled this role very adequately, mostly because they were shrewd enough to realize that their survival depended on it. When a captain approached the island, a canoe would come out bearing a scarecrow figure, longhaired and wildly bearded. Often, a small pig was tucked under his arm, as the beachcombers specialized in farming pigs for sale to the ships, living on those profits as well as what commission they could wring out of transactions made on behalf of the princes.

For the captain, it could seem a most ludicrous sight. In 1839 Commander Blake of HMS *Larne* was accosted by a "wild and savage" apparition, an Irish deserter from the American whaleship *Howard*. "His long hair hung clotted with oil; he had several wreaths of beads around his head, and was tattooed from head to foot." Yet this creature, so obviously beyond the bounds of decent society of home, was the accredited representative of the cream of society in Pohnpei.

And underneath the rags was a man who was conscientious to the extreme in his efforts to fulfill the expectations of his patron. Wiser than the captains with whom they dealt, the renegades made a genuine effort to understand and value the local way of life. Many of these washed-up vagabonds of the sea forged additional ties by marrying local women who were allied in some way to the chief, and then fathering large families of important children. Others strove to make themselves even more indispensable by establishing themselves as pilots and artisans—and this is exactly what one of William Weeks's companions, Alexander Yellott, did. While William looked for another berth, Yellott opted for settling on shore, where he made his living as a carpenter, blacksmith, and ship's pilot.

William Weeks had to contain his patience, since the harbor remained obstinately empty. It was not until November 25 that a sail appeared on the horizon, and a canoe paddled out to meet it with a beachcomber on board. The ship was the *Wilmington & Liverpool Packet*, which had left New Bedford on December 22, 1841, and was doing almost as badly as the *Sharon*, having taken less than two hundred barrels of oil in the eleven months she had been at sea.

One of the officers of the *'Packet* was twenty-three-year-old Samuel N. Brush, who came from Holmes Hole, Martha's Vineyard. He knew the Smith family well and must have been acquainted, too, with Captain Howes Norris. Samuel Brush was not enjoying his voyage; when the ship made Pohnpei he eyed the island without enthusiasm. No sooner were they floating inside the lagoon than the wind promptly changed. Unable to beat out through the gap in the reef in the face of the unfavorable gusts, the *Wilmington & Liverpool Packet* was trapped in what Brush called "this miserable hole."

The captain, thirty-one-year-old New Bedforder Gilbert Place, was equally disgruntled. When the British trader *John Bull* arrived a couple of weeks later, he marched up to the Scottish supercargo, Andrew Cheyne, with a litany of grievances. "Captain Place of the whaler informed me that the natives are very friendly and honest," wrote Cheyne. However there were about sixty runaway sailors in residence who were not desirable company at all. "Were it not for these vagabonds," Captain Place informed him, "a great many more whale ships would call at this Island." What he did not tell Cheyne was that he'd had no scruples in hiring four of these vagabond runaway whites to fill out his crew—Otis Tripp, Jack Baker, John Moore, and William Wallace Weeks.

They were hired some time between November 30 and December 11. Whatever Brush wrote in his journal during that time has been lost, though—that leaf of the journal has been deliberately cut out. Did he copy the tales he heard of the situation on the *Sharon*, and then decide it would be indiscreet to take them back to the Vineyard? It is impossible to tell. What is interesting is that soon after the *Wilmington & Liverpool Packet* got away from Pohnpei, Brush stopped filling in his journal and gave the book to William Weeks. Written boldly on the flyleaf are the words, "This Book was presented to William W. Weeks by Mr. Samuel N. Brush Chief Mate of the Ship Wilmington and Liverpool Packet of New Bedford, on March 12th 1843."

From then on, William penned the daily entries. Life on board the 'Packet was a refreshing change. William had friends, a kindly sponsor in first mate Samuel Brush, and a sociable captain who liked to gam with other ships. All in all, William was quite content—or would have been, if he had been making any money. He wrote on April 19, "4 months out from Ascension and no Oil and about 35 dollars in debt Oh! Ginger Pop."

On June 16, 1843, during a midsea visit with the *William & Eliza*, the contrast between life on the 'Packet and existence on the *Sharon* was abruptly brought home. "Heard [news] from Ship Sharon," William wrote. "Capt. Norris was killed by 3 Kanakas off of the Groups."

TEN

RETRIBUTION

NOVEMBER 5, 1842, dawned with gentle breezes. As the sun rose, it revealed a sea that was barren all the way to the horizon—no distant islands, no seabirds, no whales. The ship was rushing along in an apparently empty world. The decks were washed at early light so that the planks steamed dry in the first long rays of the sun. After that, despite the barrenness of the sea and the need to get to New Zealand quickly to recruit hands and fill the half-empty forecastle, four men clambered up the rigging and into the lookout hoops to watch out for whales. Below them, canvas billowed in a series of great white wings; all sail was set for the fastest passage possible.

Captain Norris certainly did not expect spouts to be raised. At nine in the morning, when the cry of "She blows!" echoed from the highest part of the rigging, he was in his cabin with his bottle—according to Benjamin Clough's letter to his father, the captain was already half-drunk, despite the early hour. When he heard the hail, Norris was sober enough, though, to hurry up the companionway and clamber up the rigging to look at the spouts himself. Sliding rapidly down a backstay to the deck, he would have been shouting orders as he came—"Hard down the wheel! Hoist and swing the boats!" It was then that the full realization of his shorthandedness hit home. Because so many of his oarsmen had run away, he could only lower two boats in the chase, a frustrating and infuriating reminder of his problems.

The hands did not even know which whaleboat they belonged to, so they milled about uncertainly, making Norris still more edgy. Thomas Harlock Smith and Nathan Smith shouted out names as they desperately assembled oarsmen. Clough was hurriedly given the job of Thomas Harlock Smith's boatsteerer. "I went off to steer the Larboard boat," he wrote in his log. Nathan Smith, the second mate, headed the waist boat. His boatsteerer, presumably, was Isaac Place.

Down the two whaleboats rattled. A headsman and a boatsteerer stood inside each one, handling the ropes to make sure the boats splashed evenly onto the water. The sea was always more choppy than it appeared from the deck, so Thomas Harlock Smith and Nathan Smith would have wielded their long steering oars to steady the craft. Then eight hands—four for each whaleboat—scrambled down the side of the ship and jumped into the boats as they seesawed on the waves.

The eight hands included three Kanakas—the Rotumans and one Hope Islander. The Hope Islander was in Nathan

Smith's boat, while the two Rotumans were in the other. Also assigned to Nathan Smith's boat was a man who should not have been there—Andrew White. As cooper, White should have been on board the ship getting gear ready for the work that awaited if they did indeed catch a whale. Instead, he was sent off to sweat at an oar in the hot tropical sun.

When he noted in his journal, "the Capton and the steward and 3 natives was on board," White knew this was irregular. One of the natives did have a right to be on the ship—the Ocean Islander, George Black, who was the cook. It was logical that he should remain behind, to have a hot meal waiting when the boats' crews returned. It was also routine for the steward to stay. As the boat pulled away from the ship, Manuel des Reis clambered up the rigging with his shirt stuffed with flags, ready to set signals to let the men in the boats know where the whales were rising. The other two natives left on the ship, both Hope Islanders, were ordinary foremast hands, who should have been working in the boats instead of helping the captain look after the ship. That was the job they'd been hired for.

Neither White nor Clough gave a reason for the decision to send away all the Americans and leave the natives behind. Maybe the two Hope Islanders were so weakened by the captain's beatings that they could not be depended on to do their full work at the oars. It is possible that the New Englanders raced the islanders to the boats, desperate for a break from the tension on board. Or perhaps Captain Norris preferred to be left with men he had beaten into submission—which implies that the two Hope Islanders, realizing they were to be left alone with their tormentor, felt a fear that bordered on frenzy.

• • •

Within hours the first mate's boat captured a whale. As Clough noted later in his logbook, "We struck a whale and turned him up." Benjamin Clough himself pitched the harpoon, and Thomas Harlock Smith wielded the killing lance. Then Thomas Harlock Smith ordered Clough to plant a flagged stick—a waif—in the whale's spout hole so it could be found easily later. After that, he decided to return to the hunt. Clough would have been very aware that this was a bad decision, since the dead whale presented a big enough job for a shorthanded crew, but nevertheless he obeyed when Harlock Smith ordered them all to haul on their oars in chase of another.

From the other boat, Andrew White saw the distant ship come round as Captain Norris and the natives steered for the waifed whale; he watched them as "they run down to the Whale and took him alongside." He, too, would not have felt happy that the two boats were still in the chase. Every time the whaleboat rose on the crest of one of the swells and the ship came into sight, it was a reminder of what needed to be done before the dead whale could be flensed. The grindstone had to be set up. Cutting spades had to be sharpened to a razor's edge. Sheaves of barrel staves had to be fetched from the holds where they were stowed. And, while the two Hope Islanders were struggling to cope with all this cooper's work, the cooper was still off chasing whales.

When Nathan Smith hissed a warning and the oarsmen became abruptly aware of the gasp and roar of a nearby spout, the cooper backed his oar to help stop the boat's headway as the boatsteerer balanced in the bow of the boat with his harpoon poised. White saw the whale slide under the water. The harpoon had missed, and the whale had sounded. "The wast boat went on and mised," he wrote; in Clough's logbook there is a drawing of a whale's tail, the sign of a whale that got away.

Thirty minutes later, when the whale came up, it had turned a half circle and was swimming in the direction of the ship, the rest of the pod following. Nathan Smith's whaleboat pulled around to follow the school. "The whales milled off towards the ship," wrote Andrew White, "we still chasing them up."

It was then that they saw that the ship's flag was flying at half-mast.

Thomas Harlock Smith, standing in the head of his boat, was watching the milling whales, his back turned to the distant ship, so his first warning would have been cries from the oarsmen. It would have taken only one hard stare over his shoulder to trigger the order to his men to abandon the chase and get back to the ship as fast as they could pull.

Nathan Smith was also steering for the *Sharon*. By this time, too, men in both boats had commented that the ship had been sailing erratically. For a long time it seemed as if they were getting no closer, even though the whaleboat sails were set to help the oarsmen along. Abruptly they realized that the *Sharon* was sailing away from them. "But," Andrew White recorded, "the wind being light," they slowly hauled closer. An hour dragged by as the oarsmen panted at their work. Andrew White could hear the faraway shrieks of the Portuguese steward, perched high in the rigging. More laborious sculling to bring the boat nearer, and the message became distinct.

The natives had murdered Captain Norris and taken over the ship.

THE SILENCE IN the boats was stunned. "O tis out of the power of me to relate to you the feelings there was in those 2 boats," wrote Andrew White.

It had happened at three in the afternoon, Manuel screamed; he had been waiting for them to respond to his flag of distress for nearly two hours. He had been aloft when he heard the captain's loud cry and had scrambled partway down to see what had happened. When he was within a few feet of the deck "the natives made for him with spades." Manuel had scuttled back up the rigging; as the cooper phrased it, he was "somewhat alarmed about himself as anyone of us would be placed in that situation." Trapped aloft, he had waited for the boats and watched the islanders employ the breathing space to stockpile weapons—"Cutting spades, Harpoons, hamers and other weapons," wrote Benjamin Clough, "ready to destroy the crew of the boats as soon as they should come alongside."

Manuel's hoarse shouts echoed over the water as the boats crept up to the ship. Thomas Harlock Smith bellowed back instructions to "cut the halliards," as Benjamin Clough put it, "and let the sails run down"—to halt the *Sharon* in her flight. No sooner had the words left the first mate's mouth than one of the Hope Islanders leapt onto the bulwarks. Naked, gleaming with sweat, smeared with blood, the Kanaka was almost unrecognizable as a man who had shared the forecastle with the rest of the *Sharon* foremast hands for the past seven months. He was brandishing a cutting spade and was pointing with his other hand at the Hope Islander in Nathan Smith's boat.

In his own language, he called out to him, evidently telling him to drop overboard, swim to the ship, and join the mutiny. The Hope Islander in the boat shook his head. With instant fury his fellow native seized up the cook's ax and hurled it with terrifying accuracy at his head. The Kanaka in the boat ducked in the nick of time.

The ax was followed by a hail of other missiles. Andrew White wrote, "They began to throw billets of wood," plus belaying pins, hunks of tortoiseshell, and club hammers; "and 1 ax come in the boat." The first mate's crew was belabored, too. According to Clough, the natives "commenced heaving bone belaying pins, hammers, and wood," which they had assembled "ready to use as soon as the boat should come near enough, one of them keeping to each boat when they approached the ship and the other one at the wheel."

Within minutes of the start of this deadly barrage, Thomas Harlock Smith decided that it was impossible to board the ship without losing some of their men; everyone agreed, and so the boats' crews gripped their oars and retreated for a council of war.

OBVIOUSLY, IT WAS best to wait for dark before making another attempt to recapture the ship. The problem was how to do it. Sitting in the bow of the first mate's boat and listening to the men debate ideas while the late shadows grew longer, Benjamin Clough watched the ship as she lay heavily in the glossy water. He looked at the scene so intently he was able to paint it in detail later.

In many respects Clough's painting matches his written description of what happened. The flag is at half-mast, one native is on the taffrail at the stern, another is standing at the helm, and a third is in the waist just forward of the main mast, while Manuel is on the foretopgallant yard, cutting away the foretopgallant sail. He already has done the same for the maintopgallant. As he sat and watched the ship, Benjamin Clough must have wondered why the natives were not making any attempt to flush Manuel out of the rigging, so they could fix the ropes and get the ship under way again. Indeed, back when Manuel des Reis had started cutting away the sails from the yards, a well-aimed ax could have saved them.

There are features in his painting that hint at unrecorded events. Instead of the yards being braced about and the sheets hauled aft, so that the lower sails are spread to catch the wind, the sails are brailed up. This was what was usually done to lift the canvas away from the tryworks and the blubber-cutting gear, so it looks as if the natives were getting ready for cutting in the whale when the confrontation with Captain Norris started. On the foredeck, smoke is drifting up from the galley chimney, as if a meal was being prepared when the cook—the Ocean Islander, George Black—was interrupted by the slaughter. In Clough's picture the two boats are overhauling the ship in close formation, still with their sails set and the men pulling their oars—but there is no sign of the dead whale. The natives must have cut the corpse adrift to lighten the ship while attempting to flee. But, because the breeze was so faint, and because they were not able to set the big lower sails, they had not been able to outrun the two boats.

If any of these speculations passed through Clough's mind, he never got around to writing them down. At that particular moment, it is more likely that he was totally preoccupied with the problem that faced them.

"We noed not what to do," Andrew White confessed; "we had ben without water some time and had not eaten since we eat our breakfast." And they were seven hundred miles from the nearest known land.

Finally, Benjamin Clough suggested that both boats should pull well ahead of the ship, as if they were making for some distant shore, and drop back after sunset. When it was fully dark, he told the others, he would slip into the water, swim to the stern of the ship, and climb in the cabin windows. Once there, he would find the ship's muskets and load them, and then fire a gun as a signal to the boats that it was time to board the ship. This was adopted as the most sensible plan.

At last, night descended. Andrew White began, "The Boat pulled out head of the ship and the third mate got overboard and swam to the ship and got in to the cabbing winders at the same time one of the boats kept a stern of the ship to pick up the third mate if he did not succeed in getting into the winder." Clough, in his journal, recorded likewise, "I took the boat knife in my mouth as A weapon against sharks as there was A great number around and droped silently overboard and swam for the head of the ship." According to later reports, Clough had a swim of an hour and a half to get there, while the sharks hovered menacingly close. Neither Clough nor White confirm this unlikely story, and Thomas Smith flatly contradicted it, saying that it took Clough only about ten minutes to get as far as the bow of the *Sharon*.

But what were the natives doing, while all this was happening?

Benjamin Clough must have wondered why they were not working together to get the ship away under cover of night. In the letter to his father, however, he unwittingly provided some insight into their state of mind. "When I got to the head of the ship," he wrote, "I saw 1 of the Kanakers standing between the night heads pounding on A tin pan."

The knightheads were two timbers in the bows, right at the front of the ship. It was George Black who was poised there, creating this loud, chaotic noise. He had succumbed to superstitious panic. Dark had fallen, and the dismembered body of Captain Norris was lying in a pool of congealing blood in the dense shadows of the deck. It would have been easy to believe that Norris's malevolent *'atua* was prowling the murky dark, and that it was desperately necessary to scare the frightful ghost away.

Probably because of his self-induced terror, George Black failed to glimpse Clough in the water. "He did not see me," Clough went on. "I then droped Along side of the ship, when I came to the stern I went up the Ruder and into the Cabin window."

Once inside the after cabin, which had been the captain's private sitting room, the third mate stripped naked, explaining in the letter to his father that his clothes, being wet, could have hampered him if it came to a hand-to-hand struggle. After that, he searched the dim, unfamiliar space for weapons, finding two cutlasses and putting them in the "forward cabin"—the saloon, which held the big table where he had eaten many meals with Captain Norris and the other mates. That accomplished, he "got some powder and balls and muskets and commenced loading the muskets."

Inside the saloon, it was very shadowy. Stars shone down through the skylight, making the room seem even darker. Clough could hear the natives talking; he glimpsed their shapes as they trudged round and round the after deck. He heard an odd thudding noise, like wood hitting wood, and assumed the two Kanakas were "collecting wood and other missiles to heave at the boats." If he had known the Kingsmill Islanders better, he might have wondered if the sounds were part of a traditional exorcism, as the natives drummed the planks in an ever-increasing arc around the body of the murdered captain. However, Clough was too busy loading weapons to pay much attention.

Soon two of the muskets were charged, and he had put "Powder into the third." But he had run out of ammunition. Quietly propping the guns at the foot of the companionway stairs, Clough groped his way back into the after cabin to get more musket balls. Then, "I heard someone comeing down," he wrote. Despite the noises on board the ship, his stealthy movements had been overheard.

It was one of the Hope Islanders, one of the two who had been drumming on the deck. Clough held his breath, listening to the native descend the companionway, step by slow step. All the way to the foot the Kanaka came—and fell over the muskets.

The clatter and crash was deafening. The native froze, peering into the blackness. "I could see him but not he me," wrote Clough. Characteristically, the young third mate seized the initiative. Leaping forward in the gloom without any kind of warning, Clough grabbed a cutlass "and made A thrust at him." The islander let out a great shout as blade sliced into flesh, "and reached for me and got hold of me." Struggling for the weapon, the two men plunged back and forth in the confined space, stumbling into furniture and crashing into bulkheads. The native "began to call lustily for the others to come to his help."

Wrestling desperately in the dark, knowing he was doomed if another native attacked, "I then wounded him as much as I could," Clough wrote. He forced a thumb into an eye socket and tore out one of the islander's eyes. As the Kanaka writhed in agony, Clough managed to grip the cutlass and attempted to saw off his head. The blade was very dull, but, "thinking he was about dead I got up to see if the others were A coming," wrote Clough. To his fervent relief he heard no rush of footsteps. No one came to the wounded Kanaka's aid.

Instead, the Kanaka himself jumped up, grabbed the cutlass, "and began to lay about him." Benjamin dodged about to avoid the blindly flailing blade, backing into the after cabin and crashing against the desk and settee. Chaos reigned, the cutlass clanging "against the furniture and against my flesh but he soon gave it up and I heard him breathe verry hard for A number of times and then I heard him no more."

Evidently the islander had fainted from pain and loss of blood. Clough staggered back through the saloon to the foot of the stairway, looked up, and saw a second native silhouetted at the top—the other Hope Islander, belatedly responding to his comrade's desperate shouts. Clough could see the weapon he held: "A long Cutting spade in his hands shoved about halfway down the stairs." Seizing a musket in his slashed and bleeding hands, Clough somehow squeezed the trigger. The sound was like thunder.

Despite his wounds, his aim was unerring. The native slumped on the deck at the head of the stairs. As he let go of the spade, however, it fell down the stairway, striking Clough "on the thick part of my arm above the Elbow, cutting it to the bone."

Benjamin lurched back with the force of the blow, his arm suddenly numb. He heard the native fall; he heard him groan twice. Then, silence. Clough stood there, listening intently. He heard nothing. No responsive shout, no rattle of a boat against the hull. Nothing from Manuel in the rigging. Just the slow creak as the ship rolled back and forth, the swish of the sea, and the heavy thump of his own heartbeat in his ears. A shot had been fired. All the men in the boats should have heard it. Manuel *must* have heard it. But no one made any attempt to come to Benjamin's assistance.

Instead, the third Kanaka—the Banaban cook, George Black —came to the head of the companionway. "I heard the other native coming aft and he came to the companionway and looked down." Benjamin Clough saw his dark shape against the stars; he watched him bend down to look at the huddled body of the Hope Islander he had just shot dead. Then George Black straightened to peer down the stairs. Clough saw that he, too, held a spade. "I steped back into the Cabin, the blood running from all parts of my body like a stuck dolphin," he wrote to his father; "in the dark, the boats away and one Native on deck."

The pain of his wounds was beginning to bite deeply. He was barely hanging on to consciousness. Blood spurted from the deep gash above his left elbow, dripping on the cabin floor; it seemed a ghastly possibility that an artery had been severed. When he braced himself and tried to pick up a musket, his left arm refused to bend. The cuts in his right palm had stiffened, so it would have been impossible to pull the trigger even if he had managed to aim one.

Then he heard a noise from the cabin behind him. The first islander who had attacked him was moving. "I heard the Native in the After Cabin breathe heavily," he wrote to his father. Blood dripped faster as his heart thumped.

But it was a false alarm: after that one deep groan, Clough heard no more. When he looked up at the head of the companionway again, the Ocean Islander had disappeared; George Black had quietly put down his spade and was walking back to the foredeck. Clough heard the soft footsteps retreat. At last it was safe to hail the boats.

BUT STILL THE boats did not come. Seated in the second mate's boat, Andrew White had been able to see the third native clearly—"the one that was on the Bows," the same one who had been beating on a tin. Then, at the same moment that he heard the gunshot, the cooper had watched George Black "run aft with a spade in his hand."

If White saw this, then the Smiths must have seen it, too. Instead of racing to the rescue, however, they waited and watched as George Black contemplated the dead body of the islander at the head of the companionway, peered down the stairs, and finally retreated.

Next, they heard Clough's voice, hailing the boats and asking them to come quickly, as he was badly wounded. Then the third mate slowly and painfully came onto deck, having somehow found the strength to crawl up the companionway. According to Andrew White's account, the patchy moonlight revealed a horrifying spectacle: Clough, as naked as the natives he'd fought, was liberally smeared with wet blood.

The ship had been retaken, he weakly informed the men in the boats. Two of the Kanakas were dead, and the other had run away. Yet still the Smiths did not give the order to board the ship, instead objecting that it was hard to believe that two natives were dead. Only one shot had been heard.

There had been a hand-to-hand battle, the third mate replied wearily, and he was pretty sure he had killed one islander with a cutlass. While he could not be sure he was dead, it was likely. He had heard nothing from that particular fellow for some time.

Finally the two boats' crews clambered up the side of the ship, and Manuel scuttled down from the rigging. "The steward struck fire and light a light," wrote the cooper. Holding the lamp high, the men trooped down into the cabin—to find Clough's first attacker still alive. The Hope Islander was perched on the sill of the transom window. The eye Clough had gouged out was hanging by a string from the socket. Blood ran from the ragged gash in his neck where Clough had tried to cut off his head.

The Kanaka said nothing, instead letting out a low groan. Despite his wounds, he was holding the old cutlass in one hand; the boat knife Clough had left on the sill was in the other. As the men stopped short, staring, he pushed these weapons toward them.

So Thomas Harlock Smith told the men to stand back and give him elbow room. Shuffling, they obeyed. Then he lifted a musket, took careful aim, and shot the helpless native through the heart.

The body was dragged on deck by the hair and thrown into the sea. The Hope Islander who had been shot by Clough, and whose body was slumped at the head of the companionway, was heaved overboard in the same manner. Then, with flaring torches in their hands, the crew searched the murky dark for George Black, but without success.

Instead, they stumbled over the captain's corpse. It was a grisly discovery. One slash with a whaling spade had cut his torso almost in half at the waist, while his head, nearly severed at the neck, was almost unrecognizable. According to Clough, it had been "shockingly mangled by the Hogs." The pigs were running in and out of the flickering shadows with bits of skull in their jaws.

Wincing seamen collected up the grisly remains of their captain, while others brought up a plank. Once all the pieces were found and placed on the board, the corpse was shrouded and left until daylight. This, according to Andrew White, brought the time to about ten-thirty, though he neglected to describe the scary rest of the night. Clough filled the gap, writing that they gave up the hunt for the other native until daylight, and, in the meantime, "the Watch was set the watch keeping A sharp lookout with arms in their hands." But even when the morning dawned, there was still no sign of George Black.

ELEVEN

GEORGE BLACK

"AT DAYLIGHT THE next morning all hands were called and commenced fitting the rigging it being calm," Clough recorded. Then, as soon as breakfast was over, the men were assembled to witness the burial of Captain Norris. While they stood in a huddle with their hats in their hands, Thomas Harlock Smith read a prayer, and then the shrouded corpse was launched into the ocean.

To his father, Clough simply noted, "The next morning the Captain was buried with the usual ceremonies." In his log, however, he added intriguingly, no sooner had Captain Norris's mutilated body been dropped into the deep, than "Our hogs seven in number were knocked in the head and threw overboard." These were the pigs that had been found gnawing parts of Norris's skull. While they represented several pork dinners, the men were too squeamish—or superstitious—to contemplate eating them.

The next job was to get the sails back on the yards. After that, the decks were thoroughly scrubbed to remove all traces of the bloody slaughter. It was not until that was done that the order was belatedly given to search the ship for the third native, whom by now they had identified as George Black; their erstwhile cook was apparently not a man to inspire caution, let alone fear.

Andrew White was with the group that found George cowering in a dim recess in the hold. Instead of shooting, the men told him to come out, but the native commenced "fireing woods," so the gang "punched him some with a Iron pole." After a few hard jabs the Kanaka gave himself up, after which they put him in irons. "It appears by his account," wrote Clough, "that when he came aft and saw the other native dead that he went and jumped overboard and swam away from the Ship it being calm and After the boats were hoisted up he got hold of the Eyebolt in the Rudder." George had hung on until the decks were quiet, "and then came and got on deck by the bobstays and went down into the forehole &c."

Unfortunately, Clough stopped writing at this point. Because of his wounds, for some days he was not able to hold a pen long enough to write a full account of the murder and his single-handed recapture of the ship. Giving up when he reached that enigmatic "&c.," he stuck the sheets into the appropriate place in his log with sealing wax. Any details of the assassination that George Black might have revealed went unrecorded. Still on

board were the three Kanakas who had been down in the boats
—the two Rotumans and the last Hope Islander, the one who
had been so nearly felled by the ax hurled by his fellow villager.
But Clough did not record that anyone asked them questions,
either.

The cooper was equally uncommunicative. Instead of noting
down what George Black might have had to say about the murder, he explained the unusually long entry in his journal that
spanned the fifth and sixth of November. "As the reader may
perceve," he wrote, "it is not common for us [seamen] to right
two days work together but as I had no time to right the night
before and I then thought it best to right it in one O may God
bless the little family that the Capton left at home and all the
rest," he prayed, adding, "We are bound to Bay of Islands but
we expect to stop to Rotumah to get some men and to leave two
Coonackers that we got there.

"O may we be blesed with a plesant time

"Lat By Ob. 02.20 N Long 161.15 E so ends."

TWO DAYS LATER, the chronometer stopped.

Benjamin Clough recorded that at six-thirty in the morning
someone wound the ship's clock, but when nine A.M. came
round and it was time to fix the ship's position, they "found
chronometer broke." An accurate chronometer was necessary
for correctly calculating longitude, so this was a disturbing
discovery. Clough made an attempt to find their position by
taking a lunar sight and calculating the distance between the
moon and a planet or fixed star in the moon's path, arriving at
"163:25 E 09.09 N." This was not nearly as trustworthy as a solar

reckoning, particularly when sailing at full speed through reef-strewn waters, so it was with relief, four days later, that Clough noted that the London whaleship *Bermondsey* had responded to their signal of distress.

However, when Thomas Harlock Smith went on board the other ship, he failed to return. Ostensibly he had gone to borrow a chronometer, but at sunset the first officer of the *Bermondsey* and his boat's crew arrived to spend the night on the *Sharon*, while Captain Thomas Harlock Smith and his boat's crew remained on the *Bermondsey*. The visit had turned into an all-night gam. Captain Smith, it seems, was discovering the joys of socializing with other shipmasters. In the throes of this, the plight of the *Sharon* had apparently been forgotten.

Two days later, though a chronometer had been delivered, Thomas Smith had still not returned to the *Sharon*. Because he was happily ensconced on the other ship, the two ships had to sail in company, and so the *Sharon* arrived at Pleasant Island, simply because that was where the *Bermondsey* had been headed. Still without communicating with the *Sharon*, Captain Thomas Smith accompanied his newfound friend, the captain of the *Bermondsey*, on shore. A couple more days passed while the *Sharon* tacked back and forth, waiting for Smith to remember his responsibilities as master. Then finally he arrived back on board, "bringing some fowl that he bought of the Natives and 2 hands that he shipped to go to Sidney."

While the two extra hands were very welcome, the new seamen had stipulated that they would only work on the *Sharon* for a passage to Sydney, Australia, which meant that Captain Smith had to change his mind about going to New Zealand.

Because the course would not include Rotuma, the two Rotumans could not be delivered home either. For Smith, however, it made little difference, Sydney being as good a place to find new men as the Bay of Islands. His overriding goal was to drop anchor in a port where he could fill the many gaps in his crew list, and then get back on the whaling ground.

The *Sharon* was put on a course for New South Wales, with George Black still chained to a ringbolt in the deck. Ships were spoken—the *Clarkson* of Sydney, the *Thomas Lord* of the Bay of Islands, and an unidentified French vessel. Though men who visited the *Sharon* must have asked why the islander was restrained like a dangerous animal, neither Andrew White nor Benjamin Clough mentioned him again in their journals, instead lamenting that when they raised two schools of whales, they could not lower for them, being so short of men.

Obviously, George Black was fed, presumably by one of the other Kanakas, and occasionally he would have been cleaned by having a bucket of water thrown over him. Naked when seized, he was given some clothes—perhaps the few clothes he owned, though if he had taken part in the assassination they would have been sodden with blood. Mentally, he must have been in a terrible state, having no idea of what lay in the future. Back on his home island, quarrels were settled with the traditional sport of boxing, which was ritualistic in style. Because the coconut fiber boxing gloves were studded with porcupine-fish spikes, the opponents might be quite badly hurt, but there were no hard feelings left at the end of the battle. The dispute was considered settled. Murderers and other incurably violent men were executed by being tied to a log or put in a small canoe and set adrift. While it was recognized that self-defense was an excuse for murder, the relatives of the murdered man still had the right to hunt down and kill the person who had taken the life of a member of the family. The American sailors on the *Sharon* would have considered George Black lucky not to be shot down in cold blood and dumped into the ocean. To George Black, though, swift revenge would have been much more logical than being carried off to a foreign place to be put on trial in an incomprehensible system of justice.

So it must have been with dread that he watched the approach to Sydney at sunrise on December 22. First, the headlands of Botany Bay loomed up from the predawn fog. Then, as the *Sharon* coasted along the high, dark cliffs, a sudden break presented itself like a colossal gate, beyond which glittered the bays and inlets of an enormous estuary, stretching out on every side. Observers of the time remarked on the clarity of the air and the vivid impression of brilliant color—green growth, reddish stone, white beaches, blue water. Trees and shrubs flourished among the rocks all the way to the water's edge, interspersed with clearings where English-style cottages, their facades painted white, were generously bordered with emerald lawns.

"At 10 took a Pilot," wrote the cooper. The harbor pilot conned the ship past little islands, which he would have pointed out: Garden Island, Goat Island, Pinchgut. This last was crowned with a small fort, a battery of cannon poking iron snouts out of crevices in the thick stone walls. Large vessels lay at anchor all about, while small boats and lighter barges plied the bright waters of the harbor between ship and shore. "At 3 PM come to anchor about ½ a mile from the town," White went on. This would have been opposite Fort Macquarie, built of stone by convict labor like most public buildings, and surrounded by more cannon. Behind the fort stretched the single-storied Government House, with sentries patrolling the verandah that ran the length of it. From the house and the fort a fine lawn, dotted with great trees, stretched down to the beach, where wharves poked out toward the shipping. The streets of Sydney Cove, half-seen from the deck, were a bustle of activity.

Shortly after the anchor splashed down, the harbormaster's boat arrived. According to a traveler of the time, his boat's crew were all New Zealand Maori, "fine intelligent-looking, copper-coloured fellows," stalwart, handsome men with proudly tattooed faces, wearing a Gypsy-like mixture of European and native clothing. In the boat with the harbormaster was the port physician. Both men gave Captain Thomas Smith's shipping papers just a cursory inspection, most of their attention on the prisoner as they listened to Smith's recounting of the murder of Norris and the recapture of the ship—the same story he would give to the newspapers next day. At that moment George Black, having some understanding of English, would have realized that Captain Smith was going to keep silent about Captain Norris's brutality, so that self-defense was never going to be considered as a motive for his murder. Then he watched them go away to fetch the United States consul. This was the man who would decide his immediate fate.

The consul, James Hartwell Williams, arrived in a five-oared skiff that belonged to the Sydney Water Police, and with him came the man in charge, Superintendent Browne. The force, originally called the Harbour Guard, had been founded in 1789 to foil smuggling and to prevent communication between the convicts and the crews of the sailing ships that anchored in the harbor, but attending to drunken and deserting sailors was now the heaviest part of the workload. Murder did not fit any of these categories, but Williams had persuaded Browne to find a spare cell for George Black, until he could arrange for him to be charged with murder and shifted to the Sydney Gaol on Circular Quay to await his trial.

Released from the ringbolt for the first time in over a month, George Black was shoved down the side of the ship and into the boat. Because he was in the custody of the Water Police, he was ferried to Goat Island. There, he was locked into the thick-walled, convict-built watchhouse, where he had a small cell to himself, as was the custom then.

For a man who was used to the crowded squalor of the fore-castle and the companionable bustle of his home village, this solitary confinement would have seemed a severe punishment in itself. In those days, however, being shut into a cell was not considered any kind of penalty for crime. It was merely a place where an accused criminal could be kept in seclusion until his trial. Once charged and sentenced, the real punishment began—which might include torture, mutilation, whipping, branding, or transportation to penal settlements like Norfolk Island or Van Dieman's Land. George Black was considered a murderer, so execution was the most likely outcome. On his home island, he would be set adrift, if not murdered by the victim's family first. In Sydney, he could expect to be publicly hanged.

Anchored shipping lay below the window in the sandstone wall of his cell, close and yet unattainable. As he watched, George Black would have prepared himself for death.

"THE SHARON HAS put in to obtain hands, and also on account of the murder of her late commander, Captain Norris," noted the *Sydney Morning Herald* on December 23, the day after George Black was carried off to Goat Island, following up with a long account based on details provided by Thomas Harlock Smith. The problem, according to him, had begun at Ascension Island, "where eleven of the ship's company deserted." Unfortunately, he said, they could not be retaken because of the "influence" of the "white people on the island," and so it had been Captain Norris's intention to sail as quickly as possible to the Bay of Islands or Sydney "to procure more men." However, "when in lat. 2° 20′ N., long. 162° E., they fell in with sperm whales, and being able to man only two boats, they were lowered and put off in chase, leaving on board only Capt. Norris, the apprentice boy Emanuel, and three of the natives."

For a while, Thomas Harlock Smith told the reporters, all had seemed to be going well. His boat had captured a whale and waifed it and then gone in search of more prey. However, at about five in the afternoon, "it was seen from the boats that the flag was hoisted half mast," and the boats had been forced to abandon the chase to pull for the ship as fast as possible. Nearing, the men in the whaleboats had been confronted with the alarming sight of "the three natives naked, with cutting spades, lances, &c., pointed over the side to prevent their boarding."

The boy "Emanuel" was at the masthead, and "upon being hailed to know what was the matter" had imparted the shocking news that "the natives on board had murdered the Captain with a cutting spade," and had driven him aloft.

Meanwhile, the three savages were hurling a barrage of missiles at the two boats. "The officers seeing that the mutineers were so well prepared to repel them, considered it useless to attempt boarding until dark," the newspaper report went on. According to Thomas Harlock Smith's accounting, however, the setback was only temporary. He described Clough's heroic recapture of the ship so briefly that it merited no more than a succinct paragraph that skimmed over the "severe conflict" with the first native and the shooting of the second. "The boats' crews hearing the report, jumped on deck," the interview with Thomas Harlock Smith concluded, "and the vessel was again in their possession."

The journalist made some attempt to speak with "the lad Emanuel," but to little effect; Manuel des Reis simply repeated the story he had told the men, that "he heard the captain call him to come down from aloft, but before he could reach the rail the deed was committed, and an attempt was made to stab him, but he ran aloft again." This was followed with a detailed description of the gory state of Norris's remains, along with the revelation that one of the savage murderers had been brought into port alive, though he had "offered a most violent resistance" when discovered in the hold. WATER POLICE OFFICE, ran the headline a day later:

The list of defaulters at this office yesterday, was rather heavier than usual, there having been nineteen cases: nine for drunkenness, who were severally fined in the sum of eleven shillings; either for being absent from their ship without a pass, who were fined six shillings each; one for desertion, who was sent on board his ship, and George Black, for the murder of Captain Norris, of the American whaler *Sharon*, who was remanded.

This was not quite accurate: George Black, though in custody on Goat Island, had not been charged with any crime, and therefore could not be considered remanded. Getting him arraigned was the responsibility of Consul J. H. Williams, who had assumed without a single qualm that George Black was just as guilty as Captain Smith had described, and was determined that he meet his just deserts. Because the accused, the ship, and the witnesses were all in alien territory, he had to get the local judiciary to take over the case, and so he wrote to the colonial secretary.

"The American Whaling Ship Sharon having put into this port in consequence of the murder of the Captain," he commenced, "it has become my duty to ask whether the offence is one that will come under the jurisdiction of the courts of this colony and if so whether the surviving Murderer can be brought to trial here." Then, after summarizing the circumstances of the murder, he continued, "I need not express to you my strong desire that he should speedily be brought to trial, and for this outrage against the laws of God & man should receive the punishment which the enormity of the crime demands." If there was no provision in New South Wales law for holding the trial in Australia, he concluded, "I shall be compelled to ask of his Excellency the Governor to keep him in safe custody until he can be forwarded to the United States."

The letter he received in reply was disappointing in the extreme: "regret can't help you," the colonial secretary's clerk succinctly replied. The New South Wales administration saw it as an American problem: The murder had taken place on an American ship, and the victim was American. The accused—George Black—and the primary witness—Manuel José des Reis—were not American, admittedly, but they were not British citizens, either. The judiciary not only declined to charge George Black with the murder of Captain Norris, but also refused to sanction his transfer to the Sydney Gaol. Before a man could be put behind bars, he had to be charged with a crime, the clerk declared; and because under colonial law George Black could not be arraigned, there was no way to imprison him, either.

There were some Australians who were just as outraged as the consul was at this legal prevarication. THE LAW AS REGARDS SOUTH SEA ISLANDERS, blazoned the *Sydney Morning Herald* on Monday, January 2, 1843:

> The murder of Captain NORRIS, of the American whaler *Sharon*, by a native of the Island of Ascension, and the circumstance of one of the murderers having been brought to Sydney, has raised a question of the amenability of the natives of the numerous islands of the southern seas to British law, and we regret to say that British courts have not jurisdiction over offences committed by savages, unless British interests are involved. In the case under consideration, the murder was committed on board an American ship, the murdered man was a citizen of the United States, and the murderer is a native of an island over which the British have no dominion.

"Under these circumstances," the commentator concluded, "we fear that this most atrocious murder must remain unpunished for some considerable time, as the only Court that can try the murderer is the Supreme Court of the United States, and therefore he will have to be forwarded to Washington, with the necessary witnesses, by the earliest opportunity."

Informed of this, George Black must have been both confused and despairing. Whether he had any hope of surviving the voyage to the eastern seaboard of the United States was debatable, and American justice would have been an even more terrifying unknown than incarceration on Goat Island. Meantime, however, he had gained allies on shore—because someone from the *Sharon* had gone to the Sydney Bethel and talked to one of the pastors.

The Sydney Bethel had been founded back in 1822, when a small group of quietly concerned men of good will, led by chaplains William Cowper and Richard Mill, recognized the need for a charitable institution for sailors. Bethels were (and still are) found in most major ports, attending to sailors in trouble—men who might have been rescued after shipwreck with nothing but the clothes they stood up in; who might have deserted ships because of dreadful conditions on board; men discharged sick or marooned by heartless captains. Bethels also catered to seamen who preferred reading to carousing the waterfront taverns, providing libraries and reading rooms. They held religious services and staged inspirational lectures; pious or spiritually troubled seamen could go to the Sydney Bethel to pray, or simply talk into a sympathetic ear.

In Sydney, the Bethel Union flourished despite an unusual

difficulty—the lack of a meeting house. For twenty years the good men who were willing to tend to sailors in need rowed about the ships that lay at anchor in the harbor, carrying out services on their decks, handing out books and Bibles, helping with the writing of letters, and taking down details so they could notify the families of sailors who had died. Just six months before the *Sharon* arrived, however, a wealthy Quaker, Joseph Phelps Robinson, had come to Sydney on his private steamship, *Cornuba*. Not only did he join the ranks of the mission to seamen, but he also gave them the use of the *Cornuba*, to serve as a floating chapel and reading room. By flying the white bethel flag, it signaled that troubled sailors could find comfort here, and because one or more men from the *Sharon* took advantage of the opportunity, Joseph Robinson and his fellow philanthropists learned about the plight of George Black.

Deeply concerned at what they heard, they retained a brilliant young barrister, Richard Windeyer, a handsome man with a broad, high forehead and a wide, determined mouth, who was known as much for his narrow, piercing stare as he was for ingenuity in argument. Being a pioneering agriculturalist and vintner, as well as running an immense legal practice, Windeyer found time to attend to George Black's case only because of his intense personal interest in aboriginal affairs. Just months before the *Sharon* had arrived in Sydney with George Black in irons, Windeyer had delivered a public lecture in which he discussed the ethics of the annexation of the tribal lands of Australia. In the course of his incisive argument, he had proved beyond legal doubt, with brilliant and remorseless logic, that the aboriginal natives of Australia had no right to their ancestral territory, and that the white man was justified in seizing ownership. Then, right at the end, he had revealed his true philanthropic intent, deliberately destroying his own mercilessly logical line of reasoning by meditating aloud, "Why is it our minds are not satisfied? What means this whispering in the bottom of our hearts?"—a catch-cry for humanitarians that has echoed down the years.

So, it was a subtle legal mind that examined the problem of how to save George Black. When Windeyer questioned the informants and heard about Norris's brutality and the murder of Babcock, a motive for the killing would have become horribly apparent. After interviewing George Black, he would have understood even more. According to the Sydney *Morning Herald*, George Black said the murder happened because "the captain was cross." As far as the journalist was concerned, this enigmatic statement did not need explaining. For Windeyer, however, that little word "cross" was the key.

Once he learned that Captain Norris had been beating and pounding the Kanakas, it would have been easy for him to envisage the islanders retaliating in desperation, slashing out with the deadly sharp spades that were so close to hand. Indeed, Windeyer must have wondered whether George Black had been involved in "this most atrocious murder" at all. If the cook had been busy in the galley on the foredeck when the confrontation began, by the time he arrived on the after deck the captain could well have been dead.

No one knew who had struck the first blow, but the *Sharon* informants must have had their theories. Years later, according to his grandson, Benjamin Clough mysteriously referred to

"Molino del Rey." What was possibly misheard was a suggestion that it was Manuel des Reis—a name that would sound like "Molino del Rey" to people who had never seen it written down—who had lashed out, and then thrown the blame onto the natives. Manuel was Fayal Portuguese, a race often considered second class by whalemen from New England; they were distrusted because of their foreignness, their Catholic religion, and their language. If the *Sharon* informants theorized that Manuel had started the attack, it could have been part of this common prejudice.

Windeyer may have seen the logic, though. Manuel *was* the steward—and Norris *had* beaten, tortured, and murdered the man who had previously held the job. However, the argument was academic. As long as Manuel stuck to his statement that he was aloft when he heard the captain call, and did not witness the murder, George Black's only possible plea was one of self-defense.

The problem was how to bring it. Making inquiries, Windeyer would have made certain, like U.S. consul James Hartwell Williams, that the New South Wales authorities were utterly adamant that the trial could not be held on Australian soil. Yet it was equally impossible for Windeyer to defend George Black in a courtroom in Washington, D.C. The best option by far was to have no trial at all—and Windeyer found a legal loophole that led the way to this, one that hung on the fact that while George Black had been accused of murder, he had not yet been charged with the crime. In order to take advantage of this, however, the lawyer had to wait for Captain Thomas Harlock Smith to make the first move.

Thomas Smith, meantime, had been stiffly informed that the reason George Black had not been formally charged was "in consequence of his not being a subject of the Queen," as James Hartwell Williams put it. According to the colonial secretary's clerk, the consul said, the Sydney judiciary did not even have the "power of detaining him in prison until he could be sent to the United States for trial." Williams's alternative suggestion was for Captain Smith to take the Kanaka back on board the ship and keep him there "until you can fall in with an American Man of War or other Ship that will take him to the United States where," he emphatically concluded, "he will undoubtedly meet with the punishment which his crime merits."

If Smith followed this advice, George Black was doomed; there was no way Robinson and Windeyer could save him. Smith, however, did exactly what Windeyer hoped he would. Without even considering the idea of taking the Kanaka to the United States for what would have been a very well-publicized trial accompanied by embarrassing revelations, he ordered the anchor weighed. On January 6, 1843, the *Sharon* sailed for the New Zealand whaling ground, leaving George on Goat Island, still uncharged with the crime.

The moment the *Sharon* cleared the Sydney Heads, the Supreme Court of New South Wales issued a writ of *habeas corpus*, in the name of Joseph Robinson, and at Windeyer's instigation. Directed to Superintendent Browne of the Water Police, it ordered him to produce "George, a native of one of the South Sea Islands, who had been given into his custody on a charge of having murdered one of the crew of the American whaling ship *Sharon*." Browne was to take the prisoner before the court issuing the writ without delay, and there explain why he was detained.

George Black was fetched out of his solitary cell and ferried under guard across the glittering harbor to an intersection in the busiest part of town. The Supreme Court stood on the corner of Elizabeth and King streets, a crossroads that was so cluttered with carriages, horsemen, and shouting drovers that the chief justices had repeatedly tried to persuade government officials to place barricades across Elizabeth Street so that proceedings in court could be heard above the deafening rattle of hooves and rumble of wheels. The contrast to daily life on George Black's home island could not have been greater: He had probably never seen horses before.

Inside, it was almost as crowded and noisy; at any given moment of the day as many as three hundred people were waiting to appear in court. For the past ten years the justices had been complaining constantly about the overcrowded foyers. The building itself was so unsafe that it had been necessary to brace the roof and walls with extra poles and columns, which used up still more of the space. January being high summer, the public part of the building was unbearably stuffy and hot, as well as packed with a shifting mob of people. Because of this, Mr. Justice W. W. Burton, presiding, shifted the hearing to the Judge's Rooms.

First to appear was the Quaker philanthropist, Mr. Robinson. The writ of habeas corpus having been read out, he confirmed that it had been issued at his instance. In fact, he said, he had

directed that it should be prepared well ahead of time, anticipating that the *Sharon* would leave port without George Black's
future being settled. It was because of this precaution that it
had been issued with such unusual promptness. He had retained Mr. R. Windeyer to argue the case on his behalf, he said,
and sat down.

Mr. Browne was the next to be called and must have stood
up most reluctantly, knowing he was in for judicial censure.
Consul James Hartwell Williams was not there to help the superintendent of Water Police defend his actions. He may not
have known about the hearing. Even if he had, he would have
been disinclined to place himself in the embarrassing situation
of being reprimanded by an Australian High Court judge for
not following the proper procedure.

So Browne was left to try to explain why he had thrown
George Black into prison without the necessary formality of
charging him with a crime. "Mr. H. R. Williams, the American
consul for this port," he said, getting the initials wrong in his
confusion, had delivered George Black into his custody. And
yes, he reluctantly admitted, he had been perfectly aware he
had no lawful right to put the accused behind bars, no "legal
proof of his guilt having been exhibited before him in his mag-
isterial capacity."

So why, asked Mr. Justice Burton, had the superintendent
agreed to do it?

"He had a charge of murder alleged against him," was the
lame reply.

Alleged, Mr. Windeyer pointed out sharply, might mean the

same as *accused*, but was not the same as *charged*. Had Superintendent Browne taken George Black into custody as a personal favor to the United States consul?

"No," Browne denied, mopping his brow, and went on to assert with a virtuous air that he "had taken charge of the prisoner more from charity, and to alleviate his sufferings."

"Sufferings?" queried the judge.

"Aye," Mr. Browne agreed fervently. When he had first seen the accused, "he was in a most uncomfortable condition, lashed on deck with cords in such a manner as was calculated to excite the compassion of any one who beheld him."

At that, the superintendent of Water Police was stood down, undoubtedly much to his relief, and Mr. Windeyer took his place. "I understand there is an obstacle to the prisoner's immediate discharge," the lawyer remarked by way of opening. George Black was not the person who had presented the writ, which would have been the usual custom; instead, it had been issued by a third party, to wit, Robinson. However, he went on, he had "a case in point, which would warrant the court in discharging him." Then Richard Windeyer cited the case of the Hottentot Venus, a young Khoi Khoi woman from South Africa who in 1810 had been lured to London and put on display as a freak, while humanitarians waged a court battle to save her. She, he said, "had been brought up before the Court of King's Bench in England, upon the affidavit of a third party, who merely knew that she was confined against her will."

Case history was not necessary, Mr. Justice Burton pointed out with some acerbity. The fact of the matter was that the American consul had done nothing to substantiate the allegation of murder, and the captain of the *Sharon* had sailed away without initiating any kind of official action. In view of that, he did not see that there was any legal justification for keeping George Black in custody, and so ordered his immediate release. What happened to him after that is unknown.

TWELVE

CAPTAIN THOMAS HARLOCK SMITH

WHILE RICHARD WINDEYER had been preparing his legal strategy, Thomas Harlock Smith had been preoccupied with recruiting men for the empty berths in the *Sharon*. His agents scoured the taverns and wharves on his behalf, with the result that Benjamin Clough, the officer on duty on deck, watched a motley lot of men climb the side of the ship the day before sailing, each with his sea chest or kit bag balanced on one shoulder.

At least four were Americans who were deserters from other ships. One, William Clarke, had originally shipped on the *Cherokee*, which had left New Bedford in December 1840; Henry Cooke, originally a hand on coasting schooners, had deserted the *Canton* after deeply regretting his decision to go whaling; the new carpenter, George E. Nightingale, a six-foot giant of a man from Providence, Rhode Island, had absconded from the *Hoogly*, on which he had shipped in November 1840; the cook, Francis Julian Saul, had jumped from the *Mount Vernon*. Five of the others were greenhands, so were likely to have been convicts who might or might not have worked out their sentences. But at last the forecastle was full.

"We left the 6th of Jan., the Mate Thomas H. Smith, taking command and I am second mate," wrote Clough in the letter to his father he commenced February 9. "My wounds got healed up about the time we went into Sidney. We have now about 500 Bbls of Sperm Oil on board. But how long we shall be out is more than I can say. I have enjoyed very good health since we left Sidney except my Right hand which is so that I can hardly hold a pen."

Clough, basking in the glow of his promotion to second mate, felt optimistic about the rest of the voyage. That the crew-list was complete was as pleasing to him as it was to Captain Smith: As he noted in his journal, the *Sharon* "put to Sea with A full complement of men 29 in number." In the letter he wrote, "We have got a good crew on board and I am in hopes that we shall do something." It was a new beginning.

However, disillusionment fast set in. No sooner was the ship in the Tasman Sea than whales were raised, but to Clough's chagrin they had no luck in catching them. Just three boats were lowered, which shortened their chances. This could have been because they had only three boatsteerers — Isaac Place, Andrew White (who had agreed to do that job in addition to his regular coopering), and a new man, Joseph Perry — or it could have been because Captain Thomas H. Smith declined to go down in the chase.

If Smith was not going down in his boat, Clough would have been reminded that they now had a captain who had not proved himself capable of taking charge either in the whale-boats or upon the quarterdeck. Where strength had been needed to counter Norris's violence, Thomas Harlock Smith had been weak and prevaricating. He had already demon-strated that he was scared of the whales, and now he displayed a great deal of caution about navigating unseen seas at night, ordering that canvas be taken in at sunset and set again at dawn. Norris had at least had the reputation of being a lucky captain, and so those of his men who had stayed had been able to cling to some kind of optimism, even though the voyage was doing so badly. Smith, who had no reputation at all, would not be con-sidered likely to improve their joint fortunes.

By February they were cruising about the Three Kings Is-lands, just to the north of the North Cape of New Zealand, but still had taken no whales, despite three determined attempts. Not only did the boats' crews have to find and fight the whales, but they had the terrible weather to battle, too. The notoriously stormy Tasman Sea was living up to its reputation; most of the time the weather was too horrible to lower the whaleboats. It might have been the middle of the southern summer, but for days on end the *Sharon* lay huddled under vicious gusts as the wind shrieked through the rigging and waves pounded the toss-ing hull. Any gaps in the procession of tempests were spent try-ing to fix damage to rigging, bulwarks, and sails. It was not until the seventh of that month that the first sperm whale was captured, the honor going to Benjamin Clough, who now headed the waist boat, the prerogative of the second mate.

Two more whales were taken, but one was lost when the ship gave a sudden lurch and the chains that held the carcass broke apart. On March 17, 1843, Clough wrote, "I am 24 Years Old this day," but there was little for him to celebrate. Not only were both the luck and the weather awful, but two weeks previously he had stopped noting the ship's position in his logbook, evidently because he was denied access to the chronometer. It is easy to picture the two Vineyarder cousins sequestering themselves in the after cabin with the charts and navigation instruments, isolating themselves from the rest of the ship's company and cutting Clough out of any of the decision-making.

Just two weeks later, yet another tragedy struck the ship.

Clough was sitting down to his dinner when he heard a heavy thump on the deck above his head. Dashing up the companionway, he saw men standing in a huddle on the foredeck. As he arrived, the group spread out, revealing one of the three Kanakas writhing with agony on the planks. When he crouched down by the poor fellow, Clough saw that one temple was crushed and bleeding, and the left arm was badly fractured. The ends of shattered bone protruded from the skin and flesh.

Then Clough recognized him—one of the Rotumans. He had been deranged for the past four days and confined to his berth. His shipmates should have been watching over him, but he had made an unexpected break for it, a foremast hand explained. Before anyone in the forecastle had realized what was happening, he had leapt up the ladder. Before they could stop him he had scrambled up the foremast rigging, several of the crew in hot pursuit. When one of the men caught hold of him, he had torn loose and jumped into space. His head had hit against the mast as he fell, and then his arm had smashed as he hit the deck.

Clough did his best to set the arm, "but of no avail he died about 11 last night uttering groans and cries the most of the time but not appearing to be in his right mind." At ten the following morning, Sunday, a prayer was said as the men stood around the shrouded corpse, and the Rotuman's body was committed to the sea. So another witness to Norris's reign of terror was silenced.

Yet gossip was running about the fleet. No less than twenty-eight American whaleships were cruising about the Australian coasts and calling into the ports of both Australia and New Zealand, one of them the *LaGrange*, where the men could well have heard tales of brutality from Lyman Bligh, who had joined them after running away from the *Sharon* in Rotuma. When the crews learned about the sensational murder of Captain Norris, they had many opportunities to tell and retell the melodramatic story as they gammed with other ships all about the great Pacific and gathered in the grogshops of far-flung ports. The first news of the murder and recapture reached Massachusetts when the editor of the New Bedford *Mercury* received a letter from Joseph Bailey, the first mate of the whaler *Hope*.

Captain Thomas Smith was another bearer of the tale—albeit a sanitized rendering. Just as in Sydney, he would have actively avoided any mention of Norris's brutality, but was happy to confide his version of the mutiny and murder to other captains: On May 7, the logkeeper of the whaleship *Harbinger* noted, "Spoke ship Sharon of Fairhaven, Captain Smith, 23 months out with 700 barrels. Late Captain Norris killed by the natives." By July the story, occasionally somewhat garbled, had circled the ocean. At the beginning of that month, while cruising the foggy coasts of Alaska for whales, Joseph Eayres of the *Gratitude* noted that he had "heard of the murder of Captain Lawrence of the ship Sharon of FairHaven."

In April, Clough recorded that Captain Thomas Harlock Smith had set course for the Navigators Islands—modern Samoa, a favorite place for American whalers to replenish with yams, poultry, pigs, coconuts, tropical fruit, water, and firewood, all of which were plentiful there. On May 6, 1843, a boat was sent into the Samoan island of Savai'i to trade, Clough writing, "got 9 Hogs and 1 boat load of Yams Discharged 1 man James Clark and 3 more deserted."

Next day a boat was sent in again "to try to get our men but did not succeed." The three runaways had flown. After taking a beachcomber on board to act as middleman in trading with the chiefs, Captain Thomas Harlock Smith set sail for the island of Upolu. There, Andrew White supervised the hoisting in of two casks of water, while Captain Smith asked the man who carried out the local United States consular duties to help him find replacements for the four hands he had lost in Savai'i.

This man who acted as the United States consul was John Chauner Williams, son of the influential London Missionary Society leader and no relation to James Hartwell Williams, the consul in Sydney. He had arrived in the Navigators Islands late in the 1830s, bent on a career as a "Christian trader," and then, in 1839, had been provisionally appointed U.S. consul by Lieutenant Charles Wilkes of the U.S. Exploring Expedition. While the choice seems peculiar, in those days a man did not have to have American citizenship—or even American affiliations—to act as an official representative of that country, and Wilkes's intention was to make sure that American shipmasters and traders benefited from the protection of the mission. This was after he had burned three Samoan villages to the ground, first frightening off the populace with a barrage of grapeshot, because the villagers had refused to deliver up a chief who had murdered an American some years before. The idea was to instill a comprehensive respect for American ships and captains.

John Chauner Williams, obviously, hoped to do well out of the consulship by snaring all the trade with the captains, but it turned out to be a frustrating exercise. Not only did he receive no American naval support, but his official commission did not arrive until 1848, mostly because Wilkes had forgotten to inform the U.S. State Department. Then, when his papers did come, he was not offered the job of consul, but instead the much more minor post of commercial agent. John Chauner Williams, disgusted, did not accept the position. However, he continued to act for the United States, styling himself *Fa'amasino Amelika*—which meant that he was constantly pestered by captains like Smith, who needed more men because their hands had run away.

As fast as Williams found new men for the *Sharon*, others absconded. Altogether, nine men ran away while the ship lay off

Apia and were replaced with eight. That was by no means the last of Smith's troubles in Samoa. On June 3, when all hands were called to weigh anchor, it was discovered that two more men had deserted by swimming off in the night. A third demanded his discharge, and when Thomas Smith refused to let him go on shore, the seaman produced a loaded pistol, melodramatically informing Smith that he had signed his death warrant. So John Chauner Williams was summoned yet again. After hearing the captain's side of the case, he carried the culprit off in handcuffs.

For the remnants of the crew of the *Sharon*, witnessing a man carted away in irons after threatening the captain's life was not the end of the excitement. No sooner had the pilot left the ship than Clough recorded that Smith "put 2 of the Boatsteerers on shore"—evidently Isaac Place and Joseph Perry. This meant they were marooned—cast adrift on a foreign beach for some undescribed crime. At least they were allowed to take their sea chests with them, but it still meant that they missed out on their share of the profits of the voyage.

The rashness of this action was demonstrated almost at once. The same evening, according to Clough, when sperm whales were raised two boats were lowered, but neither boatsteerer managed to get a harpoon into the quarry. Two days later, when the ship was cruising off the southern coast of Upolu, Clough saw large sperm whales pass within a mile of the ship, but, to his extreme irritation, no boats at all went down, "as the Captain was A going on shore." Smith was in quest of still more men, the cooper noting later that the captain "shipped 3 men that left the Emily Morgan of Newbedford." These were Sam

Brown, who was a boatsteerer, thirty-two-year-old seaman Stephen Knowles, and another sailor by the name of James Jackson.

THE FIRST WEEK of June 1843, they raised whales off the island of Upolu, but again Captain Smith did not give the order to lower the boats. The whales were running fast upwind, and Smith was still very short of harpooners. In fact, he had just two—Sam Brown, the ex-boatsteerer of the *Emily Morgan*, and Andrew White, who had been bribed to act as Benjamin Clough's boatsteerer. And White was in a mutinous mood.

"June 24, 1843," the cooper headed up his logbook, and proceeded to pen a long complaint. Back in January, as the *Sharon* sailed out of Sydney, Captain Smith had asked him to fill in as Benjamin Clough's harpooner; Andrew White had agreed only because he would be paid for the extra work. Since then, "he had told me several times that I should be paid for it," Andrew wrote angrily, but "when I asked him he would not." So on this date, having lost all patience, the cooper marched up to Benjamin Clough and informed him that he had to find another boatsteerer.

Clough's reaction was not recorded, but Captain Smith flew into a rage and "tolde me that he would not let me be idle a minet on deck in my watch," Andrew White wrote, concluding furiously, "I have steered A Boat 6 months for nothin and because I wont steer the rest of the voyage he is goin to work me up for it." Working up was a punishment that never got noted in the official logbooks. The chosen victim was kept busy with pointless or unnecessarily difficult tasks and constantly nagged and reprimanded, the aim being to make his life on board unbearable. Often, the intention was to force him to desert. However, Andrew White, returning to his usual laconic journal-keeping style, made no more comment. Nor did he have any intention of jumping the ship and forfeiting his lay. Instead, he remained adamant that he would steer no more, and so Captain Smith, fuming impotently, was reduced to just one harpooner.

The cruise, though extended to the waters about the Fijian Islands, was fruitless, so Thomas Smith decided to steer for Rotuma, sailing there in the company of several ships, including the *London Packet*, which had Richard Tobias Greene—the same "Toby" Greene who had sailed on the *Acushnet* with Herman Melville—in the crew. The log of the *London Packet* recorded the first encounter with the *Sharon* on July 1, off Fiji. From then on the crews of the two ships visited each other freely, exchanging yarns and gossip. On September 5, after more than a month of constant gamming, the whaleships raised Rotuma.

Unlike Norris in April 1842, Thomas Smith did not drop anchor. Instead, as Andrew White recorded, he sent a boat on shore to fetch "4 Girls to stop the night." By this time Benjamin Clough, thoroughly fed up with a captain who socialized with other ships instead of concentrating on the proper pursuit of whales, had got out of the habit of writing up his journal every day. He combined events of "September 6 and 7" into one entry, writing, "saw Whales lowered for them but got none." On the eighth, he and Nathan Skiff Smith were on shore trading with the Rotumans for provisions when whales were raised again. The third mate—a man who had been shipped in Samoa, though unrecorded in the *Sharon's* papers—lowered for them but returned to the ship after a profitless chase. Then, after this nameless officer was back on board, the whales were raised again. However, Captain Smith refused to let him have another try. Enraged by not being allowed to do what he had shipped to do—get whales and make money—the third mate mutinied: "he refused his duty." So Captain Smith retaliated by marooning him on the island.

Two days later, according to the cooper, Smith sent six more men ashore, filling up the gaps in his crew list by recruiting hands from the shifting beachcomber population. Clough noted that one was a man by the name of Robert Anderson, who had been shipped to replace the marooned third officer. Another recruit was an unnamed boatsteerer, while the rest were foremast hands, mostly Americans, including Alexander Small, a man who had been cast away when the *Benezet* was wrecked on a reef in the Fiji Islands in 1842, a deserter from the *Hesper* named Thomas Brewer, a runaway from the *William Hamilton* called James Thomson, and an American Indian by the name of Peter Daniels.

Two others were an anonymous Portuguese seaman from Fayal, and Thomas Silsby, a nineteen-year-old olive-skinned, black-haired native of Boston. This duo would have had quite a tale to relate to their new shipmates. Both had originally shipped on the *Cadmus*, commanded by Captain Mayhew, and had been cast away with all other hands at midnight on August 3, 1842, when the ship was wrecked on an uncharted and uninhabited atoll in the Tuamotu archipelago. A camp was set up on shore, and the best of the four whaleboats was packed with provisions for thirty days. Then Captain Mayhew and first mate John W. Norton, with four oarsmen, had sailed off for Tahiti, leaving the rest of the crew behind. "The reader may judge what were our feelings as we embarked," Norton wrote later, "not knowing whether we should ever reach any place where we could gain assistance." The emotions of the men left behind on the tiny waterless island can only be imagined, too.

On August 20, 1842, Mayhew and Norton had arrived at Tahiti, "after a voyage of 14 days, and sailing over a thousand miles in an open boat." The Boston schooner *Emerald*, which happened to be in port, was immediately dispatched to fetch the eighteen members of the crew that had been left behind, arriving back at the end of September. This meant that Silsby and his friend were on Tahiti when the *Lucy Ann* arrived with Herman Melville on board.

Like Melville, Silsby was finding out how heavily the system was weighted in favor of the afterdeck—Captain Mayhew and John Norton took passage to New Bedford, where they arrived in February 1843, but their crew had to find their own way out of the Pacific. If Silsby and Melville met, which seems likely, they would have had tales to tell and grievances to share. Both Silsby and his Portuguese shipmate, as events were to prove, were extraordinarily unlucky in their choice of berths.

By the time Captain Thomas Harlock Smith gave the order to set sail from Rotuma, nine of the crew had been left on shore, and twelve new hands had been taken off the beach. He charted a course for the Fiji Islands, which they raised in the third week of September, but a few days later, after capturing just one whale, Thomas Smith decided to steer south for New Zealand—and Benjamin Clough, presumably in disgust, gave up writing in his journal for the next six months, setting down his pen until April 9, 1844.

Andrew White was equally annoyed. Captain Smith was edgy and bad-tempered, and the working up had not abated. At dawn on Saturday, November 18, when all hands were called to wash down the decks, Nathan Skiff Smith ordered White to start setting up casks. Andrew objected, saying that it was impossible to straighten iron hoops on wet decks, and proposed to take the hoops and his hammer to the quarterdeck, which, being higher, was less damp. Nathan Smith sharply reminded him that the quarterdeck was not his place, "so I tolde him that he would not get any more done by setting me to work in the water before breakfast"—which led to a row, Nathan Smith snapping "that as long as there was a drop of blood in him I should not have my way."

At that stage Captain Thomas Smith arrived upon deck. Without any ado he ordered White to collect his sea chest and tools and take himself forward. Like Norris earlier, Smith was demoting him to the status of foremast hand. When he was back in his cabin, however, the captain had second thoughts: "he went down in the cabin and then sent for me," the cooper wrote. When he arrived the captain shut the door and "commenced talking to me about one thing and another," evidently trying to reason with him, saying that a ship could have only one captain, and he was that man.

White heatedly informed him that he had no ambition to be the master; he simply refused to be imposed upon by Captain

Smith or any of the officers—and if any one of them hit him, beat him, or attacked him, as had happened to other men on the ship, he, Andrew White, "would have satisfaction."

Bridling, Captain Smith demanded to know just who it was he was supposed to have mistreated. White, unintimidated, promptly produced a name: Otis Tripp, who had been beaten over the head with a heaver and had run away in Pohnpei.

"Well," said Captain Smith. "Is that all?"

"No, sir," said the cooper. There was "the steward that was kiled and Jack Baker Tom Williams and a good many more." And, Andrew White added stoutly, the mistreatment was the reason Williams and Tripp and Baker and all the others had run away from the ship, "for I hav herd them say so."

Sobered by this reminder of how vulnerable he was to gossip, Captain Smith backed off—"he then tolde me to let my things be in the cabing and go to work on the casks so ends."

So Andrew White stayed in the steerage. Meantime, he had won his point.

SIX WEEKS LATER, exactly a year after departure from Sydney, and fourteen months after the murder of Captain Norris, the ship dropped anchor at the Bay of Islands, New Zealand. No sooner had the ship been moored than Captain Thomas Smith "Poot three men in irons and floged one of them then sent them on shore to Pokey," wrote White. Again, the crime was undescribed, but obviously morale on board was at rock bottom still. Just one week later, the new third mate got drunk and demanded his discharge. "Mr Anderson come a board in Liqueur," wrote Andrew White, "and wanted his discharg and took his things and went a shore." By January 24, when the ship got ready for departure, eight more men had either quit or run away, including the American Indian Peter Daniels.

It was common enough for men to get drunk in New Zealand, and almost as common for them to desert. From its earliest days the Bay of Islands had had a close relationship with the whaling fleet, the people on shore not only catering to the appetites and thirsts of the American seamen, but demonstrating a remarkably understanding attitude, too, quite different from other anchorages in the Pacific. Nowhere else could the downbeaten foremast hand find such a sympathetic welcome — and the captains such surprising hostility.

For four decades before the arrival of the *Sharon*, American whalers had been dropping anchor here, trading with the local Maori for potatoes, peaches, pigs, spars, and flax, and writing an important page in the story of New Zealand. Through contacts with American shipmasters, the Maori gained muskets, powder, blankets, European clothing, tools, tobacco, and grog, all of which altered the balance of power between rival tribes. Chiefs organized confederations of friendly interests, whole villages moved from one location to another, and plantations of potatoes were sown and cultivated, all with the aim of gaining maximum benefit from contact with the whalers.

The missionaries had entered the scene as early as 1814, and at first had competed with local Maori for the trade in muskets and pigs with the captains, but with the arrival of a strong-minded parson, the Rev. Henry Williams, in 1823, this rivalry had lurched to a halt. Henry Williams's instructions were to shun the shipping—"Avoid as much as possible all communications with such vessels as put into your harbour, these common sinks of vice and wickedness," the directive had run, and he had followed it to the letter. This distant stance meant that the independent traders and entrepreneurs who had taken up residence with the Maori—mostly runaway convicts and seamen—had an unusually free rein. While the missionaries kept aloof in their station up the river, these beachcombers set up shop in Kororareka, on the beach.

Kororareka swiftly became notorious throughout the Pacific as a roistering sailor town, with a minimum of missionary interference. Puritanical observers of the goings-on at Kororareka were horrified. Charles Wilkes, who visited the Bay of Islands with the U.S. Exploring Expedition in 1840, described a slum town made up of "about twenty houses, scarcely deserving the name, and many shanties, besides tents. It is chiefly inhabited by the lowest order of vagabonds, mostly runaway sailors and convicts," he went on, "and is appropriately named 'Blackguard Beach.'"

American whalemen deserted their ships in droves there, and hundreds stayed to settle. At the time, New Zealand was probably the easiest place in the Pacific for runaways to decide to put down roots. The Maori were adept at learning English, and there were commercial opportunities abounding. In the Bay of Islands storekeeping promised a profit, and in the south, shore whaling stations always needed more hands. An even better reason for running away in New Zealand was that absconding seamen found a welcome not just with the tribes, but with many of the settlers as well—people who had been sickened by the tales they had been told of brutality on board. Even the missionaries, who abhorred the drunkenness, fighting, and whoring (though from a distance), thought that many American captains were unnecessarily harsh.

The United States consul for the Bay of Islands, John Brown Williams of Salem, Massachusetts, was another to share this sentiment, complaining at length in his journal about the "many ignorant whaling masters" who disgraced his homeland by "demeaning themselves in a manner unbecoming a civilized or rational being." Williams, a strapping young man over six feet tall who was known for his strength and courage, felt a great deal of sympathy for the American seamen who jumped ship on New Zealand shores, even though legislation dated July 20, 1840, made it part of his duties to reclaim deserters. The statute also stated that if it could be proved that the desertion had been caused by cruel and abusive treatment, the consul should order the discharge of the deserter, plus three months' extra pay, and J. B. Williams was one of the few to pay heed to this rule. Just a few days before the *Sharon* dropped anchor, he wrote his six-monthly report to the State Department, taking the opportunity to pen a long description of "the character and depressed condition of Americans, generally seamen, who have become exceeding numerous o'er the length and breadth of New Zealand." While some were drunken rogues, he went on, "in character they embrace every variety as they are from every condition in life, many are talented men, and with a proper field for them would be shining lights in society: others good confidential men, good mechanicks and temperate men."

The New Zealand public knew exactly what he meant. The

arrival of ships like the *Sharon* with tales of brutal discipline on board had convinced them that the average American whaling captain was a sadist, and the average American seaman was a victim. It was an attitude that proved enduring, despite all the evidence to the contrary. A full forty years after the *Sharon* sailed away from the Bay of Islands, U.S. consul Gilderoy Griffin complained bitterly to the State Department that his job was so much more difficult in New Zealand than elsewhere, because "there is a general opinion throughout the Colony that American shipmasters are proverbially cruel and brutal to their sailors"—and all because the tellers of tales of "hell-ships" like the *Sharon* found so many ready ears in grogshops, tenpin alleys, billiard rooms, clubs, and salons.

However, Captain Thomas Harlock Smith was able to fill the gaps in his crew list at the Bay of Islands, because there were more men than usual on the lookout for berths. The British had officially taken over the country on February 6, 1840, an event that had a direct impact on the American fleet. Lieutenant Charles Wilkes prophesied that the laws and taxes that the British brought with them would discourage American shipmasters from dropping anchor in New Zealand. "Our whalers are now prevented from resorting to the New Zealand ports, or fishing on the coast by the tonnage duty, port charges, &c.," he wrote. Additionally, they "are denied the privilege of disposing of anything in barter, and obliged to pay a duty on American articles of from ten to five hundred per cent."

Though Wilkes's facts were somewhat exaggerated, this prophesy turned out to be justified, partly because of native unrest when the impact of British administration was fully understood, and partly because the many American merchants who heard tales of excessive duties and taxes took fright and sent their ships to other places to refit and reprovision. By the time Thomas Harlock Smith dropped anchor, the stream of Yankee ships that called at the Bay of Islands was rapidly dwindling to a trickle, and the men who did want to ship out were getting desperate. And so Smith was able to fill his empty berths. A man by the name of Thomas Robertson was shipped as third mate in Anderson's place, and eight hands were recruited for the forecastle, all with a history of desertion. Whatever the varied backgrounds of the ragtag men Smith had managed to ship, at least the *Sharon* had a full crew list again.

But how long it was going to stay that way was quite a different matter.

AT THE BEGINNING of March the *Sharon* was back at the island of Upolu in Samoa, about to be hit by yet another tragedy. Andrew White was working on the afterdeck. The sea was moderate, and he was enjoying the fine, sunny weather. The Portuguese seaman who had been taken on at Rotuma was busy nearby, getting ready to lash spare spars to the stern of the ship, where they would be safe and out of the way. The cooper watched him lower the bundle of spars over the rail, belay it, and then clamber over the stern to secure the unwieldy lengths of wood to the hull. The black-haired head dropped out of sight, but White could still hear him as he grappled with the spars and pieces of rope.

Abruptly he heard a splash and then a muffled shout. When White ran to the rail, the dark head was bobbing in the bubbling wake of the ship, and an arm was waving desperately for help. Andrew White let out a yell, echoed by a shout from the helmsman. By the time the ship had been slowed and a boat lowered, however, the Portuguese had gone "to rise no more."

It was a sad case. The Portuguese had survived the shipwreck of the *Cadmus* and the ordeal afterward, simply to find a grave elsewhere in the ocean. Just days afterward, the carpenter ran away in Upolu—presumably the same carpenter who had been shipped here in Samoa back in May 1843—perhaps because of the gloom this had cast about the decks. Or maybe it was because the carpenter had heard that Captain Thomas Harlock Smith had made up his mind to steer for the chilly, foggy waters off the northwest coast of America and fill his empty casks with right whale oil.

WHEN THE SHIP arrived on the northwest coast in April 1844, Benjamin Clough resumed his journal, probably inspired by the prospect of some action. In a spirit of optimism, he headed the page "Journal of A Whaling Voyage kept aboard Ship Sharon of Fairhaven in the North Pacific Ocean, A Cruising for Black Whales"—a common name for right whales. Too soon, though, he found that the right whales of the North Pacific, while very plentiful, were wild and hard to strike. "Lowered for Whales but got none," he noted for the fourth time on April 13, and then added, "Spoke the Gratitude of New Bedford 30 months 1,400 of Sperm. Stetson Master."

On board the *Gratitude* was seaman Joseph Eayres, who had been intrigued by the *Sharon* ever since hearing the gossip of Norris's murder, nine months previously, in July 1843. Now, he was able to satisfy his curiosity. "Spoke the ship Sharon," he noted in his journal, going on to record that he had been one of those who went on board the ship. "I spent the evening on board the S and heard the particulars respecting the horrid death of Captain Norris formerly of the S by the natives of the Kingsmill Group," he wrote, adding, "I shall bear it in mind but it would take a dutchman's dog watch to write it."

The day after the gam, the *Sharon* hands took their first right whale, to find that while the yield—140 barrels—was much greater than that from sperm whales, it involved a lot more work. Not only did the fat have to be stripped off and boiled, but the great masses of baleen—whalebone, the real function of which was to filter krill out of the seawater—had to be ripped and heaved out of the great mouth, and then cleaned, scraped, dried, and bundled for stowing.

The *Sharon* men also found that northern right whales were very pugnacious. While they did not have the toothed jaws of sperm whales, they could fight with their great flukes, which they smashed down on attacking boats. On April 29, wrote Benjamin Clough, "the Waist Boat struck and starboard boat kiled" a whale, but during the struggle "the Waist boat got badly stove and bow boat likewise." The boat's crew was lucky that none of their number was hurt: the logbooks of the nor'west whalers are full of accounts of men "killed by a whale." This was not always with the swift blow of great flukes. Right whales rolled over and over to try to rid themselves of the painful harpoons, and men who "got afoul" of the tangled up whalelines were dragged under the water to drown like Melville's Captain Ahab, despite their desperate struggles.

Three weeks went by, of fog and hail and mending broken boats, lowering for whales without success, and scraping rancid fat and rotten shreds of meat off great masses of whalebone. Then yet another tragedy punctuated the dismal routine.

The date was May 26, 1844. Just as before, the wind was light and the weather fair. The ship was under all sail, with men on lookout in both the foremast and the mainmast rigging. Benjamin Clough was the officer on watch. Thomas Silsby, the boy from Boston who had been shipped at Rotuma, was the one in the foretopmast crosstrees. When Silsby let out a scream, everyone must have thought he had raised spouts. Instead, he fell, plunging ninety feet headlong into the ocean.

It was unpleasantly reminiscent of the day when the Portuguese had drowned. The ship was hauled aback and a boat lowered, but the boy had sunk before he could be rescued. So Silsby, too, after surviving a shipwreck and somehow getting himself from Tahiti to Rotuma, had found the same depressing end as his shipmate, the anonymous Portuguese.

Life was altogether miserable, particularly for Clough, who was lowering two or three times most days for whales, usually without success. Two weeks into July, three of the *Sharon* boats were chasing a whale that ran upwind, which meant that the men had to row in chase, not being able to use the boat sails. When at last the boats attacked, one was smashed to pieces. Nathan Smith rescued the men who were struggling for their lives in the chilly water, leaving the waist boat—which Clough headed—at the mercy of the threshing whale, "about 4 miles from the ship." If Clough had persisted in trying to kill the great creature, the result could have been disastrous. Instead, most uncharacteristically, he decided that discretion was the better part of valor and cut the whale loose.

Not long after that, he gave up writing in his journal altogether. It was the end of the first week of August 1844, and the ship was finally full of whale oil. The oil might be an inferior kind, but at least the barrels were not empty. At long, long last, Captain Smith was able to issue orders to steer for home.

THEY SAILED FIRST to the Hawai'ian Islands, to reprovision for the homeward passage, tacking into Maui on September 6, where they found just eleven ships at anchor. It was the beginning of the reprovisioning season so it was quiet. Ten days later thirty ships lay at anchor, and the town of Lahaina was abustle with business. The numbers of whaleships provisioning in the Hawai'ian Islands had started rocketing in May 1837, when Captain Barzillai Folger had arrived in Honolulu with news of a right-whaling ground off the Northwest Coast of America. Then, in 1840, with the British takeover of New Zealand, Hawai'i had become the obvious place for all American whalemen, and not just the nor'westmen, to replenish. Almost every American whaling captain steered for Honolulu or Lahaina at some time in his voyage, creating a hugely profitable market from which the chiefs and merchants benefited.

For two weeks the *Sharon*, like the other whalers in port, was cleaned and painted. Trade goods were sent on shore, and fresh water, sweet potatoes, melons, vegetables, bananas, and coconuts brought on board, much of it paid for in blackfish oil. Captain Smith was quite happy to allow the men liberty in Lahaina. In fact, it was to his advantage if a few absconded, since the ship was full, and they were owed money—money that they would forfeit if they were not on board when the *Sharon* dropped anchor in the Acushnet River.

The liberty men found a long straggling town built down one or two long streets, lined with a few American-style houses built of stone or wood, but mostly with huts made of adobe or thatch, all interspersed with gardens, taro patches, fishponds, and coconut groves. It was also a place that was dominated by missionaries, who took a lot more interest in the whaling fleet than their English counterparts in the Bay of Islands, most of them set on converting the sinners of both forecastle and cabin. However, there were plenty of grogshops, too. The crew seemed to enjoy peaceable shore leave—but when, on September 21, the order was given to weigh anchor, the sailors refused to obey.

The reason they gave, according to Andrew White, was that the ship was too short of men to make a safe passage home. It was a feeble excuse: just one man, Robert Johnstone, had run away, disappearing the day before. Sailors did occasionally abscond while their ship was provisioning for home. It is more likely, though, that Johnstone had been kidnapped by one of the many tavern keepers and boardinghouse keepers who made money out of commissions received for supplying men to the ships.

His absence, however, had given the crew of the *Sharon* an excuse to express their low opinion of the captain. Thomas Harlock Smith sent for the local U.S. consul—in this case Vice-Consular Agent Milo Calkin, a tough customer. After handcuffing all the men who had refused to obey orders and cross-examining them closely, he sorted out three ringleaders, flogged them, and then sent the bruised and smarting trio on shore. Calkin wrote an affidavit testifying that the three men had been "discharged from Ship Sharon of Fairhaven by mutual consent of parties & in accordance with the laws of the United States," but there is no record that they received any of their fairly earned money.

The ship was now short of four men, not just one, but the rest, thoroughly demoralized, went back to work. At 2 P.M. the captain returned on board, and the *Sharon* squared yards and kept off for home.

Thirteen

HOMECOMING

On January 1, 1845, the *Sharon* arrived in the North Atlantic, and, in a tradition dating back to the first American whalers that ventured into the Pacific, the tryworks furnace was broken apart and the greasy bricks thrown overboard. It was an eloquent sign that there would be no more whaling this voyage, as it was now impossible to render blubber into oil. When the ship was outfitted for the next cruise, a new tryworks furnace would be built. In the meantime the decks, rigging, and bulwarks were scrubbed and painted to make a fine show as she came up the river. Andrew White penned his last entry on February 5, and on the tenth the *Sharon* arrived at the head of Buzzard's Bay in a snowstorm.

It must have been quite a moment for all on board. Those

who were originally from New England were bound to be pensive. For those who had jumped from ship to ship in the Pacific, it might have been five or more years since they'd seen New Bedford last. Very few of the men would have received letters, and so would have had no idea what might have happened in the interval. Parents might have passed away, children been born, brothers run off to sea, sentimentally remembered sweethearts been snapped up by others; wives might have remarried, having given their husbands up as dead. Half-forgotten feuds might still be brewing. For years, the only news of the homeland would have been scraps picked up in foreign papers. When the pilot scrambled onto the after deck, Captain Smith and his officers would have plied him with questions, and his tidbits of news would have quickly flown forward.

On shore, things were good. New Bedford, booming faster than ever, was now officially recognized as the fourth largest shipping center in America, which meant she was one of the most affluent towns in the world. In fact, she was on the verge of becoming a city, her motto *Lucem Diffundo*, "We Light the World." There were nearly two hundred different stores along Union Street now. Strolling the five busiest blocks, from the waterfront to Purchase Street, the *Sharon* sailors could expect to find silversmiths, watchmakers, tailors, hatters, architects, physicians and paperhangers, ship chandlers and bootmakers, leathermakers and confectionery shops, all doing excellent trade. A fellow could now have his picture taken by one of the three daguerrotype artists who had set up in town, in a miraculous new process called photography. Great new mansions had sprung up, as rich merchants who had been strict Quakers had turned to the more liberal Unitarian Church and could now show off their wealth with good conscience. Other avenues that promised prosperity were being explored: The pilot named strange new businesses—a cordage company, a cotton textile mill; there was talk of an iron works, and a railroad for Fairhaven. So even greater changes were looming.

While the *Sharon* crew absorbed this, a big black sloop came alongside, packed with men who shouted out blandishments as they swarmed up over the rail and onto the decks of the ship. "Sharks," muttered the pilot, and spat contemptuously. The men were runners working on commission for boardinghouse keepers and tavern keepers—agents who watched for incoming ships from the cupolas set in the roofs of the shops and taverns. Once on board, they competed raucously, touting lodgings, grog, and entertainment to bewildered men who had been watching nothing but the quiet sea and the silent horizon for the past four months. The ship's officers had to yell at the hands to get them aloft and away from this demanding mob, so that the sails could be furled as the *Sharon* drifted up the ice-flecked breast of the Acushnet River toward her mooring.

On the New Bedford side there was a new place for the *Sharon* to tie up and discharge her oil—Merrill's Wharf, with a great brick building at the head. Fat oil casks lay in rows on the great squared timbers of the jetty, covered with seaweed to prevent the staves drying out and leaking—seaweed sprinkled with snow that was grimy with the smoke of prosperity. No sooner was the gangplank dropped than the rabble of runners surged down it, bearing with them the sailors they had marked as their prey. All at once, two much more respectable but equally intent figures elbowed their way through the mob—brothers Ben and Henry Lindsey. The first, Benjamin Lindsey, was the editor of the New Bedford *Daily Mercury*, a paper familiar to all those who were coming home. Brother Henry, however, was the editor of *The Whalemen's Shipping List & Merchants' Transcript*, a journal none of them would have ever heard of before. This weekly paper, the *Wall Street Journal* of the American whaling trade, had been launched in New Bedford two years earlier, while the ship was in the eastern Pacific.

The two editors knew exactly which man they wanted to speak to most—Benjamin Clough, the hero of the single-handed recapture. The sensational story of the murder and mutiny on the *Sharon* was about to be rekindled, in response to the huge public interest that was spurred by the return of the ship.

UP UNTIL THE DAY that the *Sharon* arrived home, the newspaper editors of New England had had to satisfy themselves with paraphrasing the story as it had originally appeared in the *Sydney Morning Herald*. Now, with the hero himself available, the tale could be filled out at length—if the hero could be enticed to talk. And Clough did allow himself to be interviewed. It was the older Lindsey, Benjamin, who got the scoop. The story he wrote was published in the February 27 edition of the *Mercury*, under the headline, MURDER OF CAPTAIN NORRIS OF THE WHALING SHIP SHARON OF FAIRHAVEN, AND RECAPTURE OF THE SHIP FROM MUTINEERS, BY MR. BENJAMIN CLOUGH, HER 3rd. OFFICER.

The item created a sensation. It had sounded like the same old story for the first couple of paragraphs, but then came spicy revelations concerning the conduct of Thomas Harlock Smith. As first officer of the *Sharon* and successor to the command when Captain Norris was killed, his behavior had been in shameful contrast to the courage of the dashing third mate. While lumps of wood and belaying pins were flying about the whalemen's heads, for instance, Clough had leapt up into the bow of the boat and balanced there, doing his utmost to spear the nearest native with a whaling lance. Thomas Harlock Smith had foiled this valiant attempt at counterattack by keeping the boat out of range, declaring that someone in his crew might get hurt if they came any closer, and because of this cowardice Clough had not been able to dart far enough to stab the mutineer.

Worse still was the next allegation—that Thomas Harlock Smith had decided that it would be wisest for him to stay out of harm's way if the men tried to storm the ship. Captain Norris being dead, he was the man in charge, and so he had reckoned that duty "required him to avoid all personal risk." To make sure of this, Lindsey related, the first mate had proposed that all the men should get into the second mate's whaleboat and head off for the attack, leaving him alone in his own boat to await the outcome. This proposition had "met with no favor," the report continued, "the men declaring a wish rather to start for the nearest land, five or six days' sail distant, and the second mate relishing it so little that he suffered his boat to drop astern out of talking distance." Scarcely less libelous were harrowing descriptions of Clough bleeding freely while he waited for Thomas Harlock Smith to screw up his courage to board the ship and the cold-blooded shooting of the helpless and wounded native that followed.

Naturally, when he read all this, Thomas Harlock Smith became extremely upset. Simmering, he composed a long, offended letter to the *Mercury*, which was dutifully cosigned by his cousin, Nathan. On March 10, Benjamin Lindsey printed it. "We have already published a circumstantial account of the melancholy mutiny which took place on board the ship *Sharon* on her last voyage, as related by Mr Clough the third officer on board said ship," ran his preamble. Since then, however, "Mr Smith, the 1st officer on board the *Sharon*" had asked him to print the following letter "as an act of justice to himself, in order to correct certain erroneous impressions."

Thomas Smith's letter followed. "It is not our wish to detract from the merits of Mr. Clough, or lessen the prominent part acted by him on that trying and unfortunate occasion, but to correct misrepresentations given in that article," he commenced with dignity. Then he plunged into a spirited retelling of the entire incident from his own point of view. Though he admitted that the men had shifted from one boat to another during the council of war, the allegation that he had planned to keep out of harm's way while the rest of the men attacked was nothing but a lie, and the other accusations of spinelessness did not have a shadow of truth, either. When he and Nathan Smith heard the report of the gun, they "were probably on board in ten minutes after he fired." And the native discovered on the windowsill was not harmless at all, but "armed with a cutlass and large knife, threatening the lives of all who approached him. We then shot him," Thomas Harlock Smith added, spreading the blame. There was a great deal about Mr. Clough's version that was nothing more than a bunch of fabrications, he protested, "invented to make it appear that the principal part of the officers and others were poltroons and cowards."

Unhappily for Thomas Harlock Smith, "poltroons and cowards" made much better copy than righteously offended officers. The *Mercury's* version swiftly became the accepted account, the other papers dashing in to plagiarize it word for word, as was journalistically respectable then. Henry Lindsey's *Whalemen's Shipping List*, which copied the item on March 4, did not bother to follow it up with the Smiths' side of the story, and neither did the nationally read *Littell's Living Age*. It was a tale with endurance, too: as late as March 1852 it was republished in its offensive entirety by *Hunt's Merchants' Magazine*, the story as originally written by the *Mercury* being considered "worthy of preservation and deserving of an imperishable record."

Obviously, Benjamin Clough had talked a lot during the interview with Ben Lindsey from the *Mercury*. As his journal account of his desertion from the *Rajah* and his fight with the Malay pirates illustrates, he enjoyed picturing himself as the dashing hero of dangerous adventures. Evidently, too, he had a few accounts to settle: There had been a few nasty moments during the recapture of the *Sharon* when he could have used some help; and the memory of waiting for some response after the musket had been fired certainly would have rankled. He would have resented the way he was treated after Thomas Smith had taken over the command, and it is plain that he had no respect for Smith's decisions as a whaling master, or for his courage as a whaleman.

But there is no evidence that he deliberately misled the editor. Misunderstandings are much more likely. However, the article certainly did Clough's career no harm: Not only did the insurance firms reward him with gifts of navigational instruments, but the owners, Gibbs & Jenney, passed over both Thomas Harlock Smith and Nathan Skiff Smith to give Benjamin Clough the command of the next voyage of the *Sharon*.

CLEARLY, GETTING HOME was not a happy time for Thomas Harlock Smith Jr. Harried by the press, maligned by the public, and humiliated by Gibbs & Jenney, he did, however, have the comfort that Clough had not revealed the background of the tragedy. He must have been relieved to see Benjamin Clough sail away, even if the overtalkative young man *was* in charge of the ship that Thomas Harlock Smith had had every right to expect would be his.

The *Sharon* left the Acushnet River on May 21, Gibbs & Jenney having taken just thirteen weeks to fit her out for sea again. When the pilot left the ship off Cuttyhunk, it must have been a great source of pride for Benjamin Clough to preside in the same quarters where the Smith cousins had humiliated him by not allowing him any part in the decision-making process. He must have felt gratified, too, that some of the crew who had come home on the ship had signed up for a voyage with him as master. William Leek, who had been shipped by Captain Thomas Smith at the Bay of Islands in January 1844, was the second mate; twenty-three-year-old James Johnson, who had been shipped at the same time, was a boatsteerer; Francis Saul, who had joined the *Sharon* in Sydney in December 1842, was the cook; Water Bucket, who had been taken on board in the Samoan Islands in May 1843, and Samuel Haley, a black sailor who had been shipped at Sydney, were seamen before the mast. And Andrew White was the cooper and shipkeeper. He still did not have enough money to stay home on the farm, and so was forced to return to sea. It must have been very frustrating for him to have to sail away again, though he did manage to negotiate the very good lay of 1/40. Also, by stipulating that he was to be one of those who kept ship, the cooper ensured that he would not be hauling an oar in a whaleboat when he should rightfully be on board getting ready for cutting in whales.

Despite that precaution, it does seem likely that White expected this voyage to be a lot less traumatic than the last one. Somewhat ironically, though, Benjamin Clough had to contend with a minor mutiny that was triggered by one of the shipmates who had opted to sail with him. According to the journal kept by boatsteerer James Johnson, in May 1846 two "cullard men" got into a fight, at which point "the Captin came on deck and Put one of them in irons a man by the name Of Samuel haley before the mast." Captain Clough gave Haley a choice: slush down the topmast, or be seized up for a dozen lashes — which, as Johnson went on to say, "is generley the Punishment On board of our whale ships." Then the boatsteerer added with definite bitterness, probably a reflection of the floggings he had watched Thomas Smith deal out during the previous voyage, "it shows what feeling A Man has for his fellow beings." Slushing down involved greasing the masts with the salty fat that had floated to the top of the cook's cauldrons, an unpleasant job because the salt ate into the hands and the perch was precarious.

Haley chose the flogging. Accordingly, Captain Clough "sezed him up and gave him a duzin Lashes and then all hands refused duty Before the mast but fineley our captain talked with them and they came to terms."

The men might have seen reason after Captain Clough talked it over with them, but when the *Sharon* arrived in Lahaina in November, Samuel Haley asked for his discharge. Five others went with him, and so Benjamin Clough had to look for more men. These were duly shipped, but when one of them placed his signature on the crew list, it must have brought a most unexpected reminder of terrible past events—for the name this new man gave was George Babcock.

Babcock, like George, was a common name. But surely, just for a second, Benjamin Clough's blood ran cold.

DROPPING ANCHOR AGAIN in the Acushnet River in April 1848, Clough reported a cargo of oil and bone worth just under $80,000, which meant that after expenses were subtracted and the lays apportioned out, Andrew White pocketed almost exactly one thousand dollars. At last the stalwart cooper had made enough money to swallow the anchor and head off to Tiverton, Rhode Island, to take up permanent life as a farmer.

In New Bedford and Fairhaven, Benjamin Clough, like every other homecoming whaling master, was catching up with the news. There were whispers of a great gold find in California, dismissed by most people as a baseless rumor. An ex-whaleman by the name of Herman Melville had published a book called *Typee*, a colorful tale of desertion in the Marquesas Islands that had done so well that a sequel, *Omoo*, had followed. A New Bedford blacksmith, ex-slave Lewis Temple, had created the Temple toggle iron, which promised to be one of the most significant inventions in the history of whaling. No longer would harpoons draw out of the whale in the manner that had so infuriated Captain Norris, because Temple irons incorporated a toggle that turned at right angles after piercing the blubber, lodging the harpoon securely.

Thomas Harlock Smith was also in town, having come back the previous month from a voyage in command of the Warren, Rhode Island, whaleship *Benjamin Rush*, so it is possible that the two men would have met, even if briefly, to exchange a stiff conversation concerning the events of the interval. It had taken Smith awhile to be offered a captaincy, which had meant that he had not followed Clough out of Buzzard's Bay until October 1845, a good four months after the *Sharon* had left. Clough, asking about Nathan Skiff Smith, would have learned that fate had not favored him, either. Offered nothing better, Nathan Smith had been forced to accept the job of first mate of the *Cowper* of New Bedford, and at this date was still on voyage.

Days after Clough's arrival home, flyers were put into the hands of everyone embarking on the Fairhaven ferry, and broadsides were plastered about in New Bedford and Fairhaven, advertising the first performance of a moving panorama called "A Whaling Voyage Round the World." To Clough's undoubted amazement—and Thomas Harlock Smith's definite chagrin—his famous feat was about to become more celebrated than ever, because his struggle to regain the ship was just about to hit the equivalent of the silver screen.

Static panoramas, often 360-degree vistas painted on the inside walls of specially built rotundas, had been featured in Europe for about fifty years but had never really taken off in America. Just recently, though, American entrepreneurs had improved the idea by putting the scenes on long strips of fabric, which were unscrolled from one upright roller to another within a proscenium arch, to create a vivid impression of moving through spectacular scenery. In mid-1845, New Bedforder Benjamin Russell, cooper of the whaleship *Kutusoff*, had arrived home with a sketchbook in his sea chest that he reckoned held enough material to make a panorama of his trip. So he had approached a local sign painter, Caleb Purrington, with a proposition that they should paint it jointly and then take it about the country to be shown to audiences for a fee.

It was an ambitious vision: The result was a strip thirteen hundred feet long and eight-and-a-half feet high, completely covered with paint, presenting a continuous, powerful visual narrative of a whaling voyage in the early 1840s, with views of exotic ports such as Fayal and Honolulu, dramatic whaling scenes, and vistas of island paradises. Spooled onto two ten-foot rollers, it unwound from opening scenes of the wharves at New Bedford, through the Atlantic to the Pacific and onward, accompanied by sounds of the sea and the admiring applause of the watchers. A stunning success in Fairhaven, it moved on to Boston, Cincinnati, New Bedford, and Nantucket over the following three years, and is still displayed in the New Bedford Whaling Museum.

While there is no actual record of Benjamin Clough paying over cash to have a look at this marvel, it is hard to believe he could have resisted the opportunity—particularly since the *Sharon* was featured so boldly, caught at the moment the boats had arrived to find the captain dead and the natives in control of the ship. In some respects the representation tallies with Clough's own painting of the incident. The three natives are gesticulating on the bulwarks, and Manuel des Reis is cutting away the rigging. However, the dead whale is tied up to the ship, not having been set adrift. Clough himself is featured prominently, standing in the head of one of the approaching boats, wielding a lance as he attempts to spear one of the prancing mutineers. Obviously, Purrington and Russell had taken their inspiration from the article in the *Mercury* that had lauded the heroic third mate and had been less than kind to Thomas Harlock Smith.

By legend, Melville was one of the many who viewed it. He had plenty of opportunity, since he was in New Bedford in early May to meet his young brother Tom, who was one of the crew of the incoming Westport whaler *Theophilus Chase*, and make sure he was "regularly discharged and paid," as Elizabeth Melville explained to her stepmother. He also had the opportunity while visiting in-laws in Boston, where the panorama was shown at Armory Hall. Like Benjamin Clough, Melville would have felt a natural interest, having gone through many of the same experiences in the same oceans and at the same time. And, although its publication would be preceded by three other seafaring novels, he was beginning to mull over ideas for his masterpiece, *Moby-Dick*.

• • •

AFTER A FOUR-MONTH vacation, Benjamin Clough took command of the *Frances Henrietta* of New Bedford, sailing in August and coming home in January 1851 to be regaled with more startling news — that the city fathers of New Bedford, the oil market of the world, had contracted to light the streets with gas! A textile mill was now operational, and Wamsutta shirting made in New Bedford was becoming quite famous. Of even greater moment to Clough, Congress had passed a law prohibiting flogging on board whalers and merchant ships.

This time, Captain Thomas Harlock Smith was not in port, having sailed off on another Warren ship, *Mary Frances*. Reports said that he was not doing very well. As for Nathan Skiff Smith, he was in California, chasing the elusive gold. Clough, by contrast, had made enough money to be able to afford a nine-month vacation, spending most of his time in Martha's Vineyard, where he was courting a beautiful Tisbury girl, eighteen-year-old Charlotte Chase Downs.

With strange irony, Charlotte's father was none other than Captain Charles Downs, the man who, when in command of the whaleship *Oscar*, had gammed at length with thirty-year-old Captain Howes Norris of the *London Packet* and had humiliated him with compelling evidence that his men were deliberately wasting provisions. This encounter had led directly to the mortifying mutiny on the *London Packet*, and so had contributed to the paranoia that was such a decisive factor in the violent suppression of the rebellion on the *Sharon*.

Because he was paying court to Downs's daughter, at the beginning of August Clough was on Martha's Vineyard, so would have read the report of the strange death of Elwina, Captain

Howes Norris's widow, in the *Vineyard Gazette*. She had been enjoying the company of friends for morning coffee when a storm struck. A bolt of lightning had shot down the chimney, melting the mantelpiece clock and the brass fire irons, "and is supposed to have entered her ear. It slightly scorched her neck, but there was no other trace of it on her person." Though none of her friends were hurt, Elwina Norris was instantly killed. "Mrs. Norris was about 44 years of age, a highly respected lady, and her death has cast a gloom over the circle in which she moved," the item concluded, adding, "She leaves four children to mourn her loss."

Clough also had the chance to read the first notices of a whaling novel that promised to be important. "Mr Melville will soon be again before the public," announced *The International Magazine* in July, going on to say that though the title had not yet been announced, "we believe it is in press." When Clough finally sailed away again, taking out the spanking new whaleship *Niagara* on October 9, the current issue of *Harper's New Monthly Magazine* was carrying an extract called "The *Town-Ho*'s Story." This was to be chapter fifty-four of *The Whale*, "The title of a new work by Mr. Melville, in the press of Harper and Brothers, and now publishing in London by Mr. Bentley."

When Clough arrived back in February 1854, Melville's whaling novel was old news: though everyone agreed that nothing quite like it had ever been written before, the author was so badly off that he had been forced to borrow money against the advance of a new book, *Pierre*, which was a financial and critical failure. Melville's writing career was in ruins. Clough, by contrast, was flush with success: This voyage on the *Niagara* had reaped a record-breaking total of 5,135 barrels of oil, almost half of it either sent on ahead by other ships or sold at a profit in Valparaiso. Altogether, the cargo grossed over a hundred thousand dollars, a huge fortune at the time. That whaling was falling on increasingly hard times made his report seem even more substantial. Thomas Harlock Smith's last voyage, for instance, had reaped just 850 barrels, but this kind of figure had become so typical that the owners had sent him out again.

Affluent with his share of the profits, Benjamin Clough was able to marry Charlotte in style. Unexpectedly, Captain Charles Downs arrived back from a three-year voyage the same day as the wedding. When he walked in the door, he must have been as amazed to see what was going on as the assembled guests were to see him. After hearing about his new son-in-law's wonderful whaling record, though, surely he was pleased. Benjamin Clough, too, would have shaken hands heartily, after getting over the shock.

The happy new husband bought a fine home on Main Street that overlooked the harbor and set up house with his lovely young wife — which meant that the Smiths were close neighbors. Clough must have noticed that the Smith family had done nothing to help the four children who had been orphaned by Elwina Smith Norris's sudden death. Instead, they had been fostered by Norris relatives. The two youngest, Mary and Howes, had gone to Eastville to live with their uncle, Shaw Norris, while Alonzo had been taken in by another uncle, John Norris of Bristol, Rhode Island. The eldest, Octavia, after two years of fending for herself, had married a physician. Undoubtedly Clough wondered whether the Smiths had used the chance to distance themselves from the Norris name.

In September 1855, after an eighteen-month honeymoon, Clough went back to sea on the Fairhaven whaler *General Scott*. When he left, Nathan Skiff Smith was in town, having just returned from California, and was on the hunt for a command of his own. Finally Nathan Smith achieved this, sailing off in charge of the bark *Belle* of Warren, Rhode Island, in May 1856, just one month before Thomas Harlock Smith arrived home. Captain Thomas Smith had some startling news of his own: His luck had been as poor as ever, and so he had made a most un-Vineyard-like decision—to give up whaling. Dugan and Leland, commission merchants of New York City, had offered him the command of their new 316-ton ship *Carrie Leland*, and he had grabbed the chance to get into the China trade.

When Clough got back in July 1858, Thomas Smith was long gone. He'd shifted away from the Vineyard, and then he had sailed off to the Orient, and no one had heard from him since. While his son, Alexander, was still living on Main Street with his grandfather, Thomas Harlock Smith Sr., and Thomas's brother Alphonso, Thomas and his wife, Elizabeth, had completely disappeared from the scene. Clough may have heard that Elizabeth had moved to New York, or he could have been told that she had gone along with her husband, as it was common for captains in the China trade to take their wives to sea.

Benjamin Clough stopped at home for the next six years, partly because he could afford it, and partly because the value of whale oil had slumped. Accordingly, in May 1859 he was on

Martha's Vineyard to hear about Nathan Skiff Smith's return with a scant 975 barrels of oil, nothing unusual in those days. Increasingly, captains were following Thomas Harlock Smith's lead and getting into other kinds of shipping—or, if they had the money, they stayed at home, like Benjamin Clough. This meant that Nathan Smith, despite his lackluster record, was offered the command of the New Bedford ship *Newark*. In September he sailed off, headed for the Timor Straits and the equatorial Pacific. He had been away six months when Confederate troops attacked Fort Sumter and the American Civil War began.

Then suddenly, Nathan Smith was in the news. On April 7, 1863, according to the papers, the *Newark* had been wrecked on Sandalwood Island, near Timor, and Nathan Skiff Smith and his crew had survived an open boat voyage of nine days and ten nights, with but little bread and water. No sooner was that tidbit absorbed than Clough saw Thomas Harlock Smith's name in the *Vineyard Gazette* and realized that one of the major participants in the tragedy of the *Sharon* was dead. The China coast had killed him. The issue for January 29, 1864, reported, "DIED. At Shanghai, China, Aug. 16th, Capt. Thomas H. Smith, Jr., late of bark *Copang*, aged 50 years.—Salem papers please copy."

The year 1864 was full of dire tidings. Insurance premiums had risen through the roof. Merchants were investing in factories and railroads instead of whaling ships. With so much work on shore, it was harder than ever to get hands for the long whaling voyages. Few responsible men saw the point of risking capture and imprisonment by Confederate raiders, as well as all the other more usual hazards of whaling, when more money could be safely made at home.

Then all at once the value of whale products boomed. The Industrial Age might be dragging both manpower and investment money away from the whaling trade, but factories had to be lit and machines had to be greased, creating a huge market for whale oil, which the war had made scarce. Whalebone, the spring steel of the age, was equally in demand. The prospect for profit was irresistible: Both Nathan Skiff Smith and Benjamin Clough went back to sea.

Nathan Smith departed in command of the *Java* in September, and Clough followed him in December, in charge of the *Northern Light*. Nathan Smith was headed for the Indian Ocean, and Benjamin Clough for the icy northern Pacific, beyond the Bering Straits. Clough arrived back in August 1867, but Nathan Smith did not drop anchor in the Acushnet River until October. The war was over, but their cargoes still grossed over $120,000 each. For both men, the gamble had paid off.

Nathan did not live long to enjoy his belated bonanza. He was admitted to the Massachusetts General Hospital in Boston on December 31, with massive swelling of the glands in his neck, armpits, and groin, accompanied by lassitude and "progressive general failure." Lonely for his family, he wrote two letters to his brother, Captain Pressbury Smith, the tone determinedly optimistic despite the fact that the doctors had all agreed that "they never saw such enlargement in all of their Practice, they say I must have an Iron Constitution to have stood it so long." Nathan Smith was discharged on January 6, "unrelieved," the physicians having given the condition a name—leucocythaemia—but otherwise having admitted defeat. Within weeks he was dead, at the age of fifty-one. Another witness to the murder of George Babcock was gone.

"He had been an exile from home for nearly 35 years, having passed but about 5 years of the time with his family," ran his obituary in the *Vineyard Gazette*. Having just returned from a successful voyage, the item continued, Nathan Skiff Smith had hoped to spend the remainder of his days with the loved ones at home, but instead, "he was stricken down with the disease that ended his life."

The funeral was held on March 16, 1868. It is impossible to tell if Captain Clough was one of the mourners. It is likely, though, that he attended the service, since the families were such close neighbors.

CLOUGH RETIRED PERMANENTLY, having grossed over four hundred thousand dollars in the course of a brilliant whaling career, and settled to becoming a pillar of Martha's Vineyard society. In the light of the times, it was a good decision; though whaling was still king on the Acushnet River, when New Bedford whalers returned to port they were carrying raw materials for industry as well as barrels of oil. The caulkers, riggers, sail makers, and rope makers of the Acushnet River, who had depended on the whaling fleet for their living, were doomed.

In the meantime, both Martha's Vineyard and Benjamin Clough were doing nicely. No longer focused on whaling, the island had become a fashionable—and prosperous—summer resort. A prominent Mason, Captain Clough had been made master of his lodge; he was a county commissioner, a justice of the peace, and a member of the legislature. He did not pass away until May 1889, when the *Vineyard Gazette* announced, "We are pained to chronicle the sad announcement of the death from apoplexy of Capt. Benjamin Clough."

And yet again his heroic deed was aired. "On the 6th of No., 1842, while nearly all the crew were after whales, natives on board mutinied, and killing the captain took command of the vessel," the recounting began:

> All efforts to retake the ship proved unavailing. Mr. Clough volunteered to undertake the task himself. Dropping overboard from one of the boats, after swimming for an hour and a half he climbed into the cabin window, and single-handed encountered the natives and re-took the ship. To his daring intrepidity are to be attributed the return of a valuable cargo, and what was more important, the preservation of the surviving crew from the miserable fate which would have overtaken them had they attempted to reach any of the cannibal islands in those seas.

Again, there was no hint of speculation about the reason the captain had been killed; still, it was assumed that because the natives belonged to "cannibal islands," they needed no motive to murder a man. The slain captain was not even named, let alone the interesting fact that he had been a scion of Martha's Vineyard. It was as if Norris—who had never merited an obituary of his own—had been deliberately forgotten.

If so, it had been possible only because Benjamin Clough, throughout the years of exposure to the media, had never once hinted in public at the truth of the *Sharon* tragedy. Whatever pact of silence, tacit or spoken, had been made with Thomas Harlock Smith and Nathan Skiff Smith, it had never been broken, even after their deaths. As the obituary mentioned, he had been a man of "sterling integrity."

There was one witness left—the cooper, Andrew White, still working on the farm in Tiverton, Rhode Island. White did not pass away until February 1896, when he succumbed to cancer of the stomach at the age of eighty-one. His obituary in the *Providence Journal* extolled him as one of Tiverton's oldest and most respected citizens. "At the age of 21 he went whaling, and during the nine years that he was at sea he filled the position of ship's cooper," the item related, with no mention of the *Sharon*, or the murder, or even the famous feat. While Andrew White had retained the journal where he had penned the background of the tragedy, for reasons unknown he had also kept his counsel.

And so the secret of the *Sharon* followed him to the grave.

The Crew List of the Whaleship *Sharon*

	Rank	Lay	Signed	Protection	Birthplace	Height	Skin	Hair	Eyes	Age
Norris, Howes	Captain	1/16	5/22/1841		Edgartown, MA	5' 8-½"	light	brown		38
Smith, Thomas Harlock Jr.	First officer	1/28	5/21/1841		Tisbury, MA	4'9"	light	sandy		27
Smith, Nathan Skiff	Second officer	1/48	5/21/1841		Tisbury, MA	5'4-½"	light	brown		25
Clough, Benjamin	Third officer	1/60	5/21/1841	9/10/1835	Monmouth, ME	5'6-½"	light	brown	blue	22
Tripp, Otis Jr.	Boatsteerer	1/80	5/11/1841	5/19/1841	Westport, MA	5'7"	dark	black	dark	27
Place, Isaac H.	Boatsteerer	1/90	5/11/1841	7/10/1837	New Bedford, MA	5'6"	light	light	grey	21
Wing, Leonard H.	Boatsteerer	1/85	5/21/1841	5/24/1836	Dartmouth, MA	5'2-½"	light	brown	blue	21
Hathaway, Jacob H.	Boatsteerer	1/85	5/20/1841							
Andrews, Edward A.	Greenhand	1/185	5/3/1841	5/20/1841	Portland, ME	5'7"	light	brown	blue	23
Witcher, John	Greenhand	1/185	5/3/1841	5/20/1841	Boscawen, NH	5'8"	light	light	blue	23
Sperry, Cyrus	Greenhand	1/185	5/3/1841	5/20/1841	Hartford, CT	5'9"	light	brown	blue	27
Allen, John	Greenhand	1/185	5/3/1841	5/20/1841	Utica, NY	5'4-¾"	dark	dark	black	21
White, Andrew	Cooper	1/50	5/3/1841	7/3/1837	Tiverton, CT	5'7"	light	brown	dark	26
Turner, Frederick	Carpenter	1/175	5/3/1841		Lockport, NY	5'9-½"	light	brown		27
Sweeny, William (Weeks)	Greenhand	1/210	5/3/1841	5/17/1841	Kensington, PA	5'7"	dark	dark	blue	18

	Rank	Lay	Signed	Protection	Birthplace	Height	Skin	Hair	Eyes	Age
Smith, William	Seaman	1/145	5/4/1841	5/21/1841	Newburyport, MA	5'8-3/4"	light	brown	blue	20
Leods, Samuel	Seaman	1/160	5/5/1841		New York, NY	5'6-1/4"	black	woolly		23
Mills, Henry	Cook	1/145	5/20/1841	5/20/1841	Richmond, VA	5'5"	black	woolly	black	32
Bligh, Lyman	Greenhand	1/185	5/11/1841		Lenox, NY	5'8"	light	brown		17
Yellott, Alexander	Greenhand	1/180	5/10/1841	5/17/1841	Baltimore, MD	5'10"	light	brown	blue	25
Babcock, George	Steward	1/165	5/14/1841	5/20/1841	Newport, RI	5'3-1/2"	yellow	woolly	black	18
Nichols, Samuel A.	Greenhand	1/185	5/15/1841	5/20/1841	Franklin, NY	5'8-1/2"	dark	dark	blue	22
Moore, John	Greenhand	1/185	5/15/1841	5/20/1841	Malta, NY	5'7"	light	brown	blue	19
Taylor, Sterling	Greenhand	1/185	5/15/1841	5/21/1841	Newtown, CT	5'11"	light	sandy	black	21
Davis, Thomas	Greenhand	1/185	5/20/1841	5/21/1841	Salina, NY	5'7"	light	brown	blue	19
Fugle, Henry	Greenhand	1/185	5/20/1841		Salina, NY	5'6"	dark	black		20
McQueen, John	Greenhand	1/190	5/20/1841	9/26/1835	New York, NY	5'2-1/2"	light	brown	blue	22
Baker, John	Ordinary seaman	1/170	5/22/1841	5/22/1841	Newburgh, NY	5'6-1/2"	light	brown	dark	18
Williams, Thomas	Ordinary seaman	1/175	5/22/1841	5/22/1841	New York, NY	5'6"	light	brown	blue	19
Des Reis, Manuel José	Ordinary seaman	1/175	5/22/1841		Fayal, Azores					
Bacon, John M.	Greenhand		5/21/1841	5/21/1841	Buffalo, NY	5'3-3/4"	light	brown	blue	18
Shearman, Nathaniel R.	Boatsteerer	1/85	5/24/1841	6/1/1839	Bridgeport, CT	5'3-3/4"	light	brown	grey	18

CHRONOLOGY OF MELVILLE'S SOUTH SEAS ADVENTURES AND RELEVANT PUBLICATIONS

- January 3, 1841, ships as a foremast hand on the whaleship *Acushnet*.
- July 9, 1842, deserts ship at Nukuhiva in the Marquesas Islands. Spends a month with the cannibals of the Taipi valley.
- August 9, 1842, escapes by joining the crew of the Sydney whaler *Lucy Ann*.
- October 5, 1842, placed ashore at Tahiti with ten other crewmen, and tried before the Consul for mutiny. Lightly imprisoned in Tahiti. A beachcomber on Moorea.
- November 1842, ships on whaleship *Charles & Henry*.
- May 1843, discharged at Lahaina, goes to Honolulu to work for a merchant as clerk and bookkeeper.
- August 17, 1843, enlists on U.S. Navy ship *United States*. Ship calls at Nukuhiva, Tahiti, and Callao.
- October 14, 1844, discharged from the navy at Boston.
- 1846, very successful publication of *Typee: A Peep at Polynesian Life*.
- 1847, publication of a sequel, *Omoo: A Narrative of Adventures in the South Seas*.
- 1849, publication of *Mardi*.
- 1850, publication of *White-Jacket, or The World in a Man-of-War*.
- 1851, *Moby-Dick* published to mixed reviews.

CHAPTER NOTES

INTRODUCTION

Newspaper accounts of the murder and recapture of the *Sharon* used throughout the book are: *Sydney Morning Herald* (December 23, 1842); *New Zealand Gazette and Wellington Spectator* (January 28, 1843); *Boston Courier* (June 27, 1843); *Boston Daily Atlas* (June 27, 1843); *Mercury* (New Bedford, February 27, 1845 and March 10, 1845); *Salem Observer* (March 1, 1845); *Whalemen's Shipping List & Merchants' Transcript* (New Bedford, March 4, 1845); *Essex County Whig* (Lynn, Mass., March 22, 1845); *Littell's Living Age* (New York, March 22, 1845); *Hunt's Merchants' Magazine and Commercial Review* (New York, March 1852). The dates in newspaper and logbook records occasionally differ by one day, because formal seagoing logbooks were kept in sea time, where the twenty-four hours of the day were reckoned from noon to noon instead of from midnight to midnight.

Charles Boardman Hawes's book, *Whaling,* was published in London by Heinemann in 1924. His rousing account of the murder and recapture, taken from newspaper reports of the time, is a typical rendition.

There are many worthy books and essays analyzing the plot, characters, themes, and allegories of *Moby-Dick.* A selection I found particularly inspiring and useful for the purposes of this book are:

Charles Roberts Anderson, *Melville in the South Seas*. (New York: Univ. of Columbia Press, 1939, repr. New York: Dover, 1966.)

Tyrus Hillway, *Herman Melville*. (Boston: Twayne Publishers, 1979.)

Carolyn L. Karcher, *Shadow over the Promised Land: Slavery, Race, and Violence in Melville's America*. (Baton Rouge: Louisiana State Univ. Press, 1980.)

David Kirby, *Herman Melville*. (New York: Continuum, 1993.)

Jay Leyda, *The Melville Log: A Documentary Life of Herman Melville, 1819–1891*. 2 vols. (New York: Harcourt, Brace, 1951.)

Lewis Mumford, *Herman Melville: A Study of His Life and Vision*. (New York: Harcourt, Brace, 1929.)

Herschel Parker and Harrison Hayford (eds.), *Moby-Dick as Doubloon: Essays and Extracts (1851–1970)*. (New York: W. W. Norton, 1970.)

Raymond M. Weaver, *Herman Melville: Mariner and Mystic*. (New York: George H. Doran, 1921.)

Reading Melville's correspondence also provided insight. The collection I used was *The Letters of Herman Melville* (New Haven: Yale Univ. Press, 1960), edited by Merrell R. Davis and William H. Gilman.

CHAPTER ONE: MARTHA'S VINEYARD

The details of that day in Martha's Vineyard, including the weather and the arrival of the *Champion*, come from the Jeremiah Pease diary for May 1841. This is held by the Martha's Vineyard Historical Society (henceforth MVHS), and I am grateful to Art Railton for hunting them out and transcribing them for me.

The Rev. Joseph Thaxter comments were penned in a letter to

Rev. James Freeman of Boston, dated May 1824. MVHS. The descriptions of the Thomas Smith house and Smith's Tavern were sifted from two newspaper items—"Dwelling Houses Burned in Vineyard Haven by the late first," *Vineyard Gazette*, October 10, 1883; and "Retrospect of Buildings Burning in the Great Fire of 1883," in an invitation edition of the *Vineyard Gazette*, May 6, 1966 (scrapbooks, MVHS). Further details were found in James H. K. Norton, *Walking in Vineyard Haven, MA*, page 181 (Edgartown, MA: MVHS, 2000); and Mrs. Howes Norris Jr., *Sketches of Old Homes in Our Village* (Edgartown, MA: D.A.R., 1921).

The background of the Smith family came largely from Chris Baer, "The Descendants of Capt. Jeruel West and Deborah Shaw of Frog Alley, Tisbury, MA," a manuscript in preparation. Also useful was an article by Henry Beetle Hough, "List of Vineyard Shipmasters is growing longer," *Vineyard Gazette*, October 6, 1944. The Norris genealogy comes from Elizabeth Little's compilation, as do the whaling histories of Howes Norris, Thomas Harlock Smith Jr., and Nathan Skiff Smith. I thank Catherine Mayhew, New England genealogist, for many additional family details.

The interesting information about social climbing and Eastville was provided by Art Railton, who also contributed the intriguing tidbit about Holmes Luce and his "packet." The information concerning Elwina Norris's complications after the birth of Octavia came ultimately from the Dr. LeRoy Yale diary held by MVHS. I read it first in an article by Russell Hoxsie, M.D., "Medical Tales From a Doctor's Diary, (1829–1842)," *The Dukes County Intelligencer*, 43: 2 (Nov. 2001): 51–74, 59 in particular.

Logbooks kept by Howes Norris on the *Leonidas*, July 25, 1828, to July 7, 1829, and August 12, 1829, to March 23, 1831, are held at The

Kendall Institute, New Bedford Whaling Museum (henceforth KI-NBWM), # 0739; those kept by him on the *London Packet*, November 25, 1832, to August 31, 1835, and June 5, 1836, to August 15, 1839, are also held at KI-NBWM, # 0740, # 0741. The *Leonidas* was a Fairhaven ship. There is some confusion in the records concerning the *London Packet*, most citing New Bedford as the home port for the 1832–35 voyage, and Fairhaven for the 1836–39 voyage, which could mean two different ships. However, Judith Lund, *Whaling Masters . . .*, the most recent authority and a most reliable one, gives Fairhaven as the port for both voyages.

I calculated the worth of various voyages from the tables in Starbuck, *History of the American Whale Fishery . . .*, primarily page 660, and also took the details of the *Loper* voyages (146), the 1837 voyage of the *Sharon* (336–37); and the current bad luck of the *Obed Mitchell* (also 336–37) from this book. The 1850 Federal Census noted that Elwina Norris owned real estate to the value of $2,000. Norris's take from his previous voyage — 1/16 of the net profits — would have only just covered his living expenses for twenty-six months, plus the purchase of this expensive house. It seems reasonable to deduce that he went back to sea in the hope of retrieving his fortunes.

The physical descriptions of the characters in this first chapter are extrapolated from images in the collection of MVHS. I thank Jill Bouck, curator, for kindly providing copies of these.

Chapter Two: Fairhaven

The date of Norris's arrival on board the *Sharon* was deduced from the fact that Sweeny and Yellott took out their Protections then, plus the fact that the wind changed direction that day.

CHAPTER NOTES

The *Acushnet* was constructed in 1840 at the yard owned by G. Barstow & Son, at the foot of Pearl Street, Rochester (now Mattapoisett), just up the river from Fairhaven and New Bedford. Herman Melville arrived in New Bedford on December 26, 1840, and signed onto the crew list that same day. The *Sharon*, which had arrived from the Pacific Ocean on December 10, would have been lying close by. The *Acushnet* sailed for the Pacific on January 3, 1841; unfortunately the log of the voyage, which would be immensely valuable now, was lost.

There are many books written about the history of American whaling. Alexander Starbuck's *History of the American Whale Fishery . . .* is an excellent resource, pages 4–98 being particularly relevant.

Everett S. Allen, *Children of the Night: The Rise and Fall of New Bedford Whaling and the Death of the Arctic Fleet.* (Boston: Little, Brown, 1973.)

Clifford W. Ashley, *The Yankee Whaler.* (Garden City, NY: Halcyon House, 1942.)

Judith A. Boss, with Joseph D. Thomas, *New Bedford, A Pictorial History.* (Virginia Beach, MD: The Donning Co., 1983.)

Albert Cook Church, *Whale ships and Whaling.* (New York: W. W. Norton, 1938.)

William Davis, *Nimrod of the Sea, or, The American Whaleman.* (New York: Harper Bros., 1874.)

Ernest S. Dodge, *New England and the South Seas.* (Cambridge, MA: Harvard Univ. Press, 1965.)

George Francis Dow, *Whale ships and Whaling: A Pictorial History of Whaling . . .* (Salem, MA: Marine Research Society, 1925.)

Foster Rhea Dulles, *Lowered Boats, A Chronicle of American Whaling.* (New York: Harcourt Brace, 1933.)

Samuel Eliot Morison, *The Maritime History of Massachusetts 1783–1860*. (Boston: Houghton Mifflin, 1961; repr. of 1921 edition.)

Daniel Ricketson, *The History of New Bedford* . . . (New Bedford, MA: author, 1858.)

Edouard Stackpole, *The Sea-Hunters*. (New York: Lippincott, 1953.)

Walter S. Tower, *A History of the American Whale Fishery*. (Philadelphia: Pennsylvania Univ. Press, 1907.)

The details of the *Acushnet* and the *Sharon* come from the papers for those two ships, a copy for the *Acushnet* being held at MVHS, and that for the *Sharon* at the Melville Whaling Room, New Bedford Free Public Library, henceforth NBFPL. All the details of Norris's 1832–35 *London Packet* voyage came from his private logbook, held at KI-NBWM. There is no printed evidence anywhere of the 1835 mutiny, which makes it evident that Norris did not report the incident that would have looked so bad on his record. Norris's own logbooks were private journals, meant for his eyes only and not for public release. The official logbook was traditionally kept by the first mate, who handed it to the ship's owners at the end of the voyage. The official logbooks of the two *Leonidas* voyages and the two *London Packet* voyages have been lost, as was the logbook kept by Thomas Harlock Smith on the *Sharon* up to the date of Captain Norris's death, and then kept by Nathan Smith after Thomas Smith took over the command.

The Shipping Paper for the 1832–35 voyage of the *London Packet*, held at NBFPL, lists William C. Downs (first officer), David Miller (second officer), Joseph Francis (third officer), Thomas H. Smith, Ira Crapo, John Thompson and Francis Fales (boatsteerers); Fred Stuart, George W. Dolf, John Jones, William Briggs, Frank Silver, Anton

Joseph (Antone José), David Perry, David Brown, Isaac Tucker, John R. Howard, Alexander McNeil, James B. Pittsley, Peter (illegible, but Norris notes him as Parker or Potter), William C. Dunbar, Israel Packard, Walter Willett, George Jones, John Balch, John Church. Unmentioned in the official list but noted in Norris's journal are William Hennessey (spelled Hendersy by Norris, but corrected in a later entry), Alexander Spear, Joseph King, Charles Reed, Thomas T. Dow, Frederick Cooly, Edward Pearce: evidently they were shipped during the voyage, probably at Johanna. Peter José and Emanuel José were shipped at Fayal during the Atlantic passage. John Clark, a Hawai'ian, joined the ship at Johanna by stowing away (a bad choice; he was one of the mutineers). An officer by the name of Perry was shipped at Zanzibar, along with a man named Jones. The four fore-mast hands who supported Captain Norris were William Hennessey, William Dunbar, Antone José, and Emanuel José. According to Nor-ris, the ringleaders of the mutiny were Spear, King, and Reed; Nor-ris shut himself in his cabin after Spear threatened to "see my *hearts Blood*." Thanks are due to Paul Cyr, Special Collections Librarian at NBFPL.

For the crew of the *Sharon*, the Whalemen's Shipping Paper, *Sharon* of Fairhaven, 1841, was located at NBFPL. The Seamen's Reg-ister for the same ship is owned by the New Bedford Port Society and on loan to KI-NBWM. Details were also obtained from the lists of Protection Papers held at NBFPL and also in some cases at the Rhode Island Historical Society.

Two important books read by those intrigued by whaling at the time—and used extensively by Melville as sources for the cetology sections of *Moby-Dick*—were written by two whaling surgeons, Thomas Beale, *The Natural History of the Sperm Whale* . . . (London: Jan van

Voorst, 1839; repr. Holland Press, London, 1973), and Frederick Debell Bennett, whose book *Narrative of a Whaling Voyage Round the Globe* . . . was published in London in 1840 by Richard Bentley (the man who also published the London edition of Melville's great whaling novel), and reprinted in New York by Da Capo Press in 1970. Also see Joan Druett, *Rough Medicine: Surgeons at Sea in the Age of Sail* (New York: Routledge, 2000). This book describes the surgeons' voyages and places them in the context of other whaling surgeons of the day.

The book written by Lieut. Charles Wilkes, *Narrative of the United States Exploring Expedition During the Years 1838 . . . 1842*, was published in five volumes by C. Sherman of Philadelphia in 1844. Capt. George F. Tilton's reminiscences were published as *"Cap'n George Fred" Himself* (Edgartown: Dukes County Historical Society, 1969).

The fascinating story of Ezra Rothschild Johnson, the man who witnessed the crosses made by George Babcock and Henry Mills, can be read in Kathryn Grover, *The Fugitive's Gibraltar: Escaping Slaves and Abolitionism in New Bedford, Massachusetts* (Amherst: Univ. of Mass. Press, 2001). Chapters 3, 4, and 5 (67–156) are particularly relevant.

CHAPTER THREE: INTO THE ATLANTIC OCEAN

A ruled page that Norris used as a template is in the back of the log he kept on the *London Packet* on the 1832–35 voyage. His script is so even it is reasonable to assume that he always used one. For detailed descriptions of the captain's quarters and the accommodations for the mates, along with the tradesmen's quarters in the steerage, see Joan Druett, *Petticoat Whalers* (Lebanon, NH: Univ. Press of New England, 2001).

The written description of the 1841–44 *Mercury* voyage is held at

NBFPL, while the Pacific Manuscripts Bureau (henceforth PMB) microfilm number is 363. All my quotations are taken from this. Italics indicate where Curtis underlined words in the manuscript, except for the interlocution in the captain's speech, which he penned in a different script to indicate a different font.

While the journals kept by foremast hands were almost invariably very personal records, it was common for ambitious young men to practice keeping formal logbooks once they reached some kind of rank—such as boatsteerer, or junior mate. Benjamin Clough is a good example of this. It would have been reasonable for him to guess that being able to demonstrate his logbook keeping would help him get further promotion. Benjamin Clough was unfortunate: he started to keep a formal logbook on the *Rajah* but ended up describing his own desertion from the ship; and the formal logbook on the *Sharon* turned into an eloquent record of a voyage that went badly wrong. Neither book could have been used as evidence of his dedication to a whaling career. Luckily, he did not need them.

The date of Clough's first voyage on the *Jasper* was determined by his Protection, which was taken out on September 10, 1835. He gave his age as nineteen; he was 5' 6-½" tall, light-skinned, brown-haired, and blue-eyed (Protection card, NBFPL). The *Jasper* of Fairhaven, Captain Stephen Raymond, sailed on September 13, and arrived back June 24, 1837 (Starbuck, 316–17). Logs of the voyage are held at NBFPL, KI-NBWM, and in the Nicholson Whaling Collection at the Providence (Rhode Island) Public Library (henceforth PPL); microfilms are PMB 287, 336, 870. The *Friendship* of Fairhaven, Captain Isaiah West, left on August 12, and arrived home January 22, 1838 (Starbuck, 336–37). A log is held at KI-NBWM, PMB 280. For commentaries on early American whaling in the South Island of New Zealand, see:

Captain Hempleman, *The Piraki Log*. Edited by Henry Froude. (London: Oxford Univ. Press, 1910.)

Robert McNab, *Old Whaling Days*. (Christchurch, NZ: Whitcombe & Tombs, 1912.)

Harry Morton, *The Whale's Wake*. (Dunedin, NZ: McIndoe, for Univ. of Otago, 1982.)

Rhys Richards, *Muruhiku Revisited*. (Wellington, NZ: author, 1995).

L. S. Rickard, *The Whaling Trade in Old New Zealand*. (Auckland, NZ: Minerva, 1965.)

There are also many good documentary resources, including the logs listed above. See, Joan Druett, "Americans in New Zealand and the Pacific" (work in progress, Stout Research Centre for New Zealand Studies, Victoria University, Wellington).

The *Rajah*, Captain Henry West, left New Bedford, ostensibly for New Zealand, on June 8, 1839, and arrived back May 28, 1841. Logs are held at NBFPL and KI-NBWM.

There are several good firsthand views of life in a whaler, including:

John Ross Browne, *Etchings of a whaling cruise* . . . (New York: Harper & Bros., 1846, repr. Cambridge, MA: Harvard Univ. Press, 1968.)

George A. Dodge, *A whaling voyage in the Pacific Ocean and its incidents*. Edited by Kenneth R. Martin. (Fairfield, WA: Ye Galleon Press, 1981.)

Nelson Cole Haley, *Whale hunt: the narrative of a voyage by Nelson Cole Haley harpooner* . . . (New York: Ives Washburn Inc., 1948.)

Charles Nordhoff, *Life on the Ocean: Nine Years a Sailor*. (Cincinnati: Moore, Wilstach, Keys & Co., 1874; repr. London: MacDonald and Jane's, 1974.) The second volume, *Whaling and Fishing*, is the relevant one; in the facsimile, the two volumes are bound into one. Francis Allyn Olmstead, *Incidents of a whaling voyage* . . . (New York: D. Appleton, 1841.)

An excellent background study of the Azores and whaling is Pat Amaral, *They Ploughed the Seas* (St. Petersburg, FL: Valkyrie Press, 1978).

Richard "Toby" Greene reminisced about the good times on the *Acushnet* in a letter to Melville dated April 8, 1861, and quoted on page 128 of Jay Leyda, *The Melville Log*, 2 vols. (New York: Harcourt, Brace, 1951).

CHAPTER FOUR: TOWARD THE PACIFIC

For a discussion of the different features of right whales and sperm whales, see, Joan Druett, *"She Was a Sister Sailor": The Whaling Journals of Mary Brewster, 1845–1851* (Mystic, CT: Mystic Seaport Museum, 1992), pp. 71–75.

The details of Andrew White's background come from his obituary in the *Providence Journal*, February 11, 1896. He took out his Protection on July 3, 1837, age twenty-two, giving Tiverton, Rhode Island, as his residence. His height was 5'7", he was light-skinned, brown-haired, and had dark brown eyes (Protection card, NBFPL). Coopering was heavy physical work, so he would have been strongly muscled. It is impossible to tell which ship he voyaged on first; obviously, it departed in July 1837 and returned in time for him to ship on the *Sharon* in May 1841.

The description of Kupang, Timor, is taken from a journal kept by a whaling surgeon, Dr. John Wilson of the London whaler *Gipsy.* The entry is dated October 11, 1842. *The Cruise of the 'Gipsy,'* edited by Honore Forster, (Fairfield, WA: Ye Galleon Press, 1991).

The official—and extremely misspelled—logbook of the 1839–41 *Rajah* voyage was read at NBFPL. I thank the Clough family for allowing me the privilege of reading and taking notes from Clough's remarkable record of his desertion. It is impossible to tell why he did not complete the description of his adventure. The book in which he wrote it down is not pocket-sized by any means, so it is very likely that he left it in the boat when he ran into the trees, and recovered it when he, along with an unknown number of companions, managed to escape in the boat to Bali and the *General Pike.*

While Norris's frustration is understandable, his expectations were unrealistic, because of the nature of the boatsteerer's job. Up until the instant the order to stand and face the whale was given, the boatsteerer had been setting the pace for the rest of the crew. Then, without a chance to recover from this "straining, bawling state," as Melville described, he had "to drop and secure his oar, turn round on his centre half way, seize his harpoon from the crotch, and with what little strength may remain, he essays to pitch it somehow into the whale.

"No wonder, taking the whole fleet of whalemen in a body," Melville (a boatsteerer himself for a few months on the *Charles & Henry*) went on, "that out of fifty fair chances for a dart, not five are successful; no wonder that so many hapless harpooneers are madly cursed and disrated; no wonder that some of them actually burst their blood-vessels in the boat; no wonder that some sperm whalemen are absent four years with four barrels; no wonder that to many ship owners, whaling is but a losing concern; for it is the harpooneer that makes the voyage, and if you take the breath out of his body how can you expect to find it there when most wanted!"

CHAPTER FIVE: REBELLION

Except where stated otherwise, all the quotations in this chapter come from Clough's logbook.

The "written acknowledgement" promising to behave better, signed by all the rebels, is not with the *Sharon* papers; Norris was supposed to keep such sworn statements, but either he failed to do so, or Thomas Smith destroyed it after taking over the command. The former is more likely. Clough was wise to make a copy. He signed it with the initials "B.C." Next to them is written "T.S." Thomas Smith was the only person on board with those initials.

Andrew White's account was much less descriptive than Clough's, perhaps because he was determined to disassociate himself from the violence of the quarterdeck retaliation. It is dated December 12, because White kept his journal in shore time; interestingly, it is the second entry for that date, the first being the usual brief notation of wind and weather. The second, in entirety, runs:

Sunday December 12 1841
These 24 hours light breezes from N Steering ENE nothing in sight At 5 PM the Capton seased up the Steward in the riggen and flogged him after supper he went forid the Capt called him he did not come the capton and the rest of the officers went forid and got him the foremast hands told the capton he was frade of his life and tried to prevent the capton from takin him the Capton then poot 8 of them in Irons and floged two of the[m] 24 lashes each the capton then asked the rest of them if they would go to their duty and mind the officers they said they would he then let them go it was about 11 in the night when he let them go Lat by Ob 1.22 S Long 152 55 E

It is likely that he, too, realized the necessity of keeping his own record of the rebellion, understanding that there was a strong chance of Norris not reporting it. However, he did not know enough to have it witnessed and initialed.

An excellent study of conditions and treatment of crew members on whaling vessels, including discipline, is *"Whaling Will Never Do for Me"—The American Whaleman in the Nineteenth Century,* by Briton C. Busch (Lexington: The Univ. Press of Kentucky, 1994). Professor Busch cites the interesting and relevant story of William Gamman, a black foremast hand on the bark *Shepherdess,* who in March 1849 took refuge in the forecastle after being beaten by the mate. He was dragged out, put in irons, and flogged, though the cooper, boatsteerers, and some of the foremast hands tried to stop it, "trying to rais the Devle" (Busch: 41). The log of the *Shepherdess* 1848 is held at PPL. PMB 893.

The journal kept by William A. Allen on the *Samuel Robertson* 1841–46 is held at KI-NBWM, and is also quoted and cited extensively in Busch: 18, 19, 31, 39, 40, 43, 48, 166. Melville's comment is within his review of J. Ross Browne's book *Etchings of a Whaling Cruise,* which was an effort to describe the parlous lot of the whaling hands in the forecastles, in much the same spirit as Richard Henry Dana's very successful *Two Years Before the Mast,* which drew public attention to the plight of the ordinary merchant seaman. Melville's review appeared in *The Literary World,* March 6, 1847. I read it in the Norton edition of *Moby-Dick,* cited in "Resources." The Seamen's Act is quoted in full on p. 76 of Hohman, *The American Whaleman . . . ,* also cited in "Resources."

The story of the mutiny on the *Meteor* is detailed in the New Bedford *Whalemen's Shipping List & Merchants' Transcript* for March 16, 1847.

The story of the mutiny on the *Globe* has been recounted many times. I used Alexander Starbuck's description in *History of the American Whale Fishery* . . . : 134–35. A racy book-length recounting is Edouard Stackpole, *Mutiny at Midnight, The Adventures of Cyrus Hussey of Nantucket aboard the whaleship Globe in the South Pacific, from 1822 to 1826 . . . as told by* Edouard A. Stackpole (New York: William Morrow, 1939). Two recent comprehensive studies are Thomas Heffernan, *Mutiny on the* Globe (New York: W. W. Norton, 2002); and Gregory Gibson, *Demon of the Waters* (New York: Little, Brown, 2002).

The log of the unknown ship where the "darkie" received such bad treatment on shore was read on microfilm, PMB 689. Original held at KI-NBWM.

The seafaring wife who made the comment about captains and their souls was Mary Wallis of Salem, Massachusetts. "By a Lady," *Life in Fiji* . . . (Boston: William Heath, 1851.) pp. 202–03.

CHAPTER SIX: THE GROUPS

The description of Norris's problem with islanders in the Comoros comes from his journal kept on the *London Packet*, March 22, 1834. KWI-NBWM.

Alexander Starbuck's commentary on native attack spans pages 129–31 of *History of the American Whale Fishery*.

McLaren's gory story of the cutting out of the boat's crew from the *Victoria* is held at the Alexander Turnbull Library, Wellington, New Zealand, microfilm number 386. A good account of the cutting out of the *Awashonks*, which includes a description in Silas Jones's own words, is within Theodate Geoffrey, *Suckanesset, Wherein may be read a History of Falmouth, Massachusetts* (Falmouth: Falmouth Historical Society, 1930), pp. 109–30. I thank Carolyn Partan and the Falmouth Historical Society for the opportunity to look at the memorabilia of this incident that they hold, along with documentary resources.

An important source for the discussion of conflict between the people of Oceania—and the Carolines in particular—is David Hanlon, *Upon a Stone Altar—A History of the Island of Pohnpei to 1890* (Honolulu: Univ. Hawaii Press, 1988). The intriguing comment about the names given to the first white men comes from p. 26. Another significant study of the area, focusing on the Gilberts—now known as Kiribati—is Barrie Macdonald, *Cinderellas of the Empire—Towards a history of Kiribati and Tuvalu* (Canberra: Australian National Univ. Press, 1982).

The Wilkes incident was described and quoted in Kenneth R. Martin, "Let the Natives Come Aboard: Whalemen and Islanders in Micronesia," *Glimpses of Micronesia and the Western Pacific* XVIII (3rd qt.): 38–44 (1978): 39. (The man, John Anderson by name, had tried to enter a room reserved for women, a crime for which a Tabiteuean man would also have been executed.)

I thank John Illingworth for tracking down the meaning of the obsolete word "heaver." Norris's diatribe about provisions on the *London Packet* comes from his journal, January 19, 1835.

Chapter Seven: Desertion

Three important early views of Rotuma are:

Captain Peter Dillon, *Narrative and Successful Result of a Voyage in the South Seas . . .* (London: Hurst, Chance, & Co., 1829), vol. II, pp. 91–107.

Robert Jarman, *Journal of a Voyage to the South Seas, in the* Japan, *employed in the Sperm Whale Fishery* . . . (London: Longman & Tilt, 1832), pp. 162–63; 175–87.

Edward Lucett, *Rovings in the Pacific* . . . (London: Longman, Brown, Green, 1851), pp. 157–202.

A major secondary source for the background of what the seamen found on shore is W. J. E. Eason's *A Short History of Rotuma* (Suva, Fiji: Govt. Printer, 1951). For the distinctive culture and personality of the Rotumans, I consulted Vilsoni Hereniko's inspiring study, *Woven Gods: Female Clowns and Power in Rotuma* (Pacific Islands Monograph Series, No. 12. Honolulu: University of Hawai'i Press, 1995), pp. 103–20 in particular. I owe thanks to Vilsoni Hereniko, Teresia Teaiwa, and Paul D'Arcy for their comments, hints, and lively interest.

A key study of beachcombers and deserters is contained within H. E. Maude, *Of Islands and Men* (Melbourne: OUP, 1968), pp. 134–69. Valuable background was also found in Caroline Ralston, *Grass Huts and Warehouses, Pacific Beach Communities of the Nineteenth Century* (Canberra: Australian National Univ. Press, 1977).

The fates of the men who deserted from the *Sharon* at Rotuma were deduced from details in the NBFPL Internet database of crewmen and vessels, www.ci.new-bedford.ma.us/Nav3.htm. On August 14, 1843, while the *Wilmington & Liverpool Packet* was gamming with the *Addison*, William Wallace Weeks observed that, "I saw somebody on board of the *Addison* who appeared to know me. It proved to be John Allen, a man who came out with me in the *Sharon* and left her in Rotumah."

Clough's enumeration of the men shipped at Rotuma is rather confusing, particularly as he records the shipping of five Kanakas in his journal; however, later log entries confirm that four Kanakas were recruited—two Rotumans, one Hope Islander, and one Ocean Islander. Therefore, if the missing words are supplied, the sentence in the letter to his father reads as he intended: "We shipped 2 White men, [plus] 4 Kanakas, [these comprising] 2 Rotumah men, 1 Ocean and 1 Hope Islander, the last two being left here by [the captains of] other ships." Unfortunately, it is impossible to deduce which shipmasters left the Ocean Islander and the Hope Islander on shore on Rotuma. There is no proof, either, that they were deliberately left behind; they may have been deserters themselves, particularly if they suspected that the captains were not going to return them to their home islands. It has been impossible to track down these islanders because their real names—which would have indicated their genealogy—have been lost to history.

Much of the background to the description of Ocean Island comes from H. C. and H. E. Maude, *The Book of Banaba: From the Maude and Grimble Papers; and Published Works* (Fiji: University of the South Pacific, 1994). This has a long extract from John Webster's *The Last Cruise of the Wanderer*. (Sydney: F. Cunninghame, n.d.). My quote comes from p. 79. Also useful was Ernest Sabatier, *Astride the Equator: An Account of the Gilbert Islands*, trans. Ursula Nixon (Melbourne: OUP, 1977). Of particular interest are pp. 53–60. Another view is in Sister Alaima Talu et al., *Kiribati, Aspects of History* (Suva and Tarawa: Kiribati Govt., 1984). Relevant are pp. 17–20. Very useful were early chapters of K. R. Howe, *Where the Waves Fall: A new South Sea Islands history from first settlement to colonial rule* (Sydney: George Allen & Unwin, 1984). Another background source was pp. 14–30 of Barrie Macdonald, *Cinderellas of Empire*. All of these books have some mention of the Pacific slave trade, known colloquially as "blackbirding." Also see, Thomas Dunbabin, *Slavers of the South Seas* (Sydney: Angus & Robertson, 1935). A first-person blackbirding account is William T. Wawn, *The South Sea Islanders and the Queensland Labour Trade*, edited by Peter Corris (Canberra: Australian National Univ. Press, 1973). Notorious figures in the industry were Captain Ben Pease of Martha's Vineyard and Captain William Henry "Bully" Hayes of Cleveland, Ohio.

A most illuminating modern study is R. K. (Ken) Sigrah and S. M. (Stacey) King, *Te Rii Ni Banaba, The Backbone of Banaba* (Fiji: Univ. of South Pacific, 2001). Blackbirding was not the last of the Banaban troubles. In 1901, thirty years after the whalers stopped coming, British colonists moved in to exploit the phosphate-rich soil of the island. To their horror, the Banaban people watched heavy machinery scrape away the top fifteen feet of their land. Soil that had once produced fruit and vegetables to trade with the whalers was shipped away to fertilize the farms of New Zealand and Australia, leaving the Banabans with bare coral. In 1942, after capture by the Japanese, many of the people were forcibly carried off to labor camps on other islands to grow vegetables for the Japanese forces. When the war was over, these displaced Banabans were relocated on Rabi, an island in Fiji that was purchased on their behalf with royalties that were rightfully theirs. In the 1970s, after bringing a moderately successful claim for compensation, a few Banabans began an ongoing attempt to re-create the traditional life on the last few viable acres of their devastated island.

The quotation from William Allen's journal on the *Samuel Robertson* was dated February 21, 1843. KI-NBWM.

I have taken much inspiration from a manuscript in preparation kindly shared with me by the author, Paul D'Arcy, "Forces from beyond the Horizon: The relative impact of pre-colonial European activity, indigenous intruders and natural hazards on Pacific Islanders." Also see David A. Chappell's important and seminal *Double Ghosts, Oceanian Voyages on EuroAmerican Ships.* (Armont, NY: M.E. Sharpe, 1997). Useful too is Harry Morton, *The Whale's Wake*, (Dunedin: Univ. Otago Press, 1982), particularly chapter 11, pp. 165–77.

Chapter Eight: Reign of Terror

The details of the voyage of the *Samuel Enderby* of London come from A. G. E. Jones, *Ships Employed in the South Seas Trade:* 134, 160. Logs of the *LaGrange* are held at KI-NBWM. The account book is held at the Alexander Turnbull Library, Wellington.

There are many modern studies devoted to the problem of constant exposure to the sight of evil, triggered by the disturbing clinical observation that when an atrocity is viewed repeatedly it has an emotionally numbing effect on the viewers: it is the reason people can eat their evening meals while watching famine and war on TV. One thought-provoking discussion is Fred E. Katz, *Ordinary People and Extraordinary Evil: A Report on the Beguilings of Evil* (Albany, NY: State Univ. of New York Press, 1993). Katz defines evil as "behavior that deliberately deprives innocent people of their humanity," and postulates that we become hardened when "the immediate circumstances dominate our entire field of moral vision." Particularly relevant is his observation that when the evil act is carried out by a person in authority, and the viewers are conditioned to obedience to that authority, they are less likely to intervene or even make a protest.

For racism on whalers see Busch, *Whaling Will Never do for Me*, particularly chapter 3: 32–50. Also W. Jeffrey Bolster's important study, *Black Jacks: African American Seamen in the Age of Sail* (Cambridge, MA: Harvard Univ. Press, 1997). Of interest is Eleanor E. Simpson,

"Melville and the Negro: From *Typee* to *Benito Cereno*." *American Literature* XXXXI (March 1969): 19–38. The article by William P. Powell appeared in the *National Anti-Slavery Standard* on October 29, 1846. Black activist William Powell had a highly romanticized view of life on a whaler. "The forecastles are turned into school-rooms," he wrote. "There you will see the *cook*, the *steward*, and two or three of the crew, under the tuition of their several teachers, busily engaged in their primary lessons; and others studying *navigation*, and taking *Lunars*, under the instruction of the captain or mates." Kathryn Grover, *The Fugitive's Gibraltar*, 154–55.

The description of the beachcombing situation on Nauru comes from the *Sydney Morning Herald*, September 4, 17, and 28, 1837, quoted by Saul H. Riesenberg in his introduction to James F. O'Connell's *A Residence of Eleven Years in New Holland and the Caroline Islands*, Pacific History Series 4 (Canberra: Australian National Univ., 1972), p. 16. Also see Kenneth R. Martin, "Information wanted respecting Micronesia's beach," *Guam and Micronesia Glimpses* XIX (4) 1979: 79–83.

For the formula for making a nineteenth-century adhesive plaster, as used on shipboard, see Joan Druett, *Rough Medicine: Surgeons at Sea in the Age of Sail* (New York: Routledge, 2000), p. 68.

CHAPTER NINE: DIREFUL MADNESS

Norris noted the sickness and death of William Hennesey on April 22 and 23, 1835. William Bullfinch died on May 17, 1838; Silas Smith's illness, death, and burial were recorded June 4–8, 1838. Interestingly, Norris went down in the chase after Silas Smith died, indicating that Smith, despite his youth, was either a boatsteerer or an officer and there was no one else capable of filling his place in the boat.

An illuminating discussion of the psychopathic personality—which Melville would have called "moral insanity"—can be read in Christopher D. Webster, with Grant T. Harris, Marnie Rice, Catherine Cromier, Vernon L. Quinsey, *The Violence Prediction Scheme: Assessing Dangerousness in High Risk Men* (Toronto: Center of Criminology, University of Toronto, 1994). Also see J. Reid Meloy, *Violent Attachments* (Northvale, NJ: Jason Aronson Inc., 1992). Pages 68–88 define the psychopathic personality in detail.

Whether Norris had a psychopathic personality is, of course, debatable. The most prominent signifier of a psychopath is the lack of a conscience—meaning that the person has apparently never developed the ability to empathize and sympathize with fellow human beings. Clough, a close observer, did not believe that Captain Norris felt any guilt for the murder of Babcock, which would seem to confirm the diagnosis. However, the fact that Norris took to drink and stopped lowering in the chase does hint that he might have privately agonized over what he had done. Also, psychopaths typically have disturbed childhoods, and there is nothing in the scanty Martha's Vineyard records to indicate that Norris was a juvenile offender.

If Melville indeed knew the details of the tragedy, it seems certain that he would have concluded that Norris was dangerously unbalanced—as mad, in fact, as his depiction of Captain Ahab. See Paul McCarthy, *The Twisted Mind: Madness in Herman Melville's Fiction* (Iowa City: Univ. of Iowa Press, 1990). Particularly relevant are chapters two (11–16) and five (50–73). An interesting study of Melville's own mental health is Elizabeth Renker, *Strike Through the Mask: Herman Melville and the Scene of Writing* (Baltimore, MD: Johns Hopkins University Press, 1998).

The information about the Jenney family came from *A Picture His-*

tory of Fairhaven (New Bedford, MA: Spinner Publications, 1986). I tracked down the Jenney men who were in the Pacific at the same time through the New Bedford Free Public Library crew lists site, *op cit.* H. E. Maude, *Of Islands & Men,* has much about Ichabod Handy and the coconut oil trade, pp. 233–83. For Mary Brewster's comment about Frederick Fish, see *"She Was a Sister Sailor,"* p. 30. The letter about Nathan Smith's kindness was written by an unidentified seaman on the *Gazelle,* May 15, 1865. Doris Hough Collection, MVHS. A pertinent commentary on discipline can be read in Hohman, *The American Whaleman:* 121–25. For the courts and the seamen, see 77–79.

For the story of the captain of the *Australian* who procured women for his dissident crew, see C. R. Straubel (ed.), *The Whaling Journal of Captain W. B. Rhodes, 1836–1838* (Christchurch, NZ: Whitcombe & Tombs, 1954).

Because the names of the deserters were not recorded in any of the journals, their identities had to be deduced from other sources, including Protections. Thomas Davis's misadventures after joining the *Emily Morgan* are detailed in the log of that ship. On September 27, 1843, the ship rescued a castaway by the name of Blake at Nonouti; Blake was so horrified at the conditions on board that he deserted back to the island in a canoe a couple of days later. NBFPL. PMB 323. William Weeks named Otis, Moore, and Baker in his partial journal on the *Wilmington & Liverpool Packet.* Some doubt was felt about Baker, as there was a John Baker in the original crew of the *'Packet.* However, this John Baker headed a boat, and in effect was fourth mate, while the Jack Baker who had been on the *Sharon* was a foremast hand, so it seems evident that there were two of them, John Baker being a common name.

A most interesting book on Pohnpei customs and scenery is Sibley S. Morrill, *Ponape, Where American Colonialism Confronts Black Magic, Five Kingdoms and The Mysterious Ruins of Nan-Madol* (San Francisco: Cadleon Press, 1970). Essays by Morrill (1–50) provide a modern view of magic, ruins, and medicine, while extracts from James O'Connell (Pohnpei's most famous beachcomber), Gulick (Pohnpei's most famous missionary), and F. W. Christian (*The Caroline Islands*, London, 1899) provide historical commentary. Also see H. E. Maude, *Of Islands and Men*. The pages relevant to Pohnpeian beachcombers are 238–39.

A most valuable reference is David Hanlon, *Upon a Stone Altar*. Chapters 2 and 3, pp. 26–86, are particularly relevant. Yellott (aka Zolliot, Zellet, Yelirt) was recorded by the *Novara* in 1858: on September 16, 1858, the German frigate, approaching the island, "remarked a boat of European construction" heading for them, and in it was Yellott, who "offered his services to the Commodore as pilot," proving to be a font of wisdom and advice as well. Karl Scherzer, *Narrative of the Circumnavigation of the globe by the Austrian frigate Novara . . .* (London: Saunders, Otley & Co., 3w., 1861–63). Other documentation is in *The Friend*, December 1865 and March 1875. See the compilation directed by Francis X. Hezel, "Beachcombers and Castaways in Micronesia," and also his essay, "The Role of the Beachcomber," at www.micsem.org/pubs/publications/histwork/. Also see Francis X. Hezel, *The First Taint of Civilization: A History of the Caroline and Marshall Islands in Pre-colonial Days, 1521–1885* (Honolulu: Univ. of Hawai'i Press, 1983). Yellott later married a native woman and fathered four children, one of whom became the wife of the naturalist John Kubary. He died on Pohnpei on August 25, 1874.

Andrew Cheyne's journals are published as *The Trading Voyages of*

Chapter Notes

Andrew Cheyne 1841–1844, Dorothy Shineberg, ed. (Wellington, NZ: A. H. & A. W. Reed, 1971). Pages 156–61 relate to his conversations with Captain Place. Place was instrumental in ruining Cheyne's trading career: He persuaded him to set up a trading station on the island for the convenience of the whaling fleet, but, because he continued to misunderstand and fail to adapt to the Pohnpei way of doing things, Cheyne was a comprehensive failure. He—of course—blamed the beachcombers for it.

Otis Tripp, Jack Baker, John Moore, and William Wallace Weeks were hired some time between November 30 and December 11. Whatever Samuel Brush, the twenty-three-year-old second mate of the *Wilmington & Liverpool Packet*, wrote in his journal during that time has been lost. There is the possibility that he copied down what he heard of Howes Norris's murder of the steward and then thought better of it, but it is impossible, of course, to be sure. On December 18 the ship finally worked out of the lagoon, "and we filled our way wonce more upon the Boosom of the wide Pacific," wrote Brush, who would stop writing on February 14. The explanation can be found in the next entry, dated March 14. According to this, "Nothing of any consequence" had happened in the interval, "with the exception of Mr. Brown the chief mate being put on shore at Bonin's Island by his own request on account of sickness. We got potatoes Hogs &c," the writer continued, and then signed it: "Yours &c W.W. Weeks, Jamaica LI."

Brush stepped up to the position of first officer, which meant he had to fill in the official logbook. Accordingly, he handed over the private book to Weeks. William deserted from the 'Packet in the Hawai'ian Islands in October 1843, leaving the book behind, and an unknown writer took over.

William Weeks's comment about being in debt is puzzling. When a seaman joined a ship, he owed the amount of his advance and the cost of his slops—the clothes, tobacco, soap, and so forth that he bought from the slop chest, which was the ship's store of such goods. When he ran away from the ship he left his debts as well—often a good reason for desertion. So William was not thinking about whatever he owed the *Sharon*, and must have had the debt he had accumulated since joining the *Wilmington & Liverpool Packet* in mind. Probably, Captain Gilbert Place furnished him with clothes and other necessary items. There is also the chance that William was a gambler and owed money to his new shipmates.

Chapter Ten: Retribution

There are only two more entries in Norris's logbook after the *Sharon*'s departure from Pohnpei. "All these 24 hours light breezes from N.W. steered S.E. at Noon the Island N.W. about 40 miles distant—" he wrote on the 28th, and, next day, "First part very light airs from N.W. steered S.E.—Middle and Latter parts calm Ascension still in sight bearing about N.W. nothing more worthy of remark—

"Lat. 6:07 North Long. 158.50 East."

The next twenty-four leaves are all cut out of the book. There are fragments of writing on the cut edges, but it is impossible to guess what might have been there. A note on the flyleaf signed by Howes Norris Jr.—the son who was born while Captain Norris was on the *Sharon* voyage—says, "The log is intact." That, obviously, is not so. Judging by the marks in the margins of the cut edges, the missing leaves were written on both sides. Most of the rest of the book is blank, save for some headings by Howes Jr., who collected coins and evidently intended to record them there, and barometer and weather readings in Captain Norris's hand, plus a rough crew list with marks alongside some of the names, evidently credits for whales raised during lookout. Art Railton of the MVHS also studied the cut edges, but agreed that nothing more could be deduced from them.

There was plenty of frustration to fuel Norris's brutal temper: "Nothing in sight," wrote Benjamin Clough on Friday, November 4, and, "Nothing in sight," confirmed Andrew White. According to Clough's letter, Captain Norris was "keeping drunk nearly all the time." And, as the third mate also recorded, the captain was venting his rage by "beating the Kanakas, we having 6 of them on board and but 11 of the rest of us." Clough was definitely conscious that the ratio of natives to New Englanders had changed drastically, and of the dangers inherent in this. As oblivious as always to the forces working on board his ship, however, Norris was taking out his impotent fury on the Kanakas, ignoring the fact that they now made up a significant proportion of his crew.

Andrew White's reaction to the news of the captain's murder is interesting. "O the feellings that roaled acros our breast when this awful sound reached our years [ears]," he wrote. "O tis out of the power of me to relate to you the feelings there was in thos two boats ther was some that were related to him there feelings was different from the rest." It is difficult to believe that once the initial shock was absorbed, there was not a general sense of relief. However, the immediate problem of reclaiming the ship would have been predominant.

It is impossible to tell why the three natives made the fatal error of trying to run away with the *Sharon*. The fact that at no stage was any effort made to negotiate with them indicates that they had reason to be afraid for their lives. It is significant that when the first Hope Islander descended the companionway to investigate the strange noises, he was unarmed and unready for battle, yet Benjamin Clough attacked at once, without warning. However, it must be remembered that the life of George Black was spared; most probably he owed this to the fact that he was not captured until the next day, after everyone had calmed down.

I am indebted to Mike Dyer, librarian at the Kendall Institute, New Bedford Whaling Museum, for his scholarly and illuminating analysis of Benjamin Clough's picture of the scene. The original is held by family descendants, whom I thank for permission to publish.

CHAPTER ELEVEN: GEORGE BLACK

Clough and White never referred to the Ocean Islander by name; the first mention of "George Black" is in the *Sydney Morning Herald* notice.

The description of Benjamin Clough's wounds comes from the New Bedford *Mercury*, February 27, 1845, as well as his letter to his father.

There is some confusion about the breaking of the chronometer. Clough notes that someone wound it early in the morning, but when it was checked for the 9 A.M. sight, it was found to be broken. It was unlikely to be Clough himself at fault, because of his wounded hands. Andrew White wrote that "the mate" broke it, which could mean either of the Smiths, depending on whether he meant the former first mate or the current one.

The description of traditional justice is derived from Sigrah & King, *Te Rii ni Banaba*, p. 59. I also thank Doug Munro for insight into the role played by vengeful family. The descriptions of Sydney at the time are taken from Mrs. Charles Meredith, *Notes and Sketches of New South Wales* (London: John Murray, 1844, facs. repr. Penguin Books, 1973).

The relevant issues of the *Sydney Morning Herald* are December 23, 1842; December 24, 1842 (Shipping Intelligence); December 28, 1842 (Water Police); January 2, 1843 (law as regards South Sea Islanders); January 5, 1843 (ship cleared); January 7, 1843 (shipping intelligence, writ of habeas corpus). I thank Cathi Joseph, librarian at the Mitchell Library Reading Room, Sydney, for checking all the bethel records relating to that date, including sifting for references to Joseph Phelps Robinson, a humanitarian who kept a very low profile.

The biographies of Richard Windeyer and Joseph Phelps Robinson can be read in the *Dictionary of Australian Biography* (Sydney: Angus & Robertson, 1949). One of the many works discussing Windeyer's controversial speech and its implications is Henry Reynolds, *This Whispering in Our Hearts* (St. Leonard's, NSW: Allen & Unwin, 1998). While it is known that Windeyer wrote the script of his lecture about August 1842, the date of the lecture itself is unknown; the script of the talk is held by the Mitchell Library, Sydney. The physical description of Richard Windeyer is extrapolated from a photograph of his illustrious son, Sir William Charles Windeyer, in the National Library of Australia. The documentation of the hearing of the writ of habeas corpus is held in the New South Wales State Records Office, Penrith, New South Wales, Australia. I thank Bruce Kercher for his interest and help.

The consulate papers relating to George Black are held at the National Archives, Washington, D.C., filed under the heading "Despatches from United States Consuls in Sydney, New South Wales, 1836–1906." The microfilm is no. 173, roll 1. The New South Wales responses are held by the Archives Authority of New South Wales,

4/3547: 178. As well as copy taken from the microfilm of U.S. consular records relating to New South Wales that are held at KI-NBWM, I used transcriptions made by Elizabeth Little (for her compilation) and Philip Purrington ("Anatomy of a Mutiny"), both *op cit.*

CHAPTER TWELVE:
CAPTAIN THOMAS HARLOCK SMITH

The men taken on at Sydney were: Joseph Perry, boatsteerer; George E. Nightingale, carpenter; Samuel Galen, Nicholas Samuel Haley, James Wharton, William James Clarke, Vicente Putana, Frederick Griffith, seamen; Francis Julian Saul, cook; Francis James, blacksmith; William L. Colby, W. J. Murgatroyd, William Rawson, John Fox, Henry Cook, John Manning, greenhands.

The log of the *Harbinger* is held at KI-NBWM. PMB 294.

The twenty-eight ships were counted from Nigel Wace and Bessie Lovett shipping list, *Yankee Maritime Activities and the Early History of Australia* (Canberra: Australian National University, Research School of Pacific Studies, 1973).

The background to the Samoan Islands of the time owes much to Richard P. Gilson, *Samoa 1830 to 1900: The Politics of a Multicultural Community* (Melbourne: OUP, 1970), particularly pp. 157–58 and 162–74. Gilson's voluminous research notes are held in microfilm form at both the Alexander Turnbull Library and the Victoria University Library. The relevant folders are 100–200, which include consular material. The item about Wilkes burning the three villages was in the Salem, Massachusetts, *Essex Register*, January 17, 1842. See Ward, *op cit.*

Considering the extremely rapid turnover, it is probably little wonder that Captain Thomas Smith failed to make note of the names of men discharged and shipped. Those he did manage to remember when he was testifying in front of a consul were Alexander Small, Thomas Brewer, Stephen Knowles, James Thompson, William Place, John Schuwerman, and Charles Peterson (all shipped September 11, 1843), John McReady (May 21, 1843), and Water Bucket (May 29, 1843). The consul was Milo Calkin of Lahaina, and the date of the affidavit was September 1844, so they had been on board at least a year before their presence was legally recognized. Smith had had the opportunity in January 1844, when he appeared before Consul John Brown Williams in the Bay of Islands, but neglected to take advantage of it. Presumably all the other men shipped in Rotuma and Samoa had left the ship in the meantime.

The wreck of the *Cadmus* was reported in several New England papers, including *Morning Register*, New Bedford, February 13, 1843; *Daily Herald*, Newburyport, Mass., February 14, 1843; a long report in the *Boston Daily Advertiser*, February 14, 1843; and an item in the *Salem Gazette*, February 17, 1843.

Microfilm copies of American consular records with respect to New Zealand and the Bay of Islands are held at the Library of the University of Auckland, New Zealand. I thank the staff of both the Auckland University Library and the Victoria University Library for making these available to me. The men taken on at the Bay of Islands in January 1844 were William Leek, boatsteerer, and seamen John Hays, Robert Johnson, James Johnson, and George Rothburn, all on the 15th; Thomas Robertson, third mate, and William Edwards, seaman, on the 16th; and Thomas Drake, seaman, on the 22nd.

The directive to shun the shipping was penned by the Rev. Samuel Marsden of Parramatta, New South Wales, whose correspondence is published as *The Letters and Journals of Samuel Marsden, 1765–1838*, J. R. Elder, ed. (Dunedin, New Zealand: Otago Univ. Council, 1932).

The originals, plus other Marsden material, can be studied at the Hocken Library, Dunedin. Also see Harry Morton, *The Whale's Wake*, passim, but particularly chapter 13: 196–209, and Robert W. Kenny, "Yankee Whalers at the Bay of Islands." *American Neptune* 12 (1952): 22–44.

Consul John B. Williams's journal is published as *The New Zealand Journal 1842-1844 of John B. Williams of Salem, Massachusetts*, Robert W. Kenny, ed. (Salem: Peabody Museum, with Brown University, Providence, Rhode Island, 1956). Williams's January 1, 1844, letter is included in dispatches from U.S. consuls, Bay of Islands (U.S. National Archives). Griffin's complaint was dated November 6, 1884 (U.S. National Archives). Charles Wilkes's comments regarding the British annexation of New Zealand come from *Narrative of the United States Exploring Expedition . . .* , pp. 377–78.

The description of Lahaina comes from p. 217 of Robert Elwes, *A Sketcher's Tour Round the World, 1849* (London: Hurst & Blackett, 1854).

CHAPTER THIRTEEN: HOMECOMING

A discussion of the newspaper coverage and the Smith rebuttal can be read in Philip F. Purrington, "Anatomy of a Mutiny," *The American Neptune*, XXVII : 2 (April 1967) : 98–110.

There is nothing to indicate that anyone ever tried to interview Manuel des Reis, though the correspondent to *Hunt's Merchants' Magazine* who recommended the republication of the article commented that the Portuguese boy should not have been "passed by and forgotten. He better deserves a silver pitcher than some who have obtained one," this gentleman continued, adding, "All information concerning him, now obtainable, is that he went home to the Western

Islands on the return of the *Sharon*," and that no one had heard from him since. This is hearsay: Manuel disappeared from all records, taking the secret of what he may have seen during the murder with him.

The crew list of the *Sharon* 1845 is held at NBFPL and can be read on the Internet database. Andrew White's 1/40 lay was a very generous one for a cooper. James Johnson's journal on the *Sharon* 1845 is held at KI-NBWM. He sailed two voyages on the ship and was lost on the second; his journal was kept and given to his sister when the ship got home. The six men who asked for their discharge in Lahaina in November 1846 were Westy Reese, John Griffin, John Williams, Greenleaf Goodwin, George Weeks, and Samuel Haley. Taken on in their places were George L. Babcock, George Gavitt, John Howland, and William Parker. Ship's papers, NBFPL; the spelling of Westy Reese's name is taken from a note by Clough in the back of his journal. Hohman, *American Whaleman*, p. 75, has the date of the change in the law regarding flogging.

Benjamin Clough's record as a whaling master was collated from entries in Starbuck, and also from Judith Lund, plus materials at MVHS. The story of the whaling panorama comes from an item in the New Bedford *Standard-Times*, "Exhibit takes viewers on fantastic 'voyage'," written by David B. Boyce, and published in the issue for June 21, 2001. A short biography of Benjamin Russell is held in the collection of KI-NBWM.

The genealogical details come from Elizabeth Little, Chris Baer, and Catherine Mayhew, plus sources cited in the text. There are a number of Thomas H. Smiths in the whaling records, so it took some delving to establish Thomas Harlock Smith's whaling career. The dates of the Warren ships fit information in the MVHS records and were confirmed by discussion with Judith Lund, for which I thank her. The strange coincidence of Charlotte Downs's father arriving home on the day of the wedding comes from Clough's obituary, *Vineyard Gazette*, May 17, 1889.

The details of the *Carrie Leland*, which come from the American Ship Register, were kindly located for me by Norman Brouwer, librarian at South Street Seaport Museum, New York City. It has been impossible to track down any ship by the name of *Copang*; evidently the newspaper had garbled information. Nathan Smith's last letters are in the MVHS archives; the transcript of the surgeons' report that they hold was copied from the hospital records.

While Andrew White and Benjamin Clough may have taken the secret of the *Sharon* tragedy to the grave, the two journals, plus Clough's letter to his father, survived. Suddenly, in 1919, Benjamin Clough's letter to his father appeared in print. Apparently it had never reached its intended reader, but instead had been sold to a New Bedford collector, Andrew Snow Jr., perhaps as part of the contents of a dead letter bag. Snow, recognizing its unusual interest, allowed Professor Will D. Howe, an editor with Charles Scribner's Sons of New York, to publish it. The decision was quite bizarre: The letter, edited for spelling and punctuation to make it easier to read but still detailing Norris's brutality and the sadistic murder of George Babcock, was printed in *Nineteenth Century Letters*, a schoolbook in the Modern Student's Library series.

That it received no attention from either historians of whaling or the popular press is probably no surprise, considering the nature of the publication. Consequently, the romantic story of the single-handed recapture lived on, at first exactly as it had been portrayed by the New Bedford *Mercury* and its host of plagiarists. In 1947, Clough's grandson published the account of the murder, mutiny, and recapture of the ship that Clough had stuck into his journal with sealing wax, in a collection, *The American Imagination at Work: Tall Tales and Folk Tales* (New York: Alfred A. Knopf, 1947). The item, "Saving the *Sharon*," is on pages 301–5. The interesting comment about "Molino del Roy" is within a footnote of this, as is the quoted comment about Clough choosing not to offend his neighbors.

Publishing this extract from Clough's journal without any mention of previous incidents did nothing to cast more light on the background of the tragedy. However, another collector of whaling manuscripts, Paul C. Nicholson of Providence, Rhode Island, acquired Andrew White's journal. It was in dreadful condition, but once restored, and the semiliterate entries deciphered, the story of Babcock's death was at last revealed to someone who knew whaling history and was familiar with the terminology. Commenting that at last a motive for the killing of Captain Norris had been found—"the other native sailors were literally afraid for their lives"—Nicholson compiled an eight-page abstract of the voyage and in December 1953 published it in a limited 250-copy edition.

Because this was distributed to maritime museums, and because Nicholson donated White's logbook to the Providence Public Library in 1956, the cooper's account became available to other scholars. About 1964, Philip F. Purrington, curator of the New Bedford Whaling Museum, began to make the connection between the Andrew White logbook, the Clough documents that had been published in *Nineteenth Century Letters* and *The American Imagination at Work*, and the accounts of the recapture that had been printed in the various papers, along with the logbook kept by Norris, by then held by the Martha's Vineyard Historical Society. After three years of "trying to analyze the different versions of what occurred on that unhappy voyage," in 1967 Purrington published his findings in *The American Neptune*. While this was a valuable contribution to the *Sharon* story, Purrington was careful to be circumspect, as "later generations of the Norris-Smith-Clough families, all friendly neighbors on the Vineyard, were content to draw a veil over events of *Sharon's* tragic voyage."

It is only now, because of the passage of time and the opportunity to read and utilize the journals kept by the hero of the recapture, Benjamin Clough, that the complete story of the tragic voyage of the *Sharon* can be told.

RESOURCES

Sources used throughout the book:

William A. Allen, journal kept on *Samuel Robertson* 1841–46. Held at the Kendall Whaling Institute, New Bedford Whaling Museum. Brief extracts quoted by permission.

Benjamin Clough, journal kept on whaleship *Rajah*, May 8, 1839, to March 7, 1840. Privately held. Used by permission.

Benjamin Clough, journal kept on whaleship *Sharon*, May 25, 1841, to September 21, 1843, and April 9, 1844, to August 6, 1844. Privately held. Quoted by permission.

Benjamin Clough, a long sea letter written by Benjamin Clough from the ship *Sharon* to his father, Asa Clough, commenced February 9, 1843, but retrospective, substantially based on his journal. Published in Will D. Howe (ed.), *Nineteenth Century Letters* (New York: Charles Scribner's, 1899), pp. 535–40.

Stephen Curtis Jr., *Brief extracts from the journal of a voyage performed by the whale ship M., of New Bedford, Massachusetts, commencing May 25, 1841 and terminating August 1, 1844* (Boston: Samuel L. Dickinson, 1844).

Joseph Eayres, journal kept on whaleship *Gratitude*. Kendall Institute, New Bedford Whaling Museum, reel 55. Short extracts quoted by permission.

Honore Forster, *The South Sea Whaler: An Annotated Bibliography of Published Historical, Literary and Art Material Relating to Whaling in the Pacific Ocean in the Nineteenth Century* (Sharon, MA:

The Kendall Whaling Museum with Edward J. Lefkowicz Inc. of Fairhaven, MA, 1985).

—— More South Sea Whaling: A Supplement to The South Sea Whaler . . . (Canberra: Division of Pacific and Asian History, Research School of Pacific Studies, The Australian National University, 1991).

Elmo P. Hohman, The American Whaleman, a study of life and labor in the whaling industry (New York: Longmans, Green, & Co., 1928).

Robert Langdon (ed.), American Whalers and Traders in the Pacific: A Guide to Records on Microfilm (Canberra: Pacific Manuscripts Bureau, Australian National Univ., 1984). All of the microfilms in this collection are indicated by the abbreviation PMB.

Elizabeth A. Little, "Captain Howes Norris of Holmes Hole, Martha's Vineyard and the Mutiny on the Whaleship Sharon of Fairhaven in the South Pacific in 1842." A privately printed compilation from sources at the Mitchell Library, Sydney, Australia; books; recorded family memoirs; and interviews with Deborah Champion Webster and Margaret Norris Jones Little in the 1960s. The compilation is dated 1987.

Judith Navas Lund, Whaling Masters and Whaling Voyages Sailing from American Ports: A Compilation of Sources (Massachusetts: New Bedford Whaling Museum, The Kendall Whaling Museum, and Ten Pound Island Book Co., 2001).

Herman Melville, Moby-Dick. There are many editions. One that I found particularly valuable was edited by Harrison Hayford and Hershel Parker (New York: W. W. Norton & Company, 1967), and includes letters and reviews by Melville, plus analogues, sources, and criticism.

Howes Norris, logbooks kept on *Leonidas,* July 26, 1828, to July 7, 1829, and August 12, 1829, to March 23, 1831. The Kendall Institute, New Bedford Whaling Museum. Used by permission.

Howes Norris, logbooks kept on *London Packet,* November 25, 1832, to August 31, 1835, and from June 5, 1836 to August 15, 1838. The Kendall Institute, New Bedford Whaling Museum. Used by permission.

Howes Norris, logbook kept on whaleship *Sharon,* May 25, 1841, to October 29, 1842. Held in the collections of the Martha's Vineyard Historical Society. PMB 674. Used by permission.

Philip F. Purrington, "Anatomy of a Mutiny." *The American Neptune* 27 (2): 98–110.

Stuart C. Sherman, *Whaling Logbooks and Journals 1613–1927: An Inventory of Manuscript Records in Public Collections* (New York: Garland Publishing, 1986). Originally compiled by Stuart Sherman, revised and edited by Judith M. Downey and Virginia M. Adams.

Alexander Starbuck, *The History of the American Whale Fishery* (Secaucus, NJ: Castle Books, 1989, facsimile of the 1876 edition).

Ralph G. Ward (compiler) *American Activities in the Central Pacific,* 8 vols. (Ridgewood, NJ: Gregg Press, 1966–67).

William Wallace Weeks (William Sweeny), partial journal kept on the *Wilmington & Liverpool Packet,* March 1843 to November 1843. Manuscript held in the Special Collections Room as part of the Paul Nicholson collection, Providence Public Library, Rhode Island. On microfilm as PMB 899. Quoted by permission.

Andrew White, journal kept on whaleship *Sharon,* October 3, 1841, to February 5, 1845. Also held in the Special Collections Room, Providence Public Library. PMB 893. Used and quoted by permission.

ACKNOWLEDGMENTS

The research for this book could not have been accomplished without substantial assistance from first, a Creative New Zealand grant that allowed me to commence my studies of Americans in New Zealand and the Pacific in the nineteenth century, and then the John David Stout Trust, which in 2001 gave me a most generous yearlong Research Fellowship at the Stout Research Centre for New Zealand Studies, based at Victoria University, Wellington, New Zealand. My fervent thanks to them, and also to Lydia Wevers, Director of the Stout Research Centre, and to the Stout Residents who listened with such friendly interest to the progress of the book and offered valuable advice and inspiration. Gratitude is also due to the staff of the Alexander Turnbull Library and the Victoria University Library, who made resources so readily available.

I owe a particular debt to Teresia Teaiwa, who supplied so many good hints and ideas, and allowed me to talk over the project with her students at the Pacific Studies Department of Victoria University. Others who were helpful with Pacific Island details, particularly relating to Rotuma, Banaba, Arorae, Kiribati, Samoa, and Pohnpei, were Francis X. Hezel, Doug Munro, Ken Martin, Vilsoni Hereniko, Damon Salesa, Paul D'Arcy, Stacey King, and Ken Sigrah. Over two research trips to the South Island chasing references to Benjamin Clough's early career, I was given every assistance at the Hocken Library, Dunedin, the library of the Canterbury Museum, and the reference department of the Christchurch Public Library. In Australia, as usual I was encouraged by the interest of Honore Forster; and I wish to thank the Mitchell Library, Sydney, for fielding my e-mail requests so promptly and comprehensively.

I owe a great debt to New Englanders, particularly Judith Navas Lund, who with unselfish and unflagging interest shared all she knew while delving for still more in both New Bedford and Providence. I was particularly lucky that she had so recently completed her magnum opus, *Whaling Masters*, and was so willing to share privileged background information. Likewise, without the lively interest and active help of Philip Weimerskirch, Special Collections Librarian at the Providence Public Library, Rhode Island, it would have been impossible to delve so deeply into the Andrew White and Benjamin Clough material. I also thank Richard Stattler, librarian, at the Rhode Island Historical Society.

The Clough family overwhelmed me with their generosity with the documents and images they hold. On Martha's Vineyard, Catherine Mayhew, New England genealogist, and Art Railton, editor of the *Dukes County Intelligencer*, were unfailingly forthcoming with ideas and material. Jill Bouck and the Martha's Vineyard Historical Society were wonderfully enthusiastic; and I wish to express my appreciation, too, to Ed Ambrose and Chris Baer, along with all the Vineyarders, including descendants of the Smith family, who came along to hear me talk over the *Sharon* story and to offer their ideas.

In New Bedford, Michael Dyer, librarian, and Laura Pereira, assistant librarian, were unfailingly forthcoming with both material and inspiration over two research trips, despite the fact that they were so busy with the combining and reconciling of the two big collections

ACKNOWLEDGMENTS

that had been held separately at the New Bedford Whaling Museum and the Kendall Whaling Museum, Sharon, Massachusetts, into the single collection of the Kendall Institute, New Bedford Whaling Museum. In this respect, I owe gratitude to Dr. Stuart Frank, Director of the Kendall Institute, for allowing me to invade the library when it was closed to both researchers and the public.

I thank Paul Cyr, Melville Whaling Collection Librarian at the New Bedford Free Public Library, for his interest and for fielding my queries about crew lists. Tina Furtado was also very helpful, and it was a privilege to be present when the immensely valuable crew-list database www.ci.new-bedford.ma.us/Nav3.htm that has absorbed so many hours of her time first went up on the World Wide Web — and to have the immense fun of being the first researcher to log on to it. I thank Kathryn Grover and Carl Cruz for so generously sharing their extensive knowledge of black whalemen and the fugitive slaves of Massachusetts. I am also grateful to Elizabeth Little for her generosity in sending me a copy of her valuable contribution to a Norris family history.

It would be impossible to close without acknowledging the three people who determined the ultimate shape of this book: my husband, travel companion, and illustrator, Ron Druett; my patient and dedicated editor, Antonia Fusco; and my loyal friend and diligent agent, Laura J. Langlie. All three are valued much more than they probably realize.

Index

Index

Index